·OREGON·

Majestic Mount Hood in the Cascade Range is Oregon's tallest mountain. This beautiful snow-capped peak is admired by Oregonians and visitors from all over the world. On the back cover, Mount Hood is shown overlooking Portland's skyline.

DOROTHY NAFUS MORRISON

ERIC A. KIMMEL

MACMILLAN/McGRAW-HILL SCHOOL PUBLISHING COMPANY

NEW YORK CHICAGO COLUMBUS

ABOUT THE AUTHORS

Dorothy Nafus Morrison lives on a farm outside of Portland, Oregon. She has published many books for young readers on historic subjects, including four biographies of people who were important to the development of the Northwest. Among Dorothy Morrison's published fiction is *Somebody's Horse* which was selected by Books for Young Adults as one of the outstanding books of 1988.

Eric A. Kimmel is Professor of Education at Portland State University where he teaches courses in children's literature and language arts methods. Dr. Kimmel is a past president of the Oregon Reading Association and a well-known author of books for children. One of his recent works, *Hershel and the Hanukkah Gobblins,* was a 1990 Caldecott Honor Book.

PROGRAM AUTHORS

Dr. Barry K. Beyer
Professor of Education and American Studies
George Mason University
Fairfax, Virginia

Jean Craven
Social Studies Coordinator
Albuquerque Public Schools
Albuquerque, New Mexico

Dr. Mary A. McFarland
Instructional Coordinator of Social Studies
    K-12 and Director of Staff Development
Parkway School District
Chesterfield, Missouri

Dr. Walter C. Parker
Associate Professor, College of Education
University of Washington
Seattle, Washington

CONTENT CONSULTANTS

Bruce Taylor Hamilton
Director, Oregon Historical Society Press
Portland, Oregon

Susan Booth Larson
President of the Oregon Council for the
    Social Studies
Educational Consultant
Portland, Oregon

Elaine Mattson
Social Studies Curriculum Facilitator
Beaverton School District
Beaverton, Oregon

GRADE-LEVEL CONSULTANTS

Rebecca Duncan
Fourth Grade Teacher
Buckingham Elementary School
Bend, Oregon

Dennis Hickey
Fourth Grade Teacher
Oak Grove Elementary School
Albany, Oregon

Ben Needham
Fourth Grade Teacher
Tualatin Elementary School
Tualatin, Oregon

Arleen R. Rice
Fourth Grade Teacher
Lake Grove Elementary School
Lake Oswego, Oregon

Susan Scott
Fourth Grade Teacher
Tualatin Elementary School
Tualatin, Oregon

ACKNOWLEDGMENTS

The publisher gratefully acknowledges permission to reprint the following copyrighted material:
Excerpt from "Over There" was taken from *Long Ago in Oregon.* Copyright 1987 by Claudia Lewis. Published by Harper & Row, Publishers, Inc., 10 East 53rd St., New York, NY 10022, and is reprinted with their permission. Excerpt from "OREGON, MY OREGON" Music by Henry B. Murtagh, Lyrics by J. A. Buchanan. Copyright 1973, 1974 by Barbara Roberts Oregon Secretary of State and reprinted with their permission. "Like a Godzilla Working the Forests of Oregon," *The New York Times,* December 11, 1989 is reprinted by permission of Fredric Sutherland, President of the Sierra Club Legal Fund. Excerpt from "Students try to ban paper milk cartons," was taken from *The Oregonian,* January 18, 1990. Used by permission. "Oregon: Put through the Mill," *The New York Times,* November 27, 1989 is reprinted by permission. Excerpt from "The Girl From Yamhill" by Beverly Cleary, copyright 1938 by Beverly Cleary. Used by permission of William Morrow and Company, 105 Madison Avenue, New York, NY 10016.

Macmillan/McGraw-Hill School Division
866 Third Avenue
New York, New York 10022

Printed in the United States of America
ISBN 0-02-144102-2
9 8 7 6 5 4 3 2 1

CONTENTS

UNIT 3   American Settlers Come to Oregon   104

UNIT 4   Oregon Becomes a State   150

Building Citizenship

Building Skills

Charts, Graphs, Diagrams, and Time Lines

Maps

Oregon, My Oregon

Words—J. A. Buchanan

Music—Henry B. Murtagh

Marcia *mf*

Land of the Em - pire Build - ers, Land of the Gold - en
Land of the rose and sun - shine, Land of the sum - mer's

West; _____ Con - quered and held by free men,
breeze; _____ Lad - en with health and vig - or,

f ... *mf*

Fair - est ___ and the best. _____ On - ward and up - ward
Fresh from the West - ern seas. _____ Blest by the blood of

f

ev - er, For - ward and on, and on; _____
mar - tyrs, Land of the set - ting sun; _____

ff _3_ *f*

Hail to thee, Land _ of He - roes, My O - re - gon. _____
Hail to thee, Land _ of Prom - ise, My O - re - gon. _____

WHAT IS AN
Oregonian?

Dear Student,

What does it mean to you to be an Oregonian? As you read this book keep that question in mind.

You will read about the mountains, valleys, lakes, and rivers found across Oregon. You will read about the rich history of our state—about the people who lived here hundreds of years ago and about the people who live here today.

From explorers and settlers to farmers, loggers, and office workers, it is the people who make our state special. And it is you and your classmates who will continue to make Oregon a strong, growing state.

When you finish this book, you will know more about Oregon. You will also have some new ideas about what it means to be an Oregonian.

Sincerely,

Dorothy N. Morrison

Eric A. Kimmel

Dorothy Morrison
Eric Kimmel

USING YOUR TEXTBOOK

Your textbook contains many special features that will help you to read, understand, and remember the geography, history, and people of Oregon.

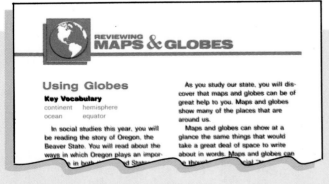

REVIEWING MAPS AND GLOBES

Reviews skills that will help you use the maps in your book

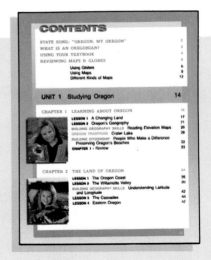

TABLE OF CONTENTS

Lists all parts of your book and tells you where to find them

LESSON OPENER

Important vocabulary, people, and places introduced in the lesson

Lesson introduction

Asks you to think about what you already know from your book or from your own experience

Question you should keep in mind as you read the lesson

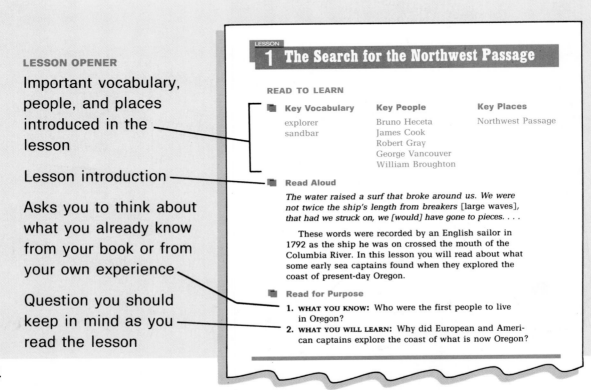

LESSON

1 The Search for the Northwest Passage

READ TO LEARN

Key Vocabulary	Key People	Key Places
explorer	Bruno Heceta	Northwest Passage
sandbar	James Cook	
	Robert Gray	
	George Vancouver	
	William Broughton	

Read Aloud

The water raised a surf that broke around us. We were not twice the ship's length from breakers [large waves], that had we struck on, we [would] have gone to pieces. . . .

These words were recorded by an English sailor in 1792 as the ship he was on crossed the mouth of the Columbia River. In this lesson you will read about what some early sea captains found when they explored the coast of present-day Oregon.

Read for Purpose

1. **WHAT YOU KNOW:** Who were the first people to live in Oregon?
2. **WHAT YOU WILL LEARN:** Why did European and American captains explore the coast of what is now Oregon?

REFERENCE SECTION

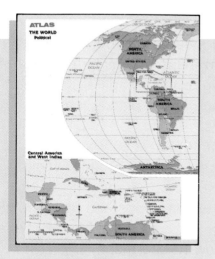

ATLAS

Maps of the world, the United States, and Oregon

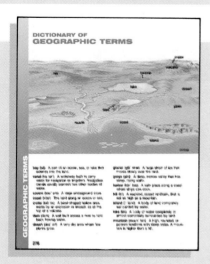

DICTIONARY OF GEOGRAPHIC TERMS

Definition, pronunciation, picture of major geographic terms

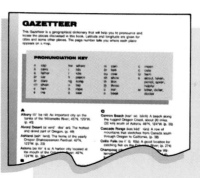

GAZETTEER

Location and pronunciation of all key places and page where each is shown on a map

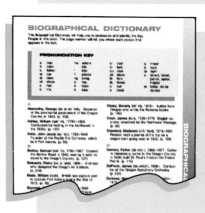

BIOGRAPHICAL DICTIONARY

Identifies and pronounces names of key people and lists first page where each is found

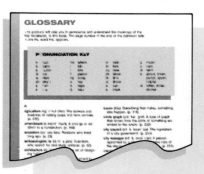

GLOSSARY

Definition and pronunciation of all key vocabulary and first page where each is found

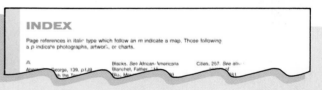

INDEX

Alphabetical list of important subjects and pages where information is found

REVIEWING
MAPS & GLOBES

Using Globes

Key Vocabulary

continent   hemisphere
ocean   equator

In social studies this year, you will be reading the story of Oregon, the Beaver State. You will read about the ways in which Oregon plays an important role in both the United States and the world.

As you study our state, you will discover that maps and globes can be of great help to you. Maps and globes show many of the places that are around us.

Maps and globes can show at a glance the same things that would take a great deal of space to write about in words. Maps and globes can be thought of as special "tools." Let's review how to use them.

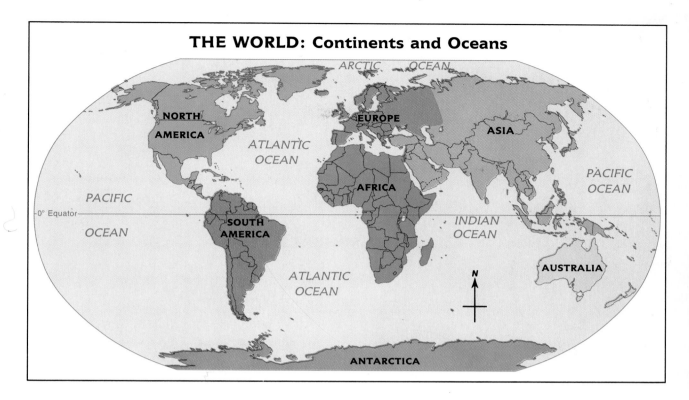

THE WORLD: Continents and Oceans

Continents and Oceans

Another word for a round body is *sphere* (sfîr). A globe, like the earth, is a sphere. A globe is a model, or small copy, of the earth, in the same way a toy train is a model of a real train. Both models are like the originals, only they are much smaller.

The students in the picture are using a globe to find the location of Oregon. By using the globe, they can also find countries, cities, rivers, lakes, and mountains.

Globes show the continents and the oceans. A continent is a very large body of land. The earth has seven continents. They are North America, South America, Europe, Africa, Asia, Australia, and Antarctica. The students in the picture learned that Oregon is located in North America.

From the map of the world, above, you can see that the continents are separated by large bodies of water. Actually, when you look closely at a globe, you will see that all the large bodies of water on the earth are part of one larger, connected body of water. This large body of water is divided into smaller parts called oceans. The earth has four oceans: the Atlantic Ocean, the Pacific Ocean, the Indian and the Arctic Oceans.

Hemispheres

No matter how you turn a globe, you can see only half of it at one time. Since a globe is a sphere, what you see is half a sphere. Another word for half a sphere is hemisphere. *Hemi* means "half."

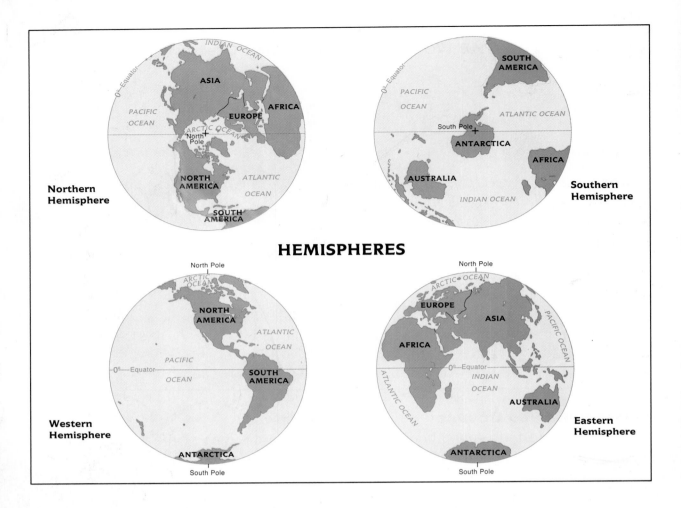

HEMISPHERES

The earth can be divided into different hemispheres. Look at the four hemisphere maps, above. Each one shows you half of the earth.

The northern half of the earth is divided from the southern half by the **equator**. The equator is an imaginary line that lies halfway between the North Pole and the South Pole. The equator divides the earth into the Northern and Southern hemispheres.

How many continents are found in the Northern Hemisphere? How many continents are found in the Southern Hemisphere? The earth can also be divided into the Eastern Hemisphere and the Western Hemisphere. Which continents are found in the Western Hemisphere? Which are found in the Eastern Hemisphere?

1. Name two things you can learn about the earth from looking at a globe.
2. What is a continent? Name two continents that border on the Atlantic Ocean.
3. What does the word *hemisphere* mean?
4. What is the equator?
5. In which two hemispheres can North America be found?

Using Maps

Key Vocabulary

compass rose

cardinal directions

intermediate directions

symbol

map key

scale

Maps are drawings that show all or part of the earth's surface. Maps are very useful. A map, unlike a globe, can show the whole earth at one time.

The Compass Rose and Directions

How can you find directions on a map? Many maps have a **compass rose**. A compass rose is a small drawing with lines showing directions.

North, east, south, and west are the **cardinal directions**, or main directions. Look at the compass rose on the map of the United States below. The letters *N*, *E*, *S*, and *W* stand for the cardinal directions.

The compass rose also has lines that mark **intermediate directions**. Intermediate directions lie halfway between the cardinal directions. Northeast is the intermediate direction between north and east. The other intermediate directions are southeast, southwest, and northwest. The letters *NE*, *SE*, *SW*, and *NW* stand for the intermediate directions. Look at the map of the United States below. In which direction is Oregon from Utah?

Not all maps have a compass rose. Instead, some maps have a north

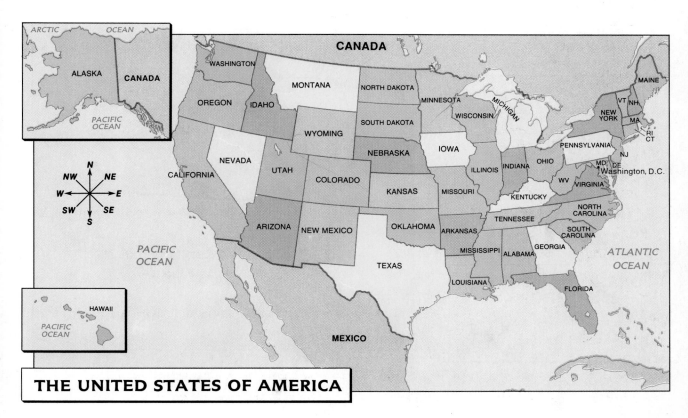

THE UNITED STATES OF AMERICA

pointer. A north pointer is an arrow that shows which direction is north on a map.

If you know where north is, you can easily find all the other directions. Look at the map titled "Oregon and Its Neighbors." In which direction is Washington from Oregon?

Symbols

Symbols are used to give information on maps. A symbol is anything that stands for something else. Symbols may be small drawings of the things they stand for. For example, a drawing of an airplane is often used to stand for an airport. Dots are often used to stand for cities and towns. Color is also used as a symbol. You may know that the color blue is usually a symbol for water.

Map Keys

To understand, or "read," a map, you must know what the symbols used on the map stand for. Most maps have a **map key**. The map key explains the meaning of symbols used on the map.

Some symbols have the same meaning on many maps. For example, ✪ often stands for a national capital and a • stands for cities.

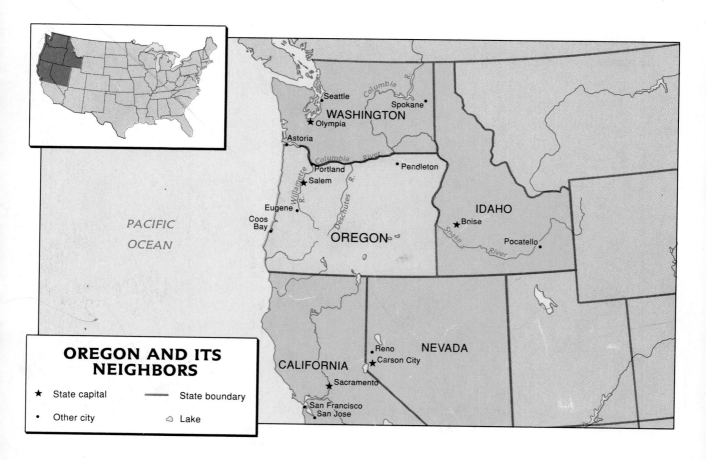

OREGON AND ITS NEIGHBORS

★ State capital   ——— State boundary

• Other city   ◡ Lake

You should always check the map key to find out what the symbols used on that map stand for. Look at the map of Oregon and Its Neighbors. What does the star stand for?

Scale

Maps do not show sizes and distances as they really are. To show real sizes and distances, maps would have to be as large as the part of the earth they show. Maps can, however, give you a very accurate idea of what the real sizes and distances are.

They do this by having short distances, such as inches or centimeters, represent much larger distances, such as miles or kilometers. Scale is the relationship between the distances shown on the map and the real distances on the earth.

In this book map scale is shown by two lines, the top one for miles and the bottom one for kilometers. Look at the map scale on this page. The scale shows you that 1 inch on the map represents 150 miles on the earth. Two centimeters on the map represent 190 kilometers on the earth.

You can use a ruler to measure the distances between places on a map. Another way to measure distances on a map is with a scale strip. Use the map scale on the map of Oregon, on this page, as a guide to making a scale strip. Take a strip of paper that has a straight edge. Place the paper below both scale lines and mark the miles and kilometers. Move the strip

OREGON:
Political

★ State capital
• Other city
— State boundary
⬭ Lake

along and continue marking distances. Your strip should look like this:

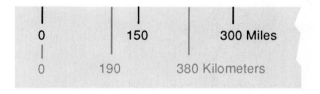

Now use the scale strip to find the distance between Eugene and Pendleton. Place the 0 (zero) edge of the scale strip on the black dot that stands for Eugene. Then read the number that is closest to Pendleton. You will see that the distance between Eugene and Pendleton is about 250 miles (410 km).

1. Why is a compass rose useful?
2. Name the cardinal and intermediate directions.
3. What does a map key show?
4. What do map scales show?

11

Different Kinds of Maps

Key Vocabulary

grid map
transportation map

There are many different kinds of maps. Some maps show continents, oceans, countries, or states. Other kinds of maps can help travelers find their way around a country, city, or national park. Each kind of map is useful and can help you better understand the places you are studying.

Map Titles

When you use a map, first look at the map title. The title tells you which part of the world is shown on the map. It may also tell you the kind of information that is shown on the map. What is the title of the map on this page?

Grid Maps

Grids make it easier to find places on the map. A **grid map** is made up of two sets of lines that cross each other to make squares. One set of lines crosses the map from left to right. The spaces between these lines are

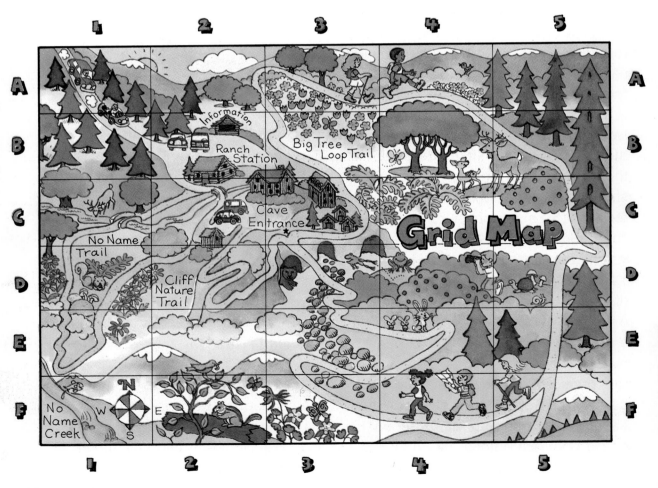

marked with letters. The other set of lines crosses the map from top to bottom. The spaces between these lines are given numbers. Each square on the map can be identified by its letter and number. This makes it easy to locate places on a map.

Look at the grid map on page 12. You can find the Ranger easily if you know that the Ranger House is located in square **B-2**. What is the letter and number of the square in which No Name Creek is located?

Transportation Maps

Suppose that you are visiting a city in Oregon for the first time. You can find your way around by using a transportation map. A transportation map shows the different ways you can travel from one place to another. Different kinds of transportation maps may show roads and railroad, subway, or bus routes.

Look at the map of the TRI-MET on this page. The TRI-MET is the name of the bus transportation system in Portland. If you live in or ever visit downtown Portland, you might use this map to help you get to the many interesting sites in this city.

The map key shows that the red line stands for the bus on the Red Fish route, and the yellow line stands for the bus on the Yellow Rose route.

Describe a route you might take from Pioneer Place to the Oregon Historical Society. Would it be faster to take the Red Fish route or the Yellow

TRI-MET BUS ROUTES IN DOWNTOWN PORTLAND

—— Yellow Rose bus route   • Yellow Rose bus stop
—— Red Fish bus route   ■ Red Fish bus stop
←— Bus direction   ● Place of interest

Rose route to get from the Oregonian Building to O'Bryant Park?

1. Look at the grid map. What is the letter and number of the square in which the cave entrance is located?
2. What is a transportation map?
3. Look at the TRI-MET bus map. Describe a route from City Hall to the Portland Art Museum.
4. Why do you think there are so many different kinds of maps?

UNIT 1

STUDYING OREGON

WHERE WE ARE

The state that we call home is in the northwest part of our country, in the region known as the West. In our state you can ski at Mount Hood, go salmon fishing along the Columbia River, swim in the Pacific Ocean, or visit the sights of Portland. Let's find out about Oregon and its people.

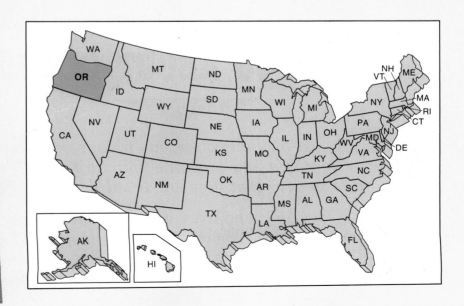

15

CHAPTER 1

LEARNING ABOUT OREGON

FOCUS

For my last birthday party, my friends and I went up to Vernonia and everyone found a fossil. It is hard to believe that they are 40 million years old.

Nicole McCord, who lives in Beaverton, has gone fossil hunting many times. She enjoys exploring for clues about Oregon's past when the land was very different than it is today. In this chapter you too will explore the land of Oregon.

1 A Changing Land

READ TO LEARN

Key Vocabulary

geography
geologist
volcano
glacier
Ice Age

Key Places

Cascade Range
Mount St. Helens
Mount Mazama
Crater Lake
Columbia River
Columbia River Gorge

Read Aloud

The flood that rushed down the Columbia was ten times the combined flow of all the world's rivers today. It would equal the force of a . . . nuclear bomb going off every four seconds for ten days.

This is the way an Oregon scientist described the flood that carved out one of our state's most beautiful places. It happened thousands of years ago and is just one event in the long and exciting history of the changing land of Oregon.

Read for Purpose

1. **WHAT YOU KNOW:** What does the land look like where you live?
2. **WHAT YOU WILL LEARN:** How did Oregon's land come to look the way it does today?

A DRAMATIC PAST

Millions of years ago Oregon looked different from the way it looks today. If you could go back in time to see Oregon the way it was then, you would find almost nothing you could recognize. That is because almost all of the land that is now Oregon was once under water. The place where your schoolyard is located was probably once ocean. Fish were most likely swimming right where you are now.

17

Oregon's geography (jē og′ rə fē) has changed a lot since that time. *Geography* is a word for the earth's land and water and its plants and animals. It also means the study of the ways in which people live on and use the land.

We know about Oregon's changing land because of the work of geologists (jē ol′ ə jists). Geologists study the earth to learn how it changes over time. They know that Oregon was once under water because they have found traces of seashells in rocks that are on land.

Volcanoes such as this one helped to form many of Oregon's mountains.

MOUNTAINS AND VOLCANOES

Over a long time the land of our state rose out of the ocean. Mountains took shape as a result of the action of volcanoes (vol kā′ nōz). A volcano is an opening in the earth's surface from which hot fiery rock, ash, and gases from inside the earth are spit out.

Volcanoes helped form the Cascade (kas kād′) Range, a row of mountains that stretches south from Canada, through Washington, and into our state before ending in California. Mount St. Helens, a mountain in this range, is still an active volcano.

Perhaps you have heard people speak of the eruption of Mount St. Helens in 1980 in Washington, our neighbor to the north. The wind carried volcanic ash for miles and dropped it like a gray snowfall. Some of the ash fell on areas of our state, such as Portland.

The people who lived near Mount St. Helens had to clean up the ash with shovels and brooms. Bulldozers were used to clear streets. Mount St. Helens is quiet now, but it still gives off smoke. Nobody knows when it might next awaken.

Among Oregon's tallest mountains in the Cascade Range are Mount Hood and Mount Jefferson. Mount Mazama (mə zäm′ ə), which was probably once the highest mountain in Oregon, erupted nearly

A man (*left*) in Oregon is cleaning off the volcanic ash that fell on his car after the volcanic eruption of Mount St. Helens in Washington (*above*).

7,000 years ago. For miles around land was covered by a blanket of rock that was 20 feet (6 m) thick—as high as a house! Lava, or red-hot melted rock, ran down the mountain's sides. Rocks exploded like bombs, and clouds of ash drifted over the earth, blocking out the sunlight for days at a time.

When the eruption stopped, the mountain looked as if its top had been sliced off. It was gray with ash and was hidden from view by smoke. At its center was a huge hole, or crater. This crater, nearly 1 mile (1.6 km) deep, became filled with water and is now beautiful, blue Crater Lake.

ICE AND WATER

Just as the extreme heat of fiery volcanoes helped to form the land of our state, extreme cold also played an important part. Thousands of years ago the earth turned extremely cold. The snow that fell did not melt. Instead, it turned into sheets of ice that built up over thousands of years. These huge sheets of ice that move very slowly are called glaciers (glā′ shərz). They covered so much of the earth that we call that period of history the Ice Age.

Though glaciers move extremely slowly, nothing can stop them. They move like bulldozers, picking up trees, large rocks, stones, and soil that carve out the land in different ways as they are dragged along.

When waters from lakes in Montana spilled over onto a glacier, the ice broke up and melted. This caused great floods of water to flow through the Columbia River. At the

19

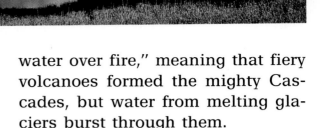

The Blue Mountains and the Columbia River Gorge were shaped by strong forces of nature.

location of present-day Portland, the water was 300 feet (91 m) deep. The floods carried gigantic pieces of ice that had broken off from the glaciers. The water and ice carved out a deep passage through the Cascade Range called the Columbia River Gorge (gôrj). A gorge is a deep, narrow opening between rocky sides of mountains.

Today you can visit this beautiful gorge. As you spread out your picnic lunch, try to imagine the floods that carved through the Cascade Range. One writer has described the formation of the Columbia River Gorge as "a victory of water over fire," meaning that fiery volcanoes formed the mighty Cascades, but water from melting glaciers burst through them.

A VARIED LAND

You have been reading about the forces of nature that formed our state. Volcanoes formed mountains where once there had been ocean. Glaciers melted, creating gorges. In the next lesson you will read more about the land of Oregon today.

 Check Your Reading

1. What is geography?
2. What great forces of nature have formed the land of Oregon?
3. What changes in the land have these forces brought about?
4. GEOGRAPHY SKILL: Use the Atlas map on page 274 to locate the Coast Range.
5. THINKING SKILL: List three questions you could ask a geologist about Oregon's volcanoes.

2 Oregon's Geography

READ TO LEARN

Key Vocabulary

region
natural feature
landform
weather
climate
natural resource
plateau
desert

Key Places

Pacific Rim
Coast Range
Columbia Plateau
Blue Mountains
Wallowa Mountains

Read Aloud

When you look out the window, or ride the bus to school, or walk to the store, do you see flat land, ocean, or mountains? In the winter does it rain where you live, or does it snow? You might see many different things in different parts of Oregon because the areas of our state are not all alike. Let's find out about these different areas of our state.

Read for Purpose

1. **WHAT YOU KNOW:** What did the land of Oregon look like long ago?
2. **WHAT YOU WILL LEARN:** Which geographic features divide Oregon into different regions?

OUR STATE AND ITS NEIGHBORS

Find our state on the United States map on page 9. Oregon is in the northwest part of the country. Look at the shape of our state. As you can see, it is almost square, but it is a little larger from east to west than it is from north to south.

Some of Oregon's borders look like straight lines. Others follow the course of winding rivers or the seacoast. Look at the map on page 23 and find the rivers that form some of Oregon's borders. What are the names of these rivers?

Another border of Oregon is the Pacific Ocean, the ocean that once covered most of our state. Find two neighboring states on the United States map on page 23 that also border the Pacific Ocean. In addition to our Pacific Coast neighbors, Washington and California, we share a border with Nevada to the south and Idaho to the east. How many of these border states have you visited?

Oregon has other neighbors that are not a part of the United States.

The Snake River forms most of Oregon's eastern border with Idaho.

They are countries that also have the Pacific Ocean as a border. These countries make up the Pacific Rim. You will be reading more about the Pacific Rim countries and their connections to Oregon later on.

WHAT IS A REGION?

Your school building is divided into areas such as a gym, a cafeteria, classrooms, and halls. Each area is different. Each has its own use. Yet all these areas are parts of the same school. In a similar way the land of our state is divided into areas, or regions. A region is a large area with common features that set it apart from other areas. Geography can help us to identify regions. Let's take a look at the different features that are used to identify regions.

LAND AND WATER

One way to identify a region is by its natural features. Natural features are the parts of the earth formed by nature. Land and water are natural features. Look at the map on the next page. It shows our state's landforms. Landforms are shapes that make up the earth's surface. In the last lesson you read about one of Oregon's important landforms—mountains. What are some other common landforms in our state?

You have already read about two important bodies of water—the Pacific Ocean and the Columbia

River. The Columbia River flows into the Pacific Ocean at the northwestern tip of our state. This link to a larger body of water makes the Columbia River a very important route for trade and transportation. There are other important rivers in our state. Two of them are the Willamette River and the Snake River. Find the Willamette River on the map on this page.

CLIMATE

Weather and **climate** are two other important parts of geography. Weather is how hot or cold and how wet or dry the air of a place is. The weather can change at any moment.

Climate is the pattern of weather over a long period of time.

Is it hot and rainy? Is it cold and dry? These are questions about weather. Weather affects the way you live day to day. Weather conditions might cause you to decide to leave your jacket at home, plan to go to the beach, or carry an umbrella.

Climate affects people's long-range plans, such as which crops to plant in an area. An area that gets plenty of both warm sunshine and rain over a long period of time has a warm, wet climate and is one that would be ideal for growing many

MAP SKILL: Through what kinds of **landforms** does the Columbia River run?

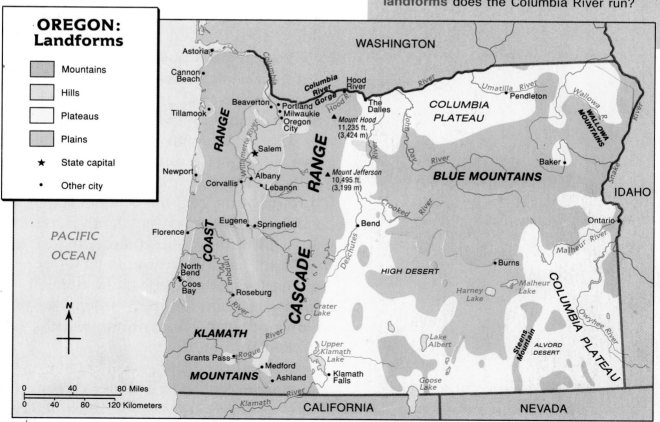

OREGON: Landforms

- Mountains
- Hills
- Plateaus
- Plains
- ★ State capital
- • Other city

kinds of crops. In the next chapter you will read about the climate of the different regions of Oregon.

NATURAL RESOURCES

Natural resources are another natural feature of a region. They are things found in nature which are useful to people. Oregon has much good farmland on which to grow crops and many forests from which to harvest wood. Other important natural resources in our state are fish and minerals.

REGIONS OF OREGON

Landforms, natural resources, and climate help us to define the four regions of our state. Look at the map on the next page to find the name and location of each one.

The Oregon Coast runs along the Pacific Ocean. This region includes beaches, a small area of flat land, and the mountainous Coast Range.

The next region, the Willamette (wə lam′ ət) Valley, has rolling hills. The Willamette River flows through this region. Much of the valley is farmland, but it also has most of the large towns of Oregon.

The Cascades region is made up of the Cascade Range, a stretch of high mountains and volcanoes. Only one river—the Columbia—has broken through them.

Beyond the Cascades is Eastern Oregon, a very large and dry region. The Columbia Plateau (pla tō′)

Farmland for growing crops such as strawberries (*top*) and lumber (*middle*), and fish (*bottom*) are important natural resources in Oregon.

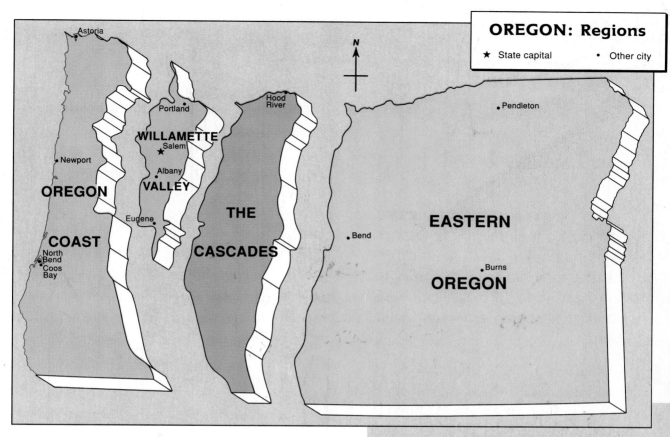

OREGON: Regions

★ State capital　　• Other city

MAP SKILL: In which region of Oregon is the city of Pendleton located?

makes up most of the northern section of Eastern Oregon. A **plateau** is a large area of high, flat land.

In the northeast corner of Eastern Oregon the **Blue Mountains** and the **Wallowa** (wä laủ′ ə) **Mountains** add variety to the region. These rugged mountains are covered with thick evergreen forests.

Oregon's **desert** makes up most of the southern part of Eastern Oregon. A desert is a hot, dry land where less than 10 inches (25 cm) of rain falls per year.

PATTERNS ON THE LAND

Each region of Oregon has its own landforms, natural resources,

and climate. In the next chapter you will take a closer look at each of Oregon's four regions.

Check Your Reading

1. What is a region?
2. Why is the Columbia River important to Oregon?
3. **GEOGRAPHY SKILL:** Name three important bodies of water that help form Oregon's borders.
4. **THINKING SKILL:** Describe how Oregon's natural resources are being used in the photographs on page 24.

Reading Elevation Maps

Key Vocabulary
elevation

In the last lesson you read about the land of our state. You learned that Oregon has many different kinds of land. The map on page 23 shows the land of our state. In this lesson you will see the land on a different kind of map.

Landforms
You know that the surface of the earth is not flat. It varies in shape from place to place. The changes in the land's shape are called landforms.

In the last lesson you read about the different landforms that are found in Oregon. Plains are landforms that are flat or nearly flat. Mountains are high, rugged landforms. Hills are landforms that are lower and less rugged than mountains.

Plains, hills, and mountains are just some of the earth's major landforms. The map on page 23 shows that all of these landforms are found in our state. Which kind of landform is found along the eastern border of our state?

Elevation
Landform maps help you to see how the land varies from one part of our state to another. But they do not show how high the mountains are or how low the plains are. They do not show anything about **elevation** (el ə vā′ shən).

Elevation is the height of land above sea level. It is usually measured in feet and meters. Elevation at sea level is 0 feet (0 m).

An Elevation Map
Look at the map on the next page. It is an elevation map of Oregon. How is this elevation map different from the landform map that is shown on page 23?

Like a landform map, an elevation map uses different colors to show different areas of land. But the colors of an elevation map only show how high the land is. They do not show what kind of land it is.

Using an Elevation Map
Look at the elevation map key. Which color is used to show elevations between 500 feet (150 m) and 1,000 feet (300 m)? Which range in elevation is shown by the color yellow?

As you can see, elevation maps can be very useful in showing what the height of the land is. They show where the land is highest, where it is lowest, and how it changes in different areas. What does this elevation map show you about the land of Oregon?

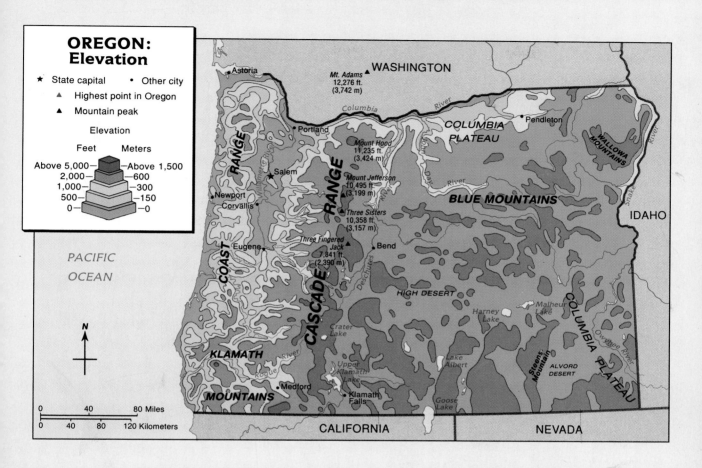

OREGON: Elevation

★ State capital   • Other city
▲ Highest point in Oregon
▲ Mountain peak

Elevation

Feet	Meters
Above 5,000	Above 1,500
2,000	600
1,000	300
500	150
0	0

Astoria
WASHINGTON
Mt. Adams
12,276 ft.
(3,742 m)
Columbia
River
COLUMBIA
PLATEAU
Pendleton
Portland
WALLOWA
MOUNTAINS
COAST
RANGE
Mount Hood
11,235 ft.
(3,424 m)
Salem
CASCADE
RANGE
Mount Jefferson
10,495 ft.
(3,199 m)
John Day
River
BLUE MOUNTAINS
Newport
Corvallis
Three Sisters
10,358 ft.
(3,157 m)
IDAHO
PACIFIC
OCEAN
Eugene
Three Fingered
Jack
7,841 ft.
(2,390 m)
Bend
Deschutes
River
HIGH DESERT
COLUMBIA
PLATEAU
Harney
Lake
Malheur
Lake
Owyhee River
N
Crater
Lake
KLAMATH
River
Rogue
Lake
Albert
Steens
Mountain
ALVORD
DESERT
MOUNTAINS
Medford
Upper
Klamath
Lake
Klamath
Falls
Goose
Lake
| 0 | 40 | 80 Miles |
| 0 | 40 | 80 | 120 Kilometers |
CALIFORNIA
NEVADA

Reviewing the Skill

Use the map above and the information in this lesson to help you to answer these questions.

1. What is the difference between a landform map and an elevation map?

2. Is Portland at a higher or lower elevation than Bend?

3. What is the approximate elevation of cities along Oregon's coast such as Astoria and Newport?

4. Which cities shown on the map have an elevation of between 500 feet (150 m) and 1,000 feet (300 m)?

5. Is any part of Oregon's land below sea level?

6. Where is the lowest point of elevation in Oregon? Where is the highest point of elevation in Oregon?

7. If you traveled from Salem to Mount Jefferson by car, would you be going mostly uphill or mostly downhill?

8. Why is it helpful to be able to read an elevation map as well as a landform map?

Oregon Traditions

READ TO LEARN

Key Vocabulary

ancestors

Read for Purpose

1. **WHAT YOU KNOW:** What happened to Mount Mazama nearly 7,000 years ago?
2. **WHAT YOU WILL LEARN:** How did the Klamath Indians explain the Mount Mazama volcano and the formation of Crater Lake?

◆ CRATER ◆ LAKE

In Lesson 1 of this chapter you read about the eruption of Mount Mazama, which occurred thousands of years ago. Did you know there were people living in Oregon at that time? These people were American Indians. They are also called Native Americans. A native is one of the first people to live in a land.

Imagine that you were one of those early Oregonians. What might you have thought was happening when the earth suddenly opened up, spitting out red-hot lava? What might you have done when you heard the thunderous roar as Mount Mazama's mighty walls collapsed?

Today there is still a lot about volcanoes that we don't know. And thousands of years ago certainly no one knew why volcanoes erupted. Early people told

stories called myths to make some sense of these frightening events in nature. The following story was told by the Klamath people, a group of Oregon Indians. Their **ancestors**, or their relatives who lived long before them, saw the fiery explosion of Mount Mazama.

HOW CRATER LAKE WAS MADE

Long ago the Chief of the Below World wished to marry a woman of the Klamath people. "If you come to live with me in my lodge inside the great mountain, you will never know sickness or death," he promised.

The woman said no. "Life without joy is an empty basket. How could I live, never to hear another bird sing? Never to feel sunshine on my face or new grass beneath my feet?"

The Chief of the Below World became very angry. He rushed through the passage leading from the Below World to the top of the great mountain. Fire burst from his throat, destroying forests and valleys.

The animals fled in terror.

The Klamath people sought shelter in Klamath Lake. Together they prayed to the Chief of the World Above, "O Great Chief, deliver us from fire!" The Chief of the World Above answered, "Only a special act of bravery can overcome the anger of the Below World Chief."

Two elder chiefs came forward. "We are honored," they said, "to offer ourselves to save our people." Together they climbed to the top of the mountain and threw themselves into the flames.

The Chief of the World Above saw what they had done and answered the people's prayer. He drove the Below World Chief back underground. Then he brought the mountain crashing on top of him, filling the passage between the two worlds so that the Below World Chief could never trouble the World Above again. All that remained of the great mountain was an enormous crater, which would soon be filled by the rains of many years. Today we call it Crater Lake.

CRATER LAKE TODAY

Crater Lake, formed in smoke and lava, is the site of one of the most beautiful of our national parks. Those who see it for the first time are astonished by its deep, clear, blue water. The shade of blue changes constantly, reflecting the sky, the time of day, and the weather. This marvelous color is caused by the lake's clearness and depth. Crater Lake is 1,932 feet (589 m) deep, the deepest lake in the United States. No streams flow into it, and none flow out. All its water has been stored up from centuries of rainfall, melting snow, and hot springs on the lake's bottom.

When visitors see Crater Lake's rare beauty, they understand what the Indians meant when they said, "Truly this is a place of magic."

Check Your Reading

1. What did the Chief of the World Above do so that another volcano would never erupt?
2. Why do you think that this legend might have made the Klamath people feel better about the Mount Mazama volcano?
3. **THINKING SKILL:** List the events of the story in the order in which they happened.

preserving
OREGON'S
beaches

In this chapter you have read about the beautiful geography of our state. The students who go to Neskowin Valley School, on the northern coast of Oregon, are very concerned about preserving the beauty and the natural resources of their town. For the last five years the students have been working on a community project that helps the local environment.

The students "adopted" the 3-mile-long beach in Neskowin and decided to take care of it. Several times throughout the year they get together to pick up any litter that has been left on the beach. They keep records of the kinds of material from which the litter is made; for example, glass, plastic, or paper. The students' records have helped to point out that plastic rings that are slipped over soda pop cans in order to keep several cans together are harmful to wildlife. Now a group called Stop Oregon Litter and Vandalism is asking can companies to make these rings out of materials that will not harm wildlife.

The Neskowin community is proud of the hard work that the students have done to preserve part of Oregon's environment. And the students know that by working together they are helping to make a difference in the community in which they live.

REVIEWING VOCABULARY

climate   natural resource
geography   region
landform

Number a sheet of paper from 1 to 5. Beside each number write the word or term from the list above that best matches the definition.

1. The earth's land, water, plants, and animals and the study of the way people live on and use the land
2. The pattern of weather over a long period of time
3. Any of the shapes that make up the earth's surface
4. A large area with common features that set it apart from other areas
5. Something found in nature that is useful to people

REVIEWING FACTS

Number a sheet of paper from 1 to 5. Beside each number write the word or term that best completes the sentence.

1. The land that is now Oregon was once _____.
2. _____ led to the creation of Crater Lake.
3. Two important rivers in Oregon are _____ and _____.
4. The region of Oregon that is home to the greatest number of people is called _____.
5. The region of Oregon that is farthest west is called _____.

WRITING ABOUT MAIN IDEAS

1. **Writing a Travel Brochure:** Choose a natural feature in Oregon that tourists might like to see. It might be a river, a mountain, a desert, or something else. Write a paragraph describing the feature. Tell where it is located, what it looks like, how it came to look that way, and any other interesting facts about it.
2. **Writing a Letter:** Imagine that you have a pen pal in another part of the United States. (Choose an area that you would like to visit.) Write to your pen pal about Oregon. Tell him or her what the different regions of our state look like. Be sure to mention at least one fact about the area in which your community is located. Ask questions about your pen pal's state and community.

BUILDING SKILLS: READING ELEVATION MAPS

1. What is an elevation map?
2. Is Eugene at a higher or lower elevation than Baker?
3. Describe a situation in which it might be helpful to know the elevation of a place.

CHAPTER 2

THE LAND OF OREGON

FOCUS

Living at the beach means that I get to go fishing and crabbing. I love finding shells and rocks on the beach and seeing the seals. The sunsets here are really nice, too.

Becky Guptill loves living in Waldport along the coast of the Pacific Ocean. In this chapter you will read more about living on the coast. You will also read about living in Oregon's other regions.

1 The Oregon Coast

Key Vocabulary

temperature
precipitation
mouth
harbor

Key Places

Astoria
Cannon Beach
Tillamook
Florence

Sea Lion Caves
Coos Bay
Rogue River
Klamath Mountains
Oregon Caves

Read Aloud

The fog deepens the magic of the coast. It has a . . . beauty that takes hold of you. When I see fog and mist, I know it's where I belong.

This is what one Oregonian had to say about his home—the coast. In this lesson you will read about the many special places that make this a region that is enchanting and beautiful.

Read for Purpose

1. WHAT YOU KNOW: What is the name of the ocean that borders the Oregon Coast?
2. WHAT YOU WILL LEARN: What are the natural features of the Oregon Coast?

WELCOME TO THE COAST

Did you know that everyone is welcome to visit any part of Oregon's 300-mile (483-km) coast? Our coast is such a special place that our state government passed a law that made the Oregon beaches open to the public.

Our coast is bordered by mountains on one side and by the Pacific Ocean on the other. These mountains are the Coast Range, and they were once heavily covered with forests. Some mountains of the Coast Range have rocky cliffs that extend down to the sea. Others are located

THE OREGON COAST

• City
■ Point of interest

MAP SKILL: What is the name of the group of mountains found in the southern part of the Oregon Coast?

farther back from the sea behind a strip of flat land. Towns have been built on some of these strips of land. You can locate the Coast Range on the map of the Oregon Coast on this page.

Between the cliffs are sandy beaches. On many of these beaches are large rocks that stand alone. Waves crash against these rocks, wearing them down and sending up clouds of ocean spray.

OUR COAST'S CLIMATE

The weather along the coast may be sunny, or rainy, or misty and gray. But it is seldom very hot, and it almost never snows. Since Oregon is located approximately halfway between the equator and the North Pole, its climate is generally mild.

The climate of the Oregon Coast is influenced by the ocean. The ocean has an affect on **temperature** (tem′ pər ə chər), or how hot or cold a place is.

In the summer ocean waters heat up more slowly than the land does. In the winter ocean waters cool off more slowly than the land does. This means that ocean breezes have a cooling effect on coastal lands in the summer. In the winter they have a warming effect on these lands. In January the average temperature is a mild 45°F. (7°C). In July the average temperature is only 60°F. (16°C).

When we examine the climate of the coast, we also examine its precipitation (pri sip i tā' shən). Precipitation is any form of water that falls to earth, such as rain, sleet, hail, or snow. As the sun heats the ocean, water evaporates (i vap' ə rāts)—or passes into the air in tiny drops called water vapor.

The air near the earth is warm. This warm air picks up the tiny water vapor drops and rises. As the warm air rises, it cools. Cool air cannot hold as much water as warm air so the water falls to the earth as rain. If the air is cold enough, the water freezes into snow, sleet, or hail. Along our coast almost all the precipitation is rain. Some places on the coast get more than 100 inches (254 cm) of rain a year. That is over 9 feet (3 m), which is higher than most classroom ceilings!

A TRIP ALONG THE COAST

Imagine that it is a clear autumn day—just the right kind of day for a trip down the coast! One way to visit our coast is to follow an old trail that is now Highway 101.

In Chapter 1 you read about the Columbia River, which forms most of the northern border of our state. Let's start our trip at the river's mouth, where the Columbia meets the Pacific Ocean. The mouth of a river is a place where the river empties into a large body of water. The mouth of the Columbia looks almost like a lake because it is 7 miles (11 km) wide.

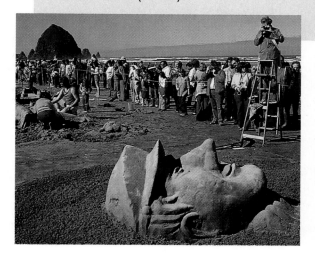

Cannon Beach is a popular place for many activities, such as the yearly sand castle contest (below).

Locate the mouth of the Columbia on the map on page 36. The city of Astoria is located here. Astoria has a harbor. A harbor is a place along a coastline where ships can dock safely.

Just over 20 miles (32 km) down the coast from Astoria is Cannon Beach. Here, without the protection of a harbor, the coast is rugged. Many people enjoy walking on the beach, collecting shells and admiring the strange rocks that jut out of the ocean.

This magnificent statue of a sea lion family sits at the entrance of the Sea Lion Caves.

About 50 miles (80 km) down the coast from Cannon Beach is the city of **Tillamook** (til' ə mək). Tillamook is known for its cheese. It is the largest dairy center in our state.

South of Tillamook, near the city of **Florence**, the ocean has carved out huge caves in some places. Just outside of Florence are the **Sea Lion Caves**. There sea lions swim in the ocean water that washes through the caves. From the cliffs off the side of Highway 101, elevators take visitors down almost 300 feet (90 m) to the edge of the sea. There people can watch the sea lions frolicking on the rocks or taking naps in the afternoon sun.

Farther south of the city of Florence is a long stretch of dunes. These dunes are piles of sand as large as hills. People can explore this area by riding in dune buggies or, in one park, by riding on camels!

Farther south of the dunes is the largest city of the Oregon Coast— **Coos** (küs) **Bay**. It is one of the world's largest centers for the shipping of forest products.

Several rivers, such as the **Rogue** (rōg) **River**, flow from the Coast Range to the ocean. The Rogue River, in the southwestern part of our state, is famous for boating, fishing, and white-water rafting. At the southern end of the Coast Range are the **Klamath** (klam' əth) **Mountains**, which are steep and covered with trees. Here you can visit the **Oregon Caves** and see their many unusual rock formations and underground streams.

OUR COAST

As you have just read, the Oregon Coast has something for everyone. Yet our coast is just one of the beautiful regions of our state. As you read the rest of this chapter, you will learn that our state has other special places with much to offer.

 Check Your Reading

1. Which natural feature do most of the cities on the coast share?
2. What is Coos Bay known for?
3. Name three activities offered by the Oregon Coast.
4. **GEOGRAPHY SKILL:** Look at the map on page 36. About how many miles (km) is Cannon Beach from Florence?
5. **THINKING SKILL:** Compare and contrast Astoria with Cannon Beach.

2 The Willamette Valley

READ TO LEARN

Key Vocabulary

tributary
transportation

Key Places

Willamette River   Corvallis
Portland   Eugene
Salem   Springfield
Albany

Read Aloud

There are so many things in the Willamette Valley that it is sometimes called the storehouse for our state. A storehouse is a building in which things are kept. In this lesson you will read about the many features of the Willamette Valley.

Read for Purpose

1. **WHAT YOU KNOW:** Which river forms much of Oregon's northern border?
2. **WHAT YOU WILL LEARN:** Which landform is located just east of the Coast Range, and why is it important?

WELCOME TO THE WILLAMETTE VALLEY

In the last lesson we toured the coast. We started our trip at the mouth of the Columbia River and headed south. Suppose that we went back to the river's mouth and traveled east up the Columbia River. What would we find? We would follow the broad Columbia River through the Coast Range, where we would see hillsides blanketed with trees and also many streams.

After more than 100 miles (160 km), we would come to the mouth of the Willamette River. The Willamette River is an important tributary (trib′ yə ter ē) of the Columbia. A tributary is a river or stream that flows into a larger river.

The Willamette River lies between the Coast Range and the Cascade Mountains. This river's northern boundary is the Columbia River. Where the Cascades and the Coast Range meet is the Willamette Val-

39

MAP SKILL: Which tributary of the Willamette flows north of Springfield?

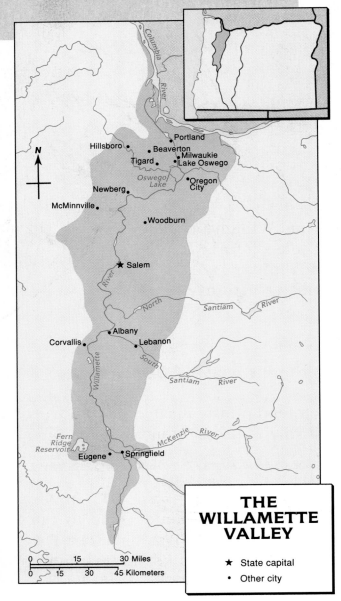

THE
WILLAMETTE
VALLEY

★ State capital
• Other city

0   15   30 Miles
0   15   30   45 Kilometers

A RICH VALLEY

People are attracted to the land of the Willamette Valley because it is neither very flat nor very mountainous. The rolling land and rich soil here are excellent for farming.

The climate of the Willamette Valley is another reason that so many people live here. As you read in Lesson 1, Oregon is located approximately halfway between the equator and the North Pole. Thus, the climate of our state is neither very hot nor very cold. Also, the ocean winds warm the Willamette Valley in winter and cool it in summer. As they blow across the Coast Range, the winds lose part of their moisture, but they still have enough to bring the valley from 30 to 60 inches (76 to 152 cm) of rain each year. During the winter and early spring a light rain falls nearly every day. This is comfortable enough for most people, and just the right amount of rain for many crops.

PORTLAND AND OTHER CITIES

The Willamette Valley is the location of our state's major cities. Look at the map on this page and find **Portland**. Portland is the largest city in Oregon.

Portland's good **transportation** (trans pər tā' shən) helped it to grow. Transportation is a way to move goods and people from one place to another. Portland is close

ley's southern boundary. Find the Willamette River and its boundaries on the map above.

The Willamette Valley is not very large; however, about two thirds of the people of our state live there. Let's find out why.

40

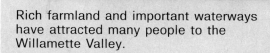

Rich farmland and important waterways have attracted many people to the Willamette Valley.

to the place where the Willamette River joins the Columbia River. As you read in the last lesson, the Columbia River flows into the Pacific Ocean. Portland's location along important waterways has helped it to become one of the largest business centers of our state. The Port of Portland welcomes ships from all over the world.

One of the state's large universities, Portland State University, is here. Several smaller colleges are also located in Portland. The other large cities of the Willamette Valley are **Salem**, **Albany**, **Corvallis** (kôr val′ əs), **Eugene** (ū jēn′), and **Springfield**. All are located on the banks of the Willamette River. Salem, the capital of Oregon, is where our state laws are made. Corvallis and Eugene are each home to large state universities. You will read more about our state government later on.

THE STOREHOUSE

Now you know why the Willamette Valley is called Oregon's storehouse. As you read on, you will find the other regions of our state are also rich in resources.

 Check Your Reading

1. What is Oregon's largest city?
2. Why does the Willamette Valley have such a mild climate?
3. Why do so many people make the Willamette Valley their home?
4. **GEOGRAPHY SKILL:** Which natural features form the boundaries of the Willamette Valley?
5. **THINKING SKILL:** Compare and contrast the Oregon Coast and the Willamette Valley.

Understanding Latitude and Longitude

Key Vocabulary

latitude   degree   prime meridian
longitude   meridian   grid
parallel

Look at the two sets of lines that cover the map on the next page. The lines that run east and west are called lines of **latitude**. The lines that run north and south are called lines of **longitude**. Together latitude and longitude can be used to help you locate places on the earth.

Using Latitude

Look at the lines of latitude below. Lines of latitude are also called **parallels**. Lines of latitude are always parallel, or the same distance apart.

Look at the equator on the globe below. It is labeled 0°. We call this zero **degrees**. A degree is a unit of measurement for latitude and longitude. The symbol ° stands for degrees. Latitudes north of the equator are labeled *N*. Those south of the equator are labeled *S*.

Using Longitude

Look at the lines of longitude, or **meridians**, on the globe below. The starting line for measuring longitude is

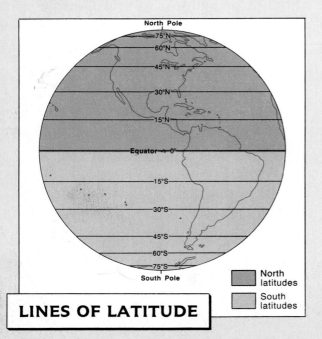

LINES OF LATITUDE

North latitudes
South latitudes

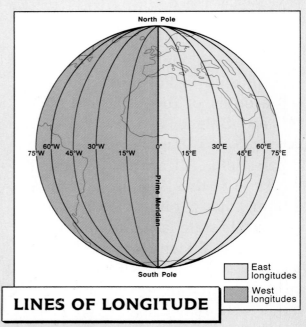

LINES OF LONGITUDE

East longitudes
West longitudes

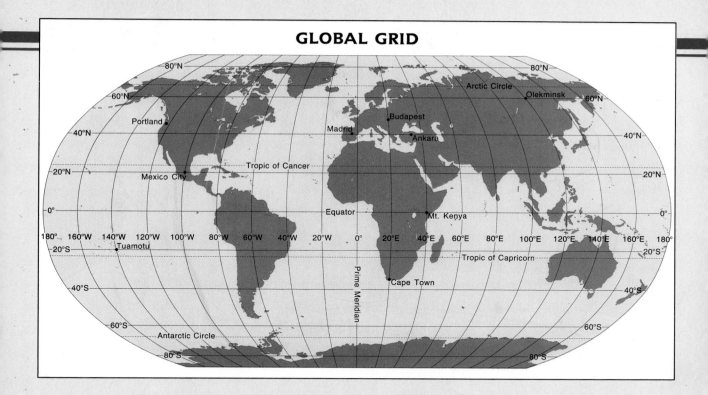

GLOBAL GRID

the **prime meridian**. The longitude of the prime meridian is 0°. Meridians west of the prime meridian are labeled *W*. Those east of the prime meridian are labeled *E*.

All meridians meet at the South Pole and the North Pole. Meridians are farthest apart at the equator. Distances between meridians become smaller as you move from the equator toward the poles.

Finding Places on a Map

Lines of latitude and longitude form a **grid**. A grid is a set of crisscrossing lines. On a map a grid makes it easy to find any place in the world if you know its latitude and longitude. For example, the location of Mexico City can be given as 20°N, 100°W. To find Mexico City on the map above, first put your finger on the point where the equator and the prime meridian cross. Now move your finger north to the 20°N parallel. Next move your finger west along this parallel to the point where it crosses the meridian labeled 100°W. Did you find Mexico City?

Reviewing the Skill

1. What are lines of latitude and longitude? What do they help you do?
2. Which city on the map is directly south of Budapest? Which latitude is it near?
3. Which city shown on the map is located at 60°N latitude, 120°E longitude?
4. To the nearest degree, what is the latitude and longitude of Portland?
5. Why is it important to understand latitude and longitude?

43

3 The Cascades

READ TO LEARN

Key Vocabulary
locks
irrigation

Key Places
Bonneville Dam
Hood River
Mount Hood

Mount Jefferson
Three Sisters
Three Fingered Jack

Read Aloud

Climb the mountains and get their good tidings. Nature's peace will flow into you as sunshine flows into trees. The winds will blow their own freshness into you, and the storms their energy, while cares will drop off like autumn leaves.

John Muir, who wrote these words, spent his life trying to save the beauty of our western mountains. Like Muir, the people who visit the mountains of the Cascades are struck by their beauty.

Read for Purpose

1. **WHAT YOU KNOW:** Which regions of our state are located west of the Cascades?
2. **WHAT YOU WILL LEARN:** What do the Cascades look like, and why are they important?

THE COLUMBIA RIVER GORGE

Let's continue our trip up the Columbia River. At first the river is broad and smooth, but it soon becomes hazardous rapids as it passes through the Cascade Mountains. People called these rapids "the cascades." Find the mountains on the map on page 45. The mountains soon began to be called by the same name.

Locks were built so that ships could travel around these rapids. Locks are narrow, concrete passages, like canals. Their water level can be raised or lowered, so boats can go through the locks and around rapids or waterfalls.

In the late 1930s **Bonneville Dam** was built just below the rapids. This great dam along the Columbia River raised the level of the river so much that the water has become smooth. Bonneville Dam is also an important source of water power for producing electricity and providing **irrigation** (ir i gā′ shən) for the Northwest. Irrigation is the watering of dry land by means of canals, ditches, or pipes.

In Chapter 1 you read about how Ice Age floods carved their way through the Cascades, forming the Columbia River Gorge. The Columbia River flows through the gorge for about 70 miles (113 km). Here there are rugged cliffs and forests, and waterfalls that thunder into cold, deep pools.

One part of the gorge, near the town of **Hood River**, is a center for wind surfing. All summer wind surfers scoot over the water, holding fast to their brightly colored sails.

People come from miles around to hike the trails that wind up the slopes of the gorge. Along the trails they stop to admire waterfalls.

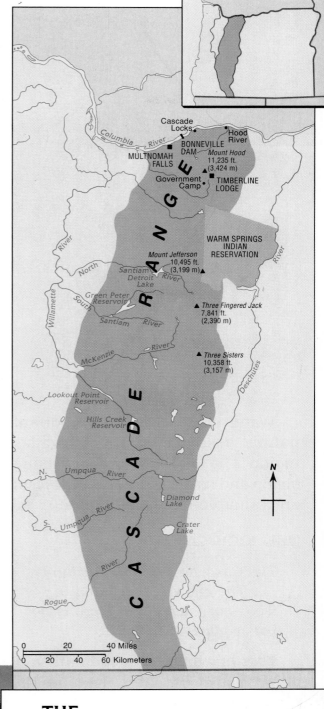

THE CASCADES

- • City
- ◢ Dam
- ▲ Mountain peak
- ■ Point of interest

MAP SKILL: What important dam, pictured at left, is found at the northern tip of the Cascades along the Columbia River?

Mount Hood, Oregon's highest peak, is a popular mountain for skiing.

Water is not the only important natural resource of the Cascades region. The land is suited for raising sheep and cattle. Pine and fir forests are valuable for their lumber.

THE HIGH CASCADES

The Cascades are tough country. . . . The snow is measured in feet—not inches. But there is no better place to live.

This is what one Oregonian said about the Cascades. Looking at Mount Hood, it is easy to understand why many Oregonians love the Cascades. During the summer ski teams come here to practice. Although Mount Hood's peak is covered with snow, there are spots that

are too hot to touch. The reason is that Mount Hood is a volcano. In fact, it may have erupted only a little over 100 years ago.

Some other interesting peaks are also found in the Cascade Range. Mount Jefferson is second in height to Mount Hood. The Three Sisters got their name because they are three mountains that are close together. Three Fingered Jack got its name because of its jagged top, which has three peaks.

A LAND OF PLENTY

In this lesson you have read about the treasures the Cascades hold. These mountains are valued for their beauty and rich natural resources. In the next lesson you will read about how these mountains greatly influence the climate of the eastern part of our state.

 Check Your Reading

1. How did the Cascade Mountains get their name?
2. What is the Bonneville Dam used for?
3. Name three natural resources found in the Cascades region.
4. **GEOGRAPHY SKILL:** Look at the map on page 45. Name the mountains that are higher than 10,000 feet (3,048 m).
5. **THINKING SKILL:** Classify the natural resources of the Cascades into three groups.

46

4 Eastern Oregon

READ TO LEARN

■ Key Vocabulary

rain shadow
canyon

Key Places

Pendleton
Newberry Crater
Bend

Alvord Desert
Klamath Lake

■ Read Aloud

The land east of the Cascades is different from the other parts of the state. It is cowboy land, wheat land, the land where the astronauts came to get ready for their trip to the moon. Here you can hunt and fish, look for fossils, or hike through mountains. Eastern Oregon has much to offer.

This is how one Oregon writer describes the eastern part of our state. In this lesson you will read about the ways in which the Cascade Mountains make the climate and land of this region altogether different from that of the western regions of our state.

■ Read for Purpose

1. **WHAT YOU KNOW:** What important natural resources are found in the Cascades?
2. **WHAT YOU WILL LEARN:** What is Oregon like to the east of the Cascades?

RAIN SHADOW

In Lesson 1 you read that air moving over the ocean picks up water vapor. This water vapor forms into clouds. Warm winds carry these clouds toward land. The diagram on page 48 shows that as the winds push the clouds up the side of the mountain, the clouds cool. Cool air cannot hold as much moisture as warm air. This means that clouds drop most of their moisture on one side of the mountain as rain or snow. When the clouds move

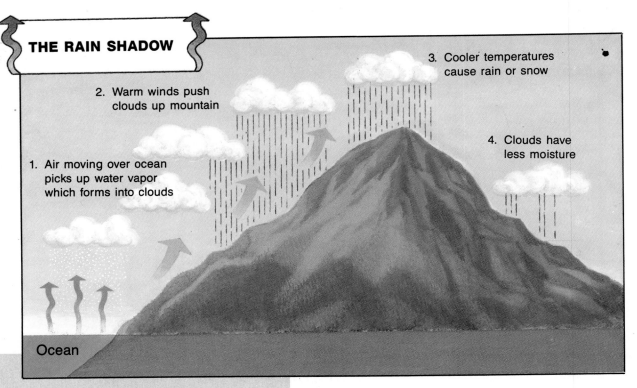

THE RAIN SHADOW

2. Warm winds push clouds up mountain

3. Cooler temperatures cause rain or snow

1. Air moving over ocean picks up water vapor which forms into clouds

4. Clouds have less moisture

Ocean

DIAGRAM SKILL: What causes rain and snow to form? Why does more rain fall on one side of the mountain?

over the other side of the mountain, little moisture remains. This drier side of the mountain is said to lie in the rain shadow.

The Coast Range mountains receive moisture from clouds that come off the Pacific Ocean. The Cascades also receive moisture from these clouds, leaving less wetness for the land on the other side.

The Cascades can be thought of as a high fence dividing Oregon in two. The west side has plenty of rain. But the east side is in the rain shadow of the mountains. If you drive through the Cascades you can see this change. On the west side

you ride through green forests of short-needled fir trees. Higher up, the forests have long-needled ponderosa pines, trees with reddish bark. On the other side there are fewer and fewer trees until you reach an area of brown hills.

The map on page 49 shows you what Eastern Oregon looks like and how it can be divided into two main parts: the Columbia Plateau and the desert. The desert is actually called the "high" desert because most of the land has an elevation of more than 4,000 feet (1,219 m). The height of a place above sea level has an effect on its climate. The greater the elevation, the colder the temperature becomes. Because of the colder temperatures there is more

48

plant and animal life in high deserts than there is in deserts at or below sea level.

THE COLUMBIA PLATEAU

As you read in Chapter 1, the Columbia Plateau covers most of the northern part of Eastern Oregon. Crossed by **canyons** (kan' yənz), or deep, narrow valleys with steep sides, the plateau lies over layers of lava that flowed out of the earth long ago.

The Columbia Plateau has hot summers, but the winters are cold. Dotting the plateau are many ranches on which wheat and cattle are raised. Since there is only a small amount of rainfall in this area, each wheat field is planted only every other year in order to store up moisture in the soil. Cattle graze on land that is too dry for the growing of wheat. If land is near a river, water can be brought to it through irrigation.

The Columbia Plateau is cowboy country. Many of the people here ride horses over the hills and know how to rope a cow. One of the largest rodeos in the nation is held in the town of **Pendleton**.

Some parts of the plateau are rocky and rough. **Newberry Crater**, near the city of **Bend**, is a volcano that erupted years ago. The explosion left a crater of jagged, hardened lava and domes of hard, glassy, black rock called obsidian

(ob sid' ē ən). Obsidian is so sharp that it tears hikers' boots. When astronauts were training to go to the moon, they went to Newberry Crater because scientists thought the surface of the land might be something like that of the moon.

THE BLUE MOUNTAINS

Eastern Oregon also has the high Blue Mountains, which are cool in summer and snowy in winter. Many

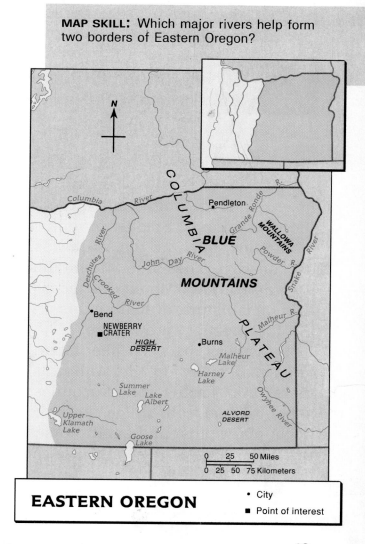

MAP SKILL: Which major rivers help form two borders of Eastern Oregon?

EASTERN OREGON
- City
- Point of interest

Lizards are well suited to the hot, dry climate of the Alvord Desert.

THE HIGH DESERT

The high desert in the southeast is even drier than the land of the Columbia Plateau. Although wheat doesn't grow here, the land has enough food for cattle. Alvord Desert in this area is probably the hottest and driest part of our state. As the manager of a nearby cattle ranch joked: "We get rainstorms now and then. Had a 10 incher last month. Between drops." In fact this area rarely gets 10 inches of rain in an entire year. Temperatures in the high desert area range from a biting −35°F. (−37°C) to a blistering 107°F. (42°C).

lakes and streams run through these mountains. Smaller groups of mountains, such as the Wallowas, are nearby. The Blue Mountains and the Wallowa Mountains receive enough moisture, even from this dry air, for forests to grow there.

In valleys between the mountains that make up the Wallowas, there are fossils of crocodiles; saber-toothed cats; huge, bearlike dogs; giant pigs; and small horses that had three toes instead of hooves. These animals lived in these valleys long ago when the area was hot and damp.

Owls, antelope, and coyotes are animals found on the high desert.

Not many people live in the high desert, but those who do live mostly on ranches. These people love the clear air and the silence. They also love the immense sky and the views of rugged rocks and mountains.

Valleys between the mountains hold shallow lakes. Birds stop on lakes, such as Klamath Lake, to rest on their long flights north or south. A flock of birds may be so large that it looks like a dark cloud crossing the sky. There are rivers, too, but they don't run to the sea. Instead, they flow into the lakes, or dry up.

The animals of the high desert include jackrabbits, lizards, coyotes, owls, and antelope. They know how to live in the dry desert climate and find food.

OUR STATE'S BEAUTIFUL LAND

Now you have read about what the four regions of our state are like. As you read the next chapter, you will learn about the people who first lived in our state.

Check Your Reading

1. Name the two main parts of Eastern Oregon.
2. Describe how the rain shadow affects the climate of Eastern Oregon.
3. Imagine that you have a pen pal in another state. How would you describe your life on a cattle ranch in the high desert?
4. **GEOGRAPHY SKILL:** What change in the types of trees do we see when we cross the Cascades? Why?
5. **THINKING SKILL:** List three ways in which Eastern Oregon is different from the western regions of our state.

51

Oregon Traditions

READ TO LEARN

📋 **Key Vocabulary**

rapids

📋 **Read for Purpose**

1. **WHAT YOU KNOW:** What are the natural resources of the Cascade Mountains?
2. **WHAT YOU WILL LEARN:** How does the Klickitat Indian legend explain the location of three Cascade mountain peaks?

THE BRIDGE OF THE GODS

As you have read, the Cascade Mountains overlook the Columbia River as it flows into the Pacific Ocean. On the Oregon side stands snowcapped Mount Hood. On the north side of the river, in Washington State, are Mount Adams and Mount St. Helens.

Thousands of years ago the Klickitat (kli′ kə tat) Indians, who lived near the Columbia River, thought of these mountains in a special way. To the Indians Mount Hood and Mount Adams were brothers, Wy'east (wī′ ēst) and Klickitat. Mount St. Helens was an old woman whom the Indians called Loo-Wit. She watched over the Bridge of the Gods, a huge stone arch that spanned the river. This is a story about the two brothers, the old woman, and the Bridge of the Gods.

WHEN MOUNTAINS MOVED

Wy'east and Klickitat fell in love with the same beautiful girl. They both came to see her. Klickitat came from the north. Wy'east came from the south. They met at the Bridge of the Gods. Each brother knew where the other was going, and their tempers flared.

Soon the brothers were roaring and stamping hard enough to shake the earth. Their anger grew so hot that they spit fire. Columns of smoke poured from their mouths.

Then Wy'east hurled a huge stone across the river at his brother. Klickitat picked up the rock and threw it back. Within minutes enormous boulders came flying through the air. Some fell on land, tearing up the earth. Others splashed into the river, causing huge waves. Still others struck the Bridge of the Gods.

Loo-Wit, the old woman who guarded the bridge, cried out, "Stop this quarrel! Put down those rocks before you destroy the bridge!"

But it was too late. With a grinding roar, the Bridge of the Gods fell into the river, taking Loo-Wit with it.

Frightened by what they had done, the brothers quickly returned home. The Bridge of the Gods sank beneath the water. Now only rushing rapids mark the spot where it had once stood. Rapids are parts of a river where the water flows swiftly.

Even the Great Spirit heard the noise of the quarrel. He came down and looked sadly at what little remained of the bridge he had made. He heard a cry from the river. Loo-Wit was clinging to a rock in the middle of the rapids! Quickly he pulled her out and dried her tears.

"The bridge is destroyed, but it is not your fault. You tried to stop the quarrel. As your reward, make any wish and I will grant it."

"I wish to be young again," Loo-Wit said. "O Great Spirit, give me the form of a young woman." So the Great Spirit gave Loo-Wit the form of a beautiful young girl. But Loo-Wit had forgotten to ask for the spirit of a young girl, so she remained old at heart. Games and dances were not for her. She cared nothing for the handsome young men who came seeking her love. Her wish had been fulfilled, but she found no happiness.

And so, sadly, she moved far to the west, away from the other mountains. There she stands to this day, Loo-Wit, or Mount St. Helens, still beautiful and distant among the Cascades. When Mount St. Helens erupts, sometimes people say it is Loo-Wit weeping.

Check Your Reading

1. How did Wy'east and Klickitat show their anger?
2. How did the Great Spirit reward Loo-Wit?
3. What do Mount Hood, Mount Adams, and Mount St. Helens have in common?
4. What natural disaster could have caused the Indians to tell the legend of the Bridge of the Gods?
5. THINKING SKILL: Predict how the Cascade Range might look today if Loo-Wit had become young at heart.

REVIEWING VOCABULARY

harbor
irrigation
mouth
rain shadow
tributary

Number a sheet of paper from 1 to 5. Beside each number write the word or term from the list above that best completes the sentence.

1. The smaller of the rivers was a ____ that flowed into the larger river.
2. The farmers used ____ to bring water to their crops.
3. The ships sailed into the ____ where they would unload their cargoes.
4. The ____ of the river is the place where it meets the sea.
5. There is less rain each year in the ____ than on the other side of the mountain.

REVIEWING FACTS

Number a sheet of paper from 1 to 10. Beside each number write the name of the region of Oregon that is described by the item.

1. harbor at Astoria
2. Columbia Plateau
3. where astronauts trained for the moon walk
4. Portland
5. Hood River windsurfing
6. Sea Lion Caves
7. cowboy country
8. Willamette River
9. Bonneville Dam
10. desert

WRITING ABOUT MAIN IDEAS

1. **Writing a Poem:** Write a poem (or the words to a song) about one of our state's regions or about one special feature of a region. The poem should tell something about what the region or feature looks like. It should also capture some of your feelings about the place.
2. **Writing a Puzzle:** Make up a crossword puzzle using important places and terms mentioned in this chapter. Based on definitions used in the text, write a clue for each word Across and each word Down.

BUILDING SKILLS: UNDERSTANDING LATITUDE AND LONGITUDE

1. What steps would you follow to find a place when you know its latitude and longitude?
2. Look closely at the map on page 43. Name two cities on the map that have the same latitude.
3. Which place is located at 20°S latitude, 140°W longitude?

REVIEWING VOCABULARY

Number a sheet of paper from 1 to 10. Beside each number write **C** if the underlined word is used correctly. If it is not, write the word that would correctly complete the sentence.

1. There is less rain in Eastern Oregon because of the <u>rain shadow</u>.
2. <u>Geography</u> is the study of the earth's land, water, plants, and animals.
3. The Willamette River is a <u>tributary</u> of the Columbia River.
4. Plateaus, mountains, and hills are examples of <u>natural resources</u>.
5. The <u>climate</u> is rainy, so take your umbrella when you go on vacation.
6. A <u>landform</u> is a large area with common features.
7. Ships can safely dock in a <u>harbor</u>.
8. Rain, sleet, and snow are examples of <u>irrigation</u>.
9. A <u>mouth</u> is a river or stream that flows into a larger river.
10. The coast is a <u>region</u> of Oregon.

✎ WRITING ABOUT THE UNIT

1. **Writing a Description:** Choose one region of Oregon and list its main features. Include its natural features and other interesting items about the region. Then write a description of the region.

2. **Writing a Newspaper Article:** Imagine that you lived long ago when Oregon's natural features were first developing. Choose an event from that time, such as the volcanic eruption that made Crater Lake possible or the flood that created the Columbia River Gorge. Write a newspaper article describing the event.

3. **Writing a Newspaper Ad:** Choose one region of Oregon. Write a newspaper ad that would make people want to visit that region. Think of a catchy slogan to use in the ad. Describe any pictures that you might want to include.

ACTIVITIES

1. **Designing a Flag:** Each state in the United States has its own flag. The design of each flag has a special meaning that is related to the history or geography of the state. Perhaps each region in Oregon should have a flag. Design a flag for a region of our state. Then write a few sentences explaining why you designed it as you did.

2. **Planning a Trip:** Plan a vacation trip to a region of Oregon other than the one in which you live. Use a road map to plan the route, or contact a bus company to see how you would get there by bus. Develop an itinerary, or list of places you will

visit, and decide how long you will stay in each place. Then imagine that you actually took the trip. Write a descriptive short story about the places you visited.

3. **Working Together to Make a Chart:** On the chalkboard make a class chart about Oregon based on the information in Unit 1. Make four columns—one for each region. Down the left-hand side of the chart, label rows with categories such as major landforms, bodies of water, cities, climate, places of interest, and so on. Work together to fill in the chart.

BUILDING SKILLS: UNDERSTANDING LATITUDE AND LONGITUDE

1. What are latitude and longitude?
2. Use the map on pages 270–271 to answer these questions. What is one line of longitude that goes through Oregon? What is one line of latitude that goes through Nevada?
3. Describe the exact location of New Orleans, Louisiana, by giving its latitude and longitude.
4. Which city is the nearest to 40°N latitude, 90°W longitude?
5. What do the lines of latitude and longitude on a map help you to do?

LINKING PAST, PRESENT, AND FUTURE

Take a minute to flip through the pictures in this unit. They show what a truly beautiful state we live in. Many of the natural sights in Oregon were formed millions of years ago by water, ice, and fire. These sights are still here for us to enjoy today. Will they still be as beautiful in the future? How can the people of Oregon make sure that their natural surroundings are protected for the future? What can the government do? What can you do?

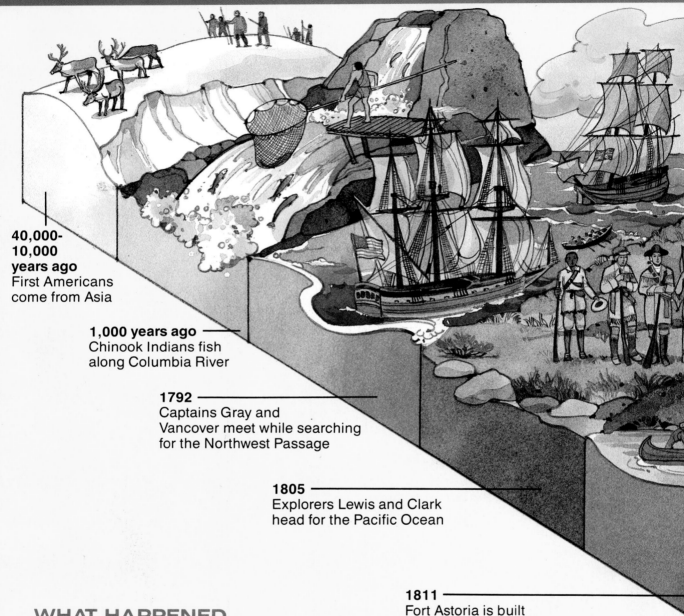

**40,000-
10,000
years ago**
First Americans
come from Asia

1,000 years ago —
Chinook Indians fish
along Columbia River

1792 —
Captains Gray and
Vancover meet while searching
for the Northwest Passage

1805 —
Explorers Lewis and Clark
head for the Pacific Ocean

1811 —
Fort Astoria is built

1824 —
The Hudson's Bay
Company opens the
Fort Vancouver
trading post

WHAT HAPPENED

The story of our state
reaches far back into the past,
and stretches far into the future.
The early part of it is the story of
Native Americans, explorers, fur trappers,
and traders. In this unit you will read about
the people who helped to settle Oregon long ago.

58

UNIT 2

EARLY OREGON HISTORY

CHAPTER 3

OREGON'S FIRST PEOPLE

FOCUS

I like being an Indian. I enjoy dancing the hoop dance at the powwows. I get to use nine hoops because I am nine years old.

Michael Tailfeathers lives on the Warm Springs Reservation. His Indian name is Old Man Eagle, which means "wise beyond his years." In this chapter you will read about the ways of life of Oregon's early Indian people.

1 Early Indians

READ TO LEARN

Key Vocabulary
migrate
artifacts
archaeologists

Key Places
Bering Strait
Beringia
Fort Rock

Read Aloud

Storms and snow, freezing nights, and days of fog and mist may have discouraged those early hunters. Furthermore, these [early people] did not know where they were going. They had no advance scouts . . . to tell them about the great prairies where their descendants would someday hunt [buffalo].

This is what one writer said about the first people to come to North America. Let's find out who these people were and how they got here.

Read for Purpose

1. **WHAT YOU KNOW:** What are some natural resources that are important to the way you live?
2. **WHAT YOU WILL LEARN:** Who were the first people to live in Oregon, and where did they come from?

A LAND WITH NO PEOPLE

When the last Ice Age began more than 70,000 years ago, many plants and animals lived on the land of present-day Oregon. But no people lived here. No men or women fished in the streams or hunted in the forests. The only human beings on earth lived on the continents of Europe, Asia, and Africa. Use the Atlas map on page 266 to locate these places. The oceans separate Europe, Asia, and Africa from the continent of North America, where we live. In this lesson you will read about how early people from Asia reached our continent.

At this Oregon site archaeologists search for clues about the past.

THE LAND BRIDGE

In Chapter 1 you read about the Ice Age. During the Ice Age so much water was frozen in glaciers that the water levels of the oceans became much lower. Places once covered by shallow seas became dry land.

Find the Bering Strait on the Atlas map on page 272. It is the narrow waterway between Asia and North America. When the water levels of the oceans dropped during the Ice Age, the floor of the Bering Strait became dry land. This dry land formed a wide land bridge that connected Asia and North America. Today scientists have named that land bridge that existed long ago Beringia (ber' ən gē ə).

Beringia was a wide plain. As herds of animals moved here to graze on grasses, they were followed by people from Asia. Hunters in fur robes may have crossed the land bridge first, carrying stone-tipped spears. Or families may have lived on the bridge, moving from one hill or valley to the next. People crossed this land bridge to migrate into North America. Migrate means to move from one country to another in order to settle there. These wandering hunters, who came to North America perhaps as long as 25,000 years ago, were the first Americans. These people from Asia were the ancestors of the American Indians.

EARLY PEOPLE IN OREGON

We know something about the lives of these first Americans because of their artifacts (är' tə fakts). Artifacts are objects left behind by people who lived long ago. Scientists who search for and study artifacts are called archaeologists (är kē ol' ə jists). These scientists look for places where people may have once lived. There, archaeologists dig very carefully, looking for signs of early people.

Sandals over 9,000 years old, made from sagebrush that grows around Fort Rock (*above*), were found in a cave.

From artifacts, such as spearheads and bits of bone, archaeologists have learned a lot about the Asians who crossed Beringia. They were hunters who used fire. They could work stone and bone into tools, such as knives and spears.

AN IMPORTANT DISCOVERY

Archaeologists made an important discovery in 1938 about the early people who lived in what is now Oregon. At Fort Rock in the high desert area of Eastern Oregon, they found more than 70 sandals made out of sagebrush. The sandals were in the back of a cave, buried by volcanic ash from the eruption of Mount Mazama. The archaeologists who examined the sandals found that they were more than 9,000 years old. This discovery proved that people had lived in the area of present-day Oregon at least 9,000 years ago.

A LAND WITH PEOPLE

No one knows exactly when the people from Asia who crossed Beringia first made their way to what is now Oregon. We do know that people have been here for at least 9,000 years. In the next lesson you will read about the ways of life of these early people who lived in different areas of our state.

Check Your Reading

1. How did the early people from Asia cross into North America?
2. Why was the discovery of sandals at Fort Rock important?
3. **GEOGRAPHY SKILL:** On the Atlas map on page 272, trace one route the people from Asia might have taken to reach the land of present-day Oregon.
4. **THINKING SKILL:** Look at the photographs on this page. How did early people use the environment to provide for their needs?

Decision Making

Key Vocabulary
decision

Imagine that you are having a test tomorrow on the early Indians of Oregon. You want to get a high score to improve your grade. You can study in the afternoon when you come home from school. Or you can play with your friends and then study after dinner.

You need to make a **decision** about what to do. Making a decision is the same thing as making a choice.

Trying the Skill
Imagine that you are an adult and that you live in a state other than Oregon. You have a job that you like, but you get an offer for a job in Oregon that you really want. Your goal is to find a happy life for yourself. You need to decide whether to move to Oregon. Listed below are some things that might happen as a result of each decision. Consider the following items and then make a decision.

- You can have a job in Oregon that you really want.
- You like the job you have now.
- Oregon is a fun and interesting place to live.
- You have many friends in the state where you live now, and you do not know many people in Oregon.

1. What is your decision?
2. What did you do to make this decision?

HELPING YOURSELF

The steps on the left will help you to make good decisions. The example on the right shows one way you might make a decision about moving to Oregon.

One Way to Make a Decision	Example
1. State your goal, or what it is you want to do.	Your goal is to find a happy life for yourself.
2. Identify some things you could do to reach your goal.	You could decide to move to Oregon or to stay where you live now.
3. Identify what might happen as a result of each choice.	You like the job you have now, but in Oregon you will be able to do something you really want to do.
4. Choose the action that is most likely to help you reach your goal.	You decide to move to Oregon.

Applying the Skill

Now apply what you have learned. Imagine that your goal is to improve life in your town. One way to make things better is to run for mayor. If you run, you will have to spend a lot of time and money on your campaign. If you win, you will have to quit your job. But you will also have the chance to make your town a better place to live. If you decide not to run, the current mayor will probably be elected again. You do not think the present mayor will improve the town.

Which decision will help you reach your goal? Answer these questions.

1. To make your decision, you should first:
   a. talk to your boss.
   b. think about your choices and the possible results of each.
   c. decide what is best for the town.

2. Your decision should help you to:
   a. reach your goal.
   b. make up your mind.
   c. win the election.

3. One reason to run for mayor is that:
   a. you do not like the present mayor.
   b. you do not like your job.
   c. if you win, you can make your town a better place.

Reviewing the Skill

1. What are some other words that mean *decision making*?
2. What steps could you follow to make a good decision?
3. Why is it important to make good decisions?

2 Indians of the Coast and River Valleys

READ TO LEARN

Key Vocabulary

environment
culture

Read Aloud

Every spring and summer huge numbers of fish moved in from the sea and crowded into the rivers and streams of the Pacific Coast. . . . It was said that you could almost walk across the rivers on the backs of the fish, they were so numerous. . . .

This is how one writer described the abundance of fish the early Indians found along the Pacific Coast. In this lesson you will read about how Indians along Oregon's coast, and along its western rivers and valleys, built a way of life by using their rich natural resources.

Read for Purpose

1. **WHAT YOU KNOW:** By which route did the early Indians come to North America?
2. **WHAT YOU WILL LEARN:** What were the ways of life of the Indians living west of the Cascades?

DIFFERENT WAYS OF LIFE

Oregon's Indians learned to live in many types of environments (en vī′ rən mənts). An environment includes the plants, animals, climate, and soil that make up an area. Because of differences in the land and how it was used, Oregon can be divided into six main Indian culture (kul′ chər) areas. A culture is a way of life of a group of people, including its customs, beliefs, and activities.

Look at the map on page 67 to find the names of the Oregon Indian groups that lived in each culture area. You will first read about three culture groups west of the Cas-

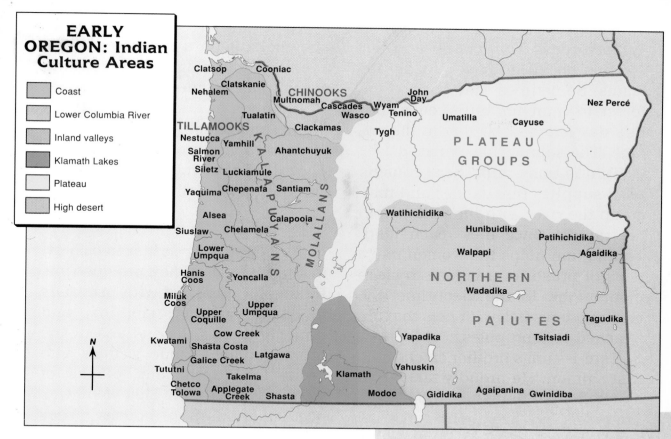

EARLY OREGON: Indian Culture Areas

Coast
Lower Columbia River
Inland valleys
Klamath Lakes
Plateau
High desert

Clatsop Cooniac
Clatskanie CHINOOKS
Nehalem Multnomah Cascades Wyam John Day
Tualatin Wasco Tenino Nez Percé
TILLAMOOKS Clackamas Tygh Umatilla Cayuse
Nestucca Yamhill Ahantchuyuk PLATEAU
Salmon River GROUPS
Siletz Luckiamule
Yaquima Chepenafa Santiam
Alsea Calapooia Watihichidika Hunibuidika Patihichidika
Siuslaw Chelamela Walpapi Agaidika
Lower Umpqua NORTHERN
Hanis Coos Yoncalla Wadadika
Miluk Coos PAIUTES Tagudika
Upper Coquille Upper Umpqua Yapadika Tsitsiadi
Kwatami Cow Creek
Shasta Costa Latgawa Yahuskin
Galice Creek Klamath
Tututni Takelma
Chetco Tolowa Applegate Creek Shasta Modoc Gididika Agaipanina Gwinidiba

MOLALLANS
KALAPUYANS

N

MAP SKILL: Which two groups of Indians lived in the Klamath Lakes culture area? In which culture area did the Clatsop Indians live?

cades—the Indians of the coast, of the lower Columbia River, and of the inland valleys.

Fishing, especially for salmon, was a way of life for the Indians of the coast and the lower Columbia River. At the same time each year, from spring through fall, millions of Chinook salmon swam in the rivers. During these "salmon runs" Indians used nets, traps, and spears to catch the swarms of fish. Salmon provided the main food of their diet.

Indians of the inland valleys also ate fish, but they depended more on plants as their main source of food. All three Indian cultures added variety to their diets by hunting animals such as deer and elk.

LIVING ON THE COAST

Let's read about an imaginary Indian family of long ago. Tsin-is-tum (sin' is təm) and her family are Tillamook (til' ə mək) Indians who live along the northern part of the Oregon coast.

Tsin-is-tum lives with her parents, brothers, and sisters in a house made of wooden planks. Her aunts, uncles, cousins, and grandparents all live in this house, too. The house is long—so long that each family group has its own fire.

67

Some days Tsin-is-tum and her cousins go to the beach to dig for clams. Sometimes they go into the forest to hunt for birds' eggs. But this day is a special day in the village. The salmon have arrived!

Tsin-is-tum and her cousins pack supplies into canoes and then go up the river with the villagers to the rapids. Once they reach land, Tsin-is-tum helps the women make tents of brush for everyone to sleep in at night. In the meantime, the men and boys fish with nets that are attached to long poles.

Tsin-is-tum's brother catches the first salmon. He proudly takes it to his mother so that she can clean it. After cleaning the salmon carefully, she cooks it on a rack over a fire. Everyone has a taste. The fishing season has begun!

In only a few days Tsin-is-tum's family has caught enough salmon to last them through the winter. They dry some fish on racks in the sun and smoke others over fires.

CEDAR RICH

Along the coast, cedar trees grew in thick forests. They provided the Indians of the coast with materials for their housing, clothing, and transportation. The Indians of the coast pounded stone wedges into cedar logs until long planks of wood were split off. This wood was used for building houses. They made canoes by hollowing out cedar logs. Cedar bark was used for clothing, mats, and blankets.

Tsin-is-tum and her relatives might have lived in a cedar long house similar to this one.

The Indian culture group on the lower Columbia River was known as the Chinook (shi nūk') Indians. The Chinooks were different from the Indians of the coast in that they traded for a living. They paddled their beautifully painted canoes up and down the Columbia River, trading salmon and whale oil.

Chinook people had foreheads that were broad and flat because as babies they spent most of their first year in a cradleboard. While the baby's head bones were still soft, the cradleboard set them in the shape that was desired without hurting the child.

A Chinook Indian woman holds her baby on a cradleboard.

INDIANS OF THE VALLEYS

The Indians of the various inland valleys, such as the Kalpuyans (kal pī' ənz) and the Molallans (mōl äl' ənz), lived too far away from the ocean to depend on fish as their main source of food. These Indians moved often in search of foods that were most important to them. They ate the roots of some plants and the bulbs of others. The women had the job of finding and gathering plants. The men were hunters. They made nets of woven grass to trap elk and deer.

The homes of the Indians of the inland valleys were built of planks and bark, with earth piled around the bottom to keep them warm. The Indians wore clothes made of grass and deerskin.

LIVING WELL

The mild climate and plentiful rainfall made the western part of Oregon a good place for the early Indians to live. In the next lesson you will read about the three Indian culture areas east of the Cascades.

 Check Your Reading

1. Why were the Chinook Indians able to become great traders?
2. Why did inland valley Indians have to move often?
3. **GEOGRAPHY SKILL:** Use the map on page 67 to name two groups of Indians who lived in each culture area west of the Cascades.
4. **THINKING SKILL:** Compare and contrast the ways of life of the Indian cultures west of the Cascades.

GRANDMA HOLT

Bertha Holt is the mother of 14 children, but to 55,000 children around the world she is known as Grandma Holt. For nearly 40 years Grandma Holt and her agency, Holt International, have been working to find families that want to adopt orphans, or children who have no parents.

It all began in 1954 when Bertha and her husband, Harry, saw a film about Korean children who became orphans because of the Korean War. They were saddened to see how many children were sick, hungry, homeless, and without families. The Holts wanted to help. First they sent money to take care of ten children. Then they decided to adopt eight children from Korea whom they brought to live with them and their six children on the Holt farm in Oregon.

But adopting eight children was just the beginning for Bertha and Harry Holt. Grandma Holt recalls, "Harry and I could not forget the tiny outstretched arms of orphans who needed to be a part of a family as much as our children needed to be." In 1956 the Holts began an adoption agency to help find homes for other orphans. Although Harry Holt died in 1964 during a trip to Korea, Bertha continued working for what they both believed in.

Today at age 85 Grandma Holt is still helping to make a difference in the lives of children. Her agency, Holt International, continues to find homes for children from around the world.

3 Indians of Eastern Oregon

READ TO LEARN

Key Vocabulary

tepee

Key Places

Celilo Falls

Read Aloud

Numbers of us went to see him and we all admired him. He put us in mind [reminded us] of a deer that had lost his horns, and we did not know what name to give him. But as he was a slave to Man, like the dog which carried our things, he was named the Big Dog.

This is what an Indian of the Columbia Plateau thought the first time he saw a horse. Horses would become very important to these Indians who traveled from place to place in search of food. In this lesson you will read about the Indians of the plateau and two other Indian groups east of the Cascades—the people of the high desert and those of the Klamath Lakes.

Read for Purpose

1. **WHAT YOU KNOW:** If you drew a picture of a plateau and of a desert, what would they look like?
2. **WHAT YOU WILL LEARN:** What were the three main Indian culture areas east of the Cascades?

INDIANS OF THE PLATEAU

The Indians of the plateau lived in a very different environment from that of the Indians west of the Cascades. Locate the plateau culture area on the map on page 67. As you have read, this area receives little rainfall because it lies to the east of the Cascade Mountain rain shadow. The temperatures of the plateau are more extreme than those in the western part of our state. In the summer the days are extremely hot. The winters are long and cold. Life for many of the Indians of this area was not easy.

The Nez Percé (nez' pûrs'), Cayuse (kī üs'), Umatilla (ū mə til' ə), Tenino (te nīn' o), and Tygh (tī) Indians lived in the plateau area. These Indians lived in groups in long houses, much like the families of the western groups. But because there was not much wood available in the plateau area, these Indians usually made frames of poles and covered them with grass mats.

Indians of the plateau had to move each season to find food. At different times of the year they walked to various food-gathering places, hunting grounds, and fishing spots. The chart on the next page shows the cycle they traveled.

In the spring and summer during the fish runs, they gathered at the best fishing spots on the Columbia River, such as Celilo Falls (sə lī' lō fôlz). During the winter months the Indians of the plateau usually stayed in one place and ate mostly stored foods. They spent the winter months making and repairing tools, telling stories, and taking part in religious ceremonies. Toward the coming of spring, the Indians of the plateau camped in the mountains. They hunted elk and deer and gathered nuts, roots, and berries.

For thousands of years, the Indians of the plateau followed their seasonal route on foot. They used dogs to pull their belongings on sleds made of poles. But around the year 1740, the Indians of the plateau finally obtained horses through trade with the Plains Indians. The Plains Indians lived to the east across the Rocky Mountains. Horses brought great changes to the lives of the Indians of the plateau. They were able to travel much farther in search of food.

Like the Plains Indians, the Indians of the plateau hunted buffalo and learned how to build tepees (tē' pēz). A tepee is a cone-shaped tent that can be put up and taken down quickly.

As the painting on the tepee lining (inset) shows, horses were important to the Nez Percé way of life.

The circular chart shows the following months and activities:

- DECEMBER
- JANUARY — Toolmaking
- FEBRUARY — Hunting
- MARCH
- APRIL — Gathering
- MAY — Fishing and Gathering
- JUNE — Fishing and Gathering
- JULY — Trading
- AUGUST
- SEPTEMBER — Fishing and Gathering
- OCTOBER
- NOVEMBER — Preparation for winter

CHART SKILL: During which months did the Indians of the plateau hunt for animals such as deer?

INDIANS OF THE DESERT

The Indians of the high desert lived in the most difficult environment of any of the Oregon Indians. The high desert receives the least rainfall and has the most extreme changes in temperature of any area in Oregon. The Northern Paiutes (pī üts′) who lived here wore little clothing in summer and rubbed mud on their skin to keep mosquitoes away. In the winter they wore robes of rabbit fur.

They ate seeds, nuts, bulbs, roots, insects, rabbits, and fish. Sometimes they hunted antelope.

Since the Northern Paiutes had little wood and few animal skins, they built their houses of willow frames covered with reed mats. When they ran out of food in one place, they would move to another place, finding new reeds with which to build other houses.

The Klamath Indians used tule to make boats, decoys, mats, and houses.

THE KLAMATH LAKES

The Klamath (klam′ əth) Indians and the Modoc (mōd′ ok) Indians lived in the Klamath Mountains and along the shores of the Klamath Lakes and Tule Lake. Their great resource was water. They ate water birds and their eggs, and food plants from these shallow, marshy lakes. The Klamath Indians wove tule (tü′ lē), or tall reeds, together to make boats.

They also lured ducks with decoys. Decoys are models of ducks. The Klamaths made decoys out of tule and decorated them with feathers and paint. They floated them among the reeds and hid nearby, waiting for the real ducks to come.

The Klamaths and Modocs were sometimes called "pit Indians" because of the type of houses they built. They dug shallow pits over which they laid a rounded framework of poles covered with tule mats and a thick layer of earth.

INDIAN NAMES

Reminders of Oregon's first people are everywhere in our state. If you live in Tillamook, Clatskanie, Klamath Falls, Yamhill, or Coos Bay, your home has taken its name from the languages of early Oregon Indians. What are some other Oregon place names you can think of that were named for Indians?

The varied ways of life of the six Indian cultures you have just read about were shaped by their different environments. In the next chapter you will read about other people who started to come to the land of present-day Oregon.

Check Your Reading

1. Which Indian culture areas were located east of the Cascades?
2. How did horses change the lives of the Indians of the plateau?
3. **GEOGRAPHY SKILL:** Use the map on page 67 to name two groups of people who lived in each of the three Indian culture areas east of the Cascades.
4. **THINKING SKILL:** In what ways were the lives of the Indians of the plateau and the Indians of the high desert alike? In what ways were they different?

Oregon Traditions

READ TO LEARN

Key Vocabulary
sweat lodge

Read for Purpose
1. **WHAT YOU KNOW:** Why is fire so important to people?
2. **WHAT YOU WILL LEARN:** How did the Nez Percé use a story to explain an event that changed their history?

In Lesson 2 you read about the Indian girl, Tsin-is-tum, and how important fire was to her family. To have fire meant to be warm and to be able to cook food. No one knows exactly how and when Native Americans discovered the way to make fire. But the Nez Percé, who called themselves the *Nimipu* (nim′ i pü), which means "people," told this story to explain it.

THE FIRE FROM THE SKY

A long time ago the Nimipu had no fire. They ate their food raw, like the bears and foxes did. In winter they huddled together in their shelters, their teeth chattering, their skin blue with cold. Life was hard for the Nimipu then.

They knew about fire. They had seen it flashing in the sky high above their heads. Fire belonged to the Great Spirit, who kept it tied up in black storm bags. These bags tore whenever they bumped together. Then fire could be seen flashing through the holes.

The Nimipu looked at the fire in the sky and thought that it would be a good thing to have. Their leaders tried to call the fire down. They fasted and danced and beat their magic drums for days. But they failed, and fire remained in the sky.

Then a boy appeared. None of the Nimipu knew his name. No one had ever seen him before, but he spoke their language. He said to the Nimipu, "I will bring fire down from the sky."

Some leaders raised angry voices. How could this boy, a stranger, do what they could not with all their magic power? Even so, the Nimipu decided to give the boy a chance.

The boy prepared himself carefully. First he fasted for many days. Then he sat in the **sweat lodge** for a day and a night. A sweat lodge is a small hut in which cold water is poured upon heated rocks to make steam. After that he bathed in the icy waters of a mountain pool. When he finished, he rubbed himself all over with fir tree branches. Then he put on white deerskin clothing that was embroidered with porcupine quills. He looked so handsome and shining that the sight of him gladdened the hearts of the Nimipu.

The boy strung his bow with a new bowstring. He cut some bark from a cedar tree and tied it around the head of his straightest arrow. He placed the bow and arrow on the ground. Beside them he laid a creamy white abalone (ab ə lō′ nē) shell, or shell of a sea snail, that was beautiful in shape and color. Then the boy prayed.

"Let my arm be strong. Let my bow be powerful. Let my arrow fly straight to heaven. Let it bring the Great Spirit's fire back to earth."

Black storm clouds gathered. Thunderheads rolled across the sky. When one came directly overhead, the boy raised his bow and fired his arrow up into the sky.

A clap of thunder shook the heavens. The fire bag ripped open. Fire poured out in great flashes. The boy's burning arrow fell back to earth like a shooting star. It struck the shell. Sparks in the cedar bark made a small flame.

The Nimipu dashed forward with sticks and bark. They caught bits of flame from the fire in the shell, then rushed back with it to their huts. Soon every family had its own fire. The Nimipu laughed with joy. They put on their best clothes. They danced and sang. No longer would they have to eat their food raw. No longer would they have to spend the long winters huddling together to keep warm. Now they had the Great Spirit's fire, brought down from the sky by the brave boy.

The boy! Where was he? The Nimipu started looking for him at once, but they could find no trace of him. No one knew where he had gone. His bow lay on the ground next to the shell. The strongest of the Nimipu men picked up the bow. Not one could bend it.

The Nimipu never saw the boy again. But the fire he brought still burns in their lodges. And his beautiful shell, the abalone, still shimmers with the changing colors of the fire.

Check Your Reading

1. What was life like for the Nimipu before they had fire?
2. What did the boy do to prepare himself in order to bring fire down from the sky?
3. What do you think the fire that poured out of the thundercloud was?
4. **THINKING SKILL:** Predict what might have happened to Oregon's Indians if they hadn't learned to make fire.

REVIEWING VOCABULARY

artifact   environment
archaeologist   tepee
culture

Number a sheet of paper from 1 to 5. Beside each number write the word from the list above that best matches the definition.

1. A scientist who looks for and studies artifacts
2. The way of life of a group of people, including their customs, beliefs, and activities
3. A cone-shaped tent built by certain Oregon Indians
4. An object left behind by people who lived long ago
5. Surroundings, including the plants, animals, climate, and soil of an area

REVIEWING FACTS

1. How do we know that there were people in Oregon at least 9,000 years ago?
2. For what purpose did Indians along the coast use cedar?
3. What were the main foods of the Indians of the inland valleys?
4. Why was life harder for Indians who lived east of the Cascades?
5. How did the Klamath and Modoc Indians make use of their greatest resource—water?

WRITING ABOUT MAIN IDEAS

1. **Writing Clues:** Make up the clues for a "Who Am I?" game about the Indian culture groups of Oregon. Write at least three clues about each group. Each clue should apply to only one culture group.
2. **Writing a Paragraph:** How did environment influence the development of the ways of life of the Indian groups in Oregon? Write a paragraph that answers this question. Mention all the Indian groups that you have read about in this chapter and make a list of at least three facts about each group to support your answer.

BUILDING SKILLS: DECISION MAKING

1. Name some steps you could take that would help you to make good decisions.
2. Think of a decision that you must make soon. For instance, are you deciding whether or not to try a certain after-school activity? Use the decision-making steps to reach a decision.
3. When you are making a decision, why is it important to think of several different actions you could take to reach your goal?

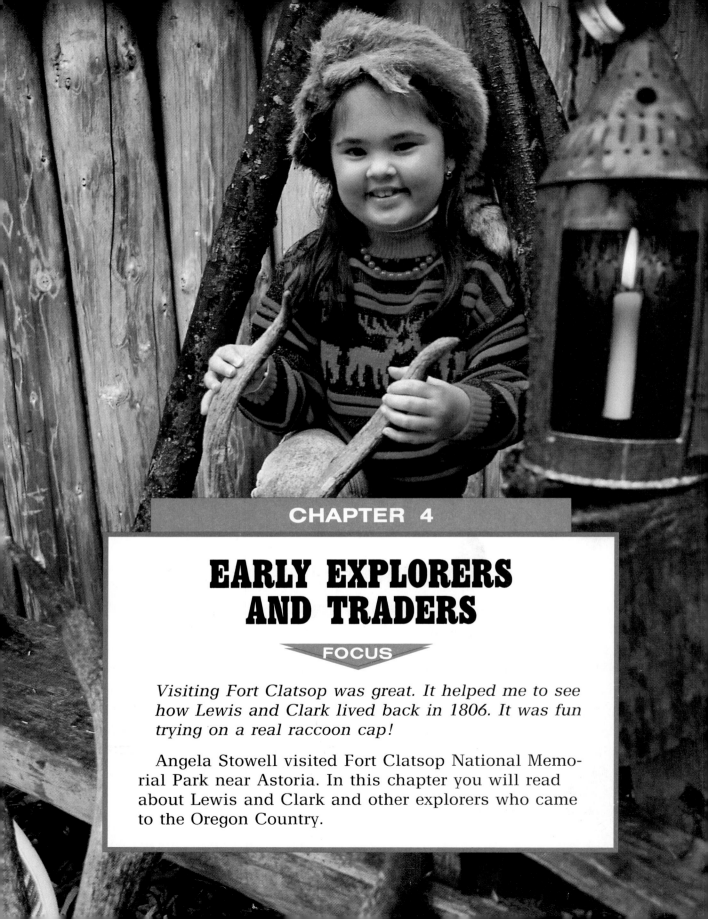

CHAPTER 4

EARLY EXPLORERS AND TRADERS

FOCUS

Visiting Fort Clatsop was great. It helped me to see how Lewis and Clark lived back in 1806. It was fun trying on a real raccoon cap!

Angela Stowell visited Fort Clatsop National Memorial Park near Astoria. In this chapter you will read about Lewis and Clark and other explorers who came to the Oregon Country.

1 The Search for the Northwest Passage

READ TO LEARN

Key Vocabulary
explorer
sandbar

Key People
Bruno Heceta
James Cook
Robert Gray
George Vancouver
William Broughton

Key Places
Northwest Passage

Read Aloud

The water raised a surf that broke around us. We were not twice the ship's length from breakers [large waves], that had we struck on, we [would] have gone to pieces. . . .

These words were recorded by an English sailor in 1792 as the ship he was on crossed the mouth of the Columbia River. In this lesson you will read about what some early sea captains found when they explored the coast of present-day Oregon.

Read for Purpose

1. **WHAT YOU KNOW:** Who were the first people to live in Oregon?
2. **WHAT YOU WILL LEARN:** Why did European and American captains explore the coast of what is now Oregon?

THE NORTHWEST PASSAGE

Imagine that it is the year 1775 and you are the captain of a ship. Your job is to find the shortest way to sail from the Atlantic Ocean to the Pacific Ocean. Which way would you go? What dangers might you meet along the way?

These are some of the questions that early explorers asked themselves. An explorer is a person who travels to unknown lands.

During the late 1700s many countries along the Atlantic Ocean, such as Britain, Spain, and the United States, sent ships to Asia to

The British **explorer** Captain Cook came to North America in search of the Northwest Passage.

The Granger Collection

THE EARLY EXPLORERS

In 1775 **Bruno Heceta** (brü′ nō e se′ tə), a Spanish captain, came to the west coast of North America. He wanted to find the Northwest Passage. Sailing near the shore, he saw "the mouth of some great river, or of some passage to another sea."

Was this the Northwest Passage? Actually, it was the mouth of the Columbia River. But Captain Heceta could not explore the river further. His crew was too sick to enter the river and so they left the area. However, Captain Heceta is remembered in Oregon today. You may have heard about or visited Heceta Head on our coast, which was named after him.

In 1776 Britain sent Captain **James Cook** to search for the Northwest Passage. Cook was an experienced sea captain who had already been on two voyages around the world. While sailing along the coast of North America, he drew maps that were used by later explorers.

Captain Cook never found the Northwest Passage; therefore, he decided it didn't exist. However, while he was exploring the coast, he traded with the Indians for otter fur, a valuable kind of animal skin. Word soon spread throughout many countries about the fortune in furs to be found along the west coast of North America. Now explorers had another reason to find the Northwest Passage.

trade for goods. Asia had many goods that other countries did not have, such as tea, spices, and silk.

The trip was long and hard, sometimes taking two or three years. Sailing around Cape Horn, at the tip of South America, was especially dangerous. The waters were rough, and the winds were fierce.

If a captain could find a sea passage through North America, it would mean a shorter and safer journey to the Pacific Ocean. This waterway was called the **Northwest Passage** because seamen hoped it would lead them across North America to Asia.

Many sea captains came to the coast of what is now Oregon in search of the Northwest Passage.

THE COLUMBIA RIVER

In 1792 two ships came to what is now the Oregon coast at almost the same time. The American ship *Columbia* was commanded by Captain Robert Gray. In April Gray saw the mouth of a large river as he explored the coast. But he sailed on because the weather was stormy.

The second ship, the British ship *Discovery*, was under the command of Captain George Vancouver (van kü′ vər). When he came upon the mouth of the same river, Vancouver wrote, "The sea had now changed from its natural [color] to river-colored water." But because he was headed farther north, Vancouver decided not to explore the river.

In May Captain Gray passed the mouth of the river again, and this time he decided to enter. On May 11, 1792, he took his ship across the large sandbar at the river's mouth.

A sandbar is a ridge of sand built up from the ocean floor by the action of waves. It can be very dangerous to cross.

As the American crew sailed up the river, they traded with the groups of Indians they met. They exchanged one nail for two salmon; one sheet of copper for four otter skins; and large nails, for one beaver skin.

On May 20 Captain Gray and his crew headed back to the Pacific Ocean. But before they did, Gray named the river Columbia after his ship. It has been called the Columbia River ever since.

Captain Vancouver soon heard that Captain Gray had entered the river and named it, so he decided to explore it, too. He sent in his smaller ship, under the command of Lieutenant William Broughton.

Groups of Indians came to meet Captain Gray and his crew as his ship sailed up the Columbia River.

Like Gray, Broughton also had to cross the dangerous sandbar. The waves pushed the ship back as it tried to sail forward. If the ship's bottom became wedged in the sand, it might never get loose. "I never felt more alarmed and frightened in my life," a sailor wrote in his journal.

Following Captain Vancouver's instructions, Lieutenant Broughton traveled upstream about 200 miles (320 km). He stayed for three weeks to explore and claim all the land on either side of the Columbia River for Great Britain.

Captain Vancouver and the *Discovery* crew were determined to claim the Columbia River and the land for Britain.

AN IMPORTANT WATERWAY

In this lesson you have read how explorers from different countries searched for the Northwest Passage. Although a water route across North America was never found, Captains Gray and Vancouver explored an important waterway. The Columbia River gave these explorers an opportunity to travel through a new land.

The United States later used Gray's trip to claim the land for itself. And, as you have read, Captain Vancouver also claimed this area for Britain. You have also read, in Chapter 3, how groups of Native Americans had depended on this river and the land for thousands of years. What would happen now that the Columbia River was an important waterway for three groups of people? In the next lesson you will learn how the United States tried to strengthen its claim in this area.

Check Your Reading

1. Why were sea captains looking for a Northwest Passage?
2. Name two ship captains who sailed the Columbia River.
3. **GEOGRAPHY SKILL:** What was dangerous about the entrance to the Columbia River?
4. **THINKING SKILL:** Predict what might have happened if Captain Heceta had explored the Columbia River.

2 The Lewis and Clark Expedition

READ TO LEARN

Key Vocabulary
Louisiana Purchase
expedition
frontier
slave

Key People
Thomas Jefferson
Meriwether Lewis
William Clark
Sacajawea
Ben York

Key Places
Louisiana
    Territory
Missouri River
St. Louis
Fort Clatsop
Lewis and
    Clark Trail

Read Aloud

We would have spent . . . [Christmas] in feasting, had we anything . . . to raise our spirits. . . .

An army captain used these words to describe Christmas dinner at a fort on the coast of present-day Oregon during the winter of 1805. He was one of the first Americans to cross the country and reach the Pacific Ocean. Can you imagine what it would have been like to have gone with him?

Read for Purpose

1. **WHAT YOU KNOW:** Why was the Columbia River an important discovery for the United States?
2. **WHAT YOU WILL LEARN:** How did Lewis and Clark explore a land route to Oregon?

THE LOUISIANA PURCHASE

In 1803 the border of the United States extended only as far west as the Mississippi River. The country bordered on a large area owned by France, called Louisiana. **Thomas** Jefferson, President of the United States, feared that France might try to close the Mississippi River to American trade. He asked the leaders of France if the United States could buy part of Louisiana. The

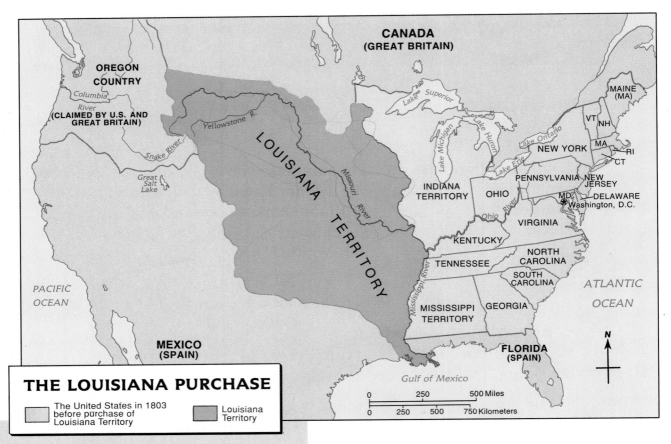

THE LOUISIANA PURCHASE

The United States in 1803 before purchase of Louisiana Territory

Louisiana Territory

MAP SKILL: How many countries claimed land in North America?

map above shows the land owned by the United States and France.

To Jefferson's surprise the French offered to sell all of Louisiana for $15 million. Here was a chance to double the size of the United States. The sale was called the **Louisiana Purchase** and it took place in 1803.

LEWIS AND CLARK

Maps of the time showed that the **Louisiana Territory**, as it was now called, stretched from the Mississippi River to the Rocky Mountains.

Flowing through this territory was the **Missouri River**. Jefferson decided to send a group of explorers on an **expedition** to the Pacific Ocean. An expedition is a journey made for a special purpose. An expedition also means the people making such a journey. Jefferson chose **Meriwether Lewis** as the leader of the group. Lewis then asked his friend **William Clark** to join the expedition as a co-leader.

Jefferson told Lewis and Clark to "explore the Missouri River . . . across the continent." He also told them to bring back information about the land, the wildlife, and the people they saw.

In the spring of 1804, Lewis and Clark began their trip at St. Louis on the American frontier (frun tîr´). A frontier is the settled region of a country lying along the border of an unsettled area. Beyond the frontier is the wilderness. Look at the map of Lewis and Clark's journey westward below. You may refer back to this map as we trace their trip.

SACAJAWEA

The expedition traveled up the Missouri River, where it spent the winter with the Mandan Indians. There a Shoshone Indian named Sacajawea (sak ə jə wē´ ə), joined the expedition. Sacajawea had been a slave of the Mandan Indians. A slave is a person who is owned by another person. Lewis and Clark hoped that Sacajawea would act as a translator for them when they reached Shoshone country.

OVERLAND TO OREGON

In April of 1805, the explorers continued west along the Missouri River. There were 33 people, including Sacajawea and Clark's slave, Ben York. In his journal Clark wrote:

The men are in the water from morning until night, hauling the boats, walking on sharp rocks and round slippery stones. . . .

MAP SKILL: Did the Lewis and Clark expedition spend more time traveling by river or traveling by land?

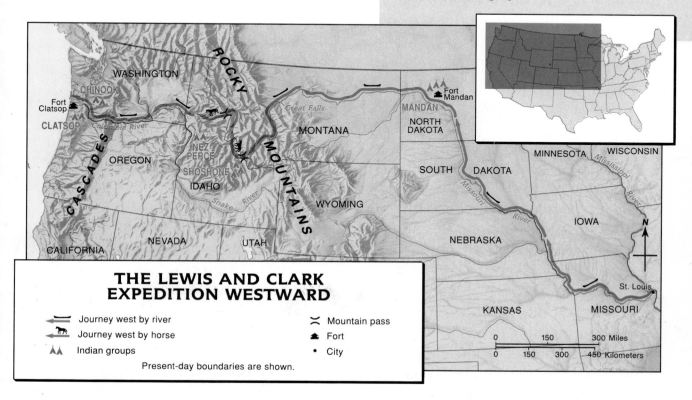

THE LEWIS AND CLARK EXPEDITION WESTWARD

- Journey west by river
- Journey west by horse
- Indian groups
- Mountain pass
- Fort
- City

Present-day boundaries are shown.

Sacajawea led the way as Lewis and Clark, York, and the expedition crossed the Rocky Mountains.

When the expedition reached the Great Falls of the Missouri River, the explorers had to climb around the falls in order to reach calm waters again. This meant loading everything on their backs, including the boats.

By August the explorers saw the snow-covered peaks of the Rocky Mountains. For Sacajawea, this was the land of her childhood, the home of the Shoshone Indians.

One day a group of Shoshone approached. Clark watched as Sacajawea began "to dance with joy." She had found her people, and her brother was now their chief. Sacajawea acted as translator for the expedition. With her help, Lewis and Clark obtained horses in order to continue their trip. The explorers and their horses then followed a path through the Rocky Mountains.

From the Rockies, Lewis and Clark followed the Snake River and then the Columbia River to the sea. Finally, in November of 1805, they reached the Pacific Ocean. "Great joy in camp," Clark wrote in his journal. "We are in view of this great Pacific Ocean which we have been so long anxious to see."

FORT CLATSOP

Now that winter was upon them again, the expedition didn't dare start back home. However, the men were miserable. The winds were fierce, the ocean roared, and the rain seemed endless. Their clothing was soaked and rotted.

Clark realized that they had to shoot animals for food and use the hides for new clothes. If they didn't, they might not survive the winter.

Another problem was the Chinook Indians. In the past fur traders treated them terribly. It was now hard for them to trust anyone, and they tried to steal from the Lewis and Clark party.

It was important to set up a camp where the expedition would be safe. The group cut timber and built a small fort in the forest, near the mouth of the Columbia River. They named it Fort Clatsop because the Clatsop Indians lived nearby. The men lived in Fort Clatsop during the heavy winter rains, feeding themselves with the meat of animals that they hunted.

THE RETURN

In the spring of 1806, the Lewis and Clark party loaded their canoes with supplies for the long trip home. They went up the Columbia River, passed the Cascades, and rode horses over the Rocky Mountains.

At last, on September 23, 1806, the expedition returned to St. Louis. The people of the town gave them a hearty welcome. "We had been long since given up by the people of the U.S. generally, and almost forgotten," wrote Clark. They had been gone for more than two years.

A GREAT ADVENTURE

This expedition made Lewis and Clark famous. The route they took became known as the Lewis and Clark Trail. They were the first explorers from the United States to explore the land that we now know as Oregon. Later on, many others would come, following in

Today you can visit Fort Clatsop. It has been rebuilt near the city of Astoria along the coast.

their footsteps. Lewis and Clark had shown that it could be done.

Check Your Reading

1. Why was the Louisiana Territory an important purchase for the United States?

2. In what way did Lewis and Clark expect Sacajawea to help them on the expedition?

3. **GEOGRAPHY SKILL:** Order the following parts of the Lewis and Clark Trail from east to west: Rocky Mountains; Missouri River; St. Louis; Columbia River.

4. **THINKING SKILL:** What questions might you have asked Lewis and Clark to find out more about their expedition west?

Reading Time Lines

Key Vocabulary

time line

As you were reading about the early explorers of our state, you came across a number of phrases that told you when important events took place. These phrases may have provided actual dates, such as *in 1775*. Or they may have given you other time clues, such as *one year later* or *a few days later*. To understand the history of our state you need to know when different events happened.

Because time is hard to picture we use **time lines** to help us keep track of events. A time line is a diagram that shows when events took place. It also shows the order in which events happened and the amount of time that passed between them.

Reading a Time Line

The time line below shows some of the important events in the history of the exploration of our state. The name of each event is written beneath the date on which it happened. The earliest event is at the left. The latest event is at the right.

A time line is divided into equal parts. Each part of the time line represents a time period. The time period can be short, such as one month. It can also be long, such as 100 years. What is the length of each time period in the time line below?

To read a time line, begin by looking for the earliest and latest events. Which is the first event shown on the time line below? Which is the last event? What happened between the years 1800 and 1805?

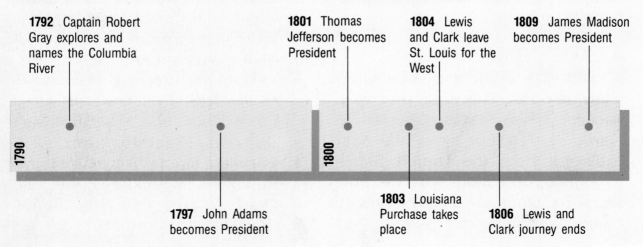

1792 Captain Robert Gray explores and names the Columbia River

1801 Thomas Jefferson becomes President

1804 Lewis and Clark leave St. Louis for the West

1809 James Madison becomes President

1790

1800

1797 John Adams becomes President

1803 Louisiana Purchase takes place

1806 Lewis and Clark journey ends

90

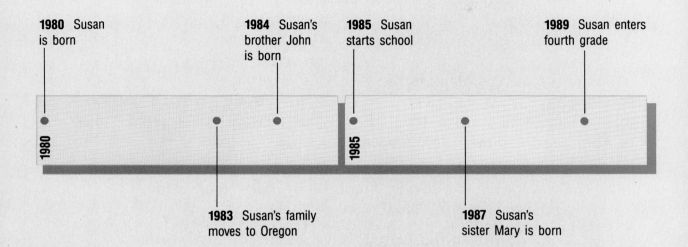

1980 Susan is born

1984 Susan's brother John is born

1985 Susan starts school

1989 Susan enters fourth grade

1980

1985

1983 Susan's family moves to Oregon

1987 Susan's sister Mary is born

Look again at the time line on page 90 to see the order in which events took place. Did Lewis and Clark leave St. Louis before or after Captain Robert Gray explored the Columbia River?

Making a Time Line

Time lines can be made for many different purposes. The time line above shows the life of Susan, a young girl growing up in Oregon today. How many years are shown on the time line?

Make a time line of your life. Divide it into two-year periods. Make the year you were born the first date. Include the year you started school and the year you entered fourth grade. Also include at least two other important events. Use the time line above as a guide, but include only events from your own life.

Reviewing the Skill

Use the information in this lesson and the time line on page 90 to answer the following questions.

1. What is a time line?
2. Between which years did the Lewis and Clark journey take place?
3. How many years are shown on the time line on page 90?
4. When did Captain Gray name the Columbia River?
5. Why is it important to know how to use a time line?

3 Fur Traders

READL2LEARN

Key Vocabulary

fur trapper
trading post
Pacific Fur
  Company
joint occupation

Key People

John Jacob Astor
Jonathan Thorn
William Black

Key Places

Oregon Country
Fort Astoria
Fort George

Read Aloud

Is this the fort I've heard so much about? Why, . . . I could knock it down in a couple of hours with a four-pounder [small cannon]*!*

A captain of the British navy shouted these words when he first saw the American fort at the mouth of the Columbia River. Prepared for a great battle, he was shocked to discover how tiny the fort was.

Read for Purpose

1. **WHAT YOU KNOW:** Which famous explorers came to Oregon by land?
2. **WHAT YOU WILL LEARN:** How did Fort Astoria begin as a trading post, and what happened to the fur trading company that built it?

THE OREGON COUNTRY

The success of the Lewis and Clark expedition in 1806 brought good news for American **fur trappers**. A fur trapper is someone who traps wild animals for their fur. Beaver fur was very valuable. It was used to make men's hats. Fur trading com-panies hired fur trappers to follow the Lewis and Clark Trail to the **Oregon Country** and search for beaver. The Oregon Country was the American name for the land that stretched from the Rocky Mountains to the Pacific Ocean.

Fur trappers searched for beaver along the Lewis and Clark trail.

ASTOR'S FUR COMPANY

John Jacob Astor was born in Germany and came to the United States when he was 20 years old. By 1800 he was one of the wealthiest fur traders in New York. In 1808 Astor read about the Lewis and Clark expedition and the newly opened Louisiana Territory. He wanted to build a United States trading post near the mouth of the Columbia River. A trading post was built like a fort. It was a place to which fur trappers and Indians could bring their furs and exchange them for goods or money.

Astor formed the Pacific Fur Company in 1810. He decided to send two expeditions to the Oregon Country. Because he wanted to make sure that his fort would be built, Astor sent one expedition by sea and the other by land.

THE *TONQUIN*

The sea expedition set out from New York in 1810 on Astor's ship, the *Tonquin*. It was commanded by Captain Jonathan Thorn. After a journey of many thousands of miles, the *Tonquin* reached the sandbar at the mouth of the Columbia River. The waves were rough, and they tossed the ship around.

Captain Thorn commanded five sailors to row across the sandbar in a small boat. The sailors refused. They feared for their lives because the water was too rough.

However, Captain Thorn threatened to sail back to New York if the crew didn't do as he commanded. The sailors boarded the tiny boat and were lowered over the side of the ship. The rest of the crew watched as the men rowed toward the wild waters. All of a sudden there was an explosion of waves and white foam. The boat disappeared. Ten minutes passed, then twenty minutes passed. But the boat never reappeared.

An explosion of waves crashed against the *Tonquin* and the small rowboat as they tried to cross the Columbia River's sandbar.

Captain Thorn was determined to get across the sandbar. He sent out another boat. It too was lost in the waves, never to be seen again. Captain Thorn then decided to sail the *Tonquin* across the sandbar. Waves crashed against the side of the ship, rocking it from side to side. It was difficult to move forward. Finally, the *Tonquin* managed to cross the sandbar and sail into the Columbia River. However, eight men had lost their lives while trying to get there.

FORT ASTORIA

Once they were on dry land, the men of the Pacific Fur Company began to search for a place to build their fort. We began "clearing away brush and rotten wood for a spot to land on," one man wrote.

They chose a site on a hill with a fine view of the river. There the men began to build the trading post, which they named Fort Astoria. It was named for their company's owner, John Jacob Astor.

Meanwhile, Captain Thorn and the crew of the *Tonquin* had sailed north. While he was trading with the Chinook Indians there, Captain Thorn insulted the chief. Soon a fight broke out between the sailors and the Indians. The *Tonquin* was destroyed, and the crew and all but one Indian were killed. This was a terrible loss for the Indians and for the men at Fort Astoria. The *Tonquin* was supposed to bring supplies back to the fort.

ASTORIA BY LAND

On September 3, 1810, Astor's second expedition left St. Louis and traveled to the Columbia River by land. After more than one year of traveling, the group still had not reached the Columbia River. Supplies were almost gone. The group decided to divide themselves into two groups. Each group would make its way to Fort Astoria separately.

In February 1812 the first group arrived at Fort Astoria. In May the second group arrived. There were now more men at Fort Astoria than there had been before. They had few supplies and there was no ship to help them. How was Astor's Pacific Fur Company going to survive?

94

FORT GEORGE

When news of the events at Fort Astoria reached John Jacob Astor, he could do little to help his men. A conflict, the War of 1812, had broken out between Great Britain and the United States. The British had sent their warship *Raccoon*, commanded by Captain William Black, to capture Astor's fort.

However, before the ship *Raccoon* arrived, another group reached the fort. This group consisted of Canadians from the North West Company, which was owned by people in Canada. Canada at this time was a colony of Great Britain. This meant that whatever possessions belonged to Canada also belonged to Great Britain.

The men at Fort Astoria thought that the Canadians would try to capture their fort. But, to the surprise of Astor's men, the Canadians offered to buy Fort Astoria from them. The Americans decided to sell.

When Captain Black and the men of the *Raccoon* arrived, they were ready for a battle. However, they were too late. The Americans had already sold Fort Astoria to the Canadians. This news made Captain Black very angry. You read his comments about Fort Astoria in the Read Aloud of this lesson. He realized that he had sailed all the way around Cape Horn for nothing. Fort Astoria was now in British hands.

Fort Astoria, a trading post built along the Columbia River, was named for John Jacob Astor.

The Granger Collection

Today you can visit Astoria and see where Fort Astoria once stood. Part of it has been rebuilt on the original site.

Captain Black raised the British flag over the fort. He changed its name to Fort George.

Following the War of 1812 Great Britain and the United States signed a treaty. This treaty said that both countries were to have joint occupation of the Oregon Country. This meant that they were to share the land between the Rocky Mountains and the Pacific Ocean.

FORT ASTORIA TODAY AND YESTERDAY

Today you can visit the city of Astoria and see where the fort stood that Captain Black claimed was so small. Part of it has been rebuilt on the site of the original fort. As you have read, John Astor's fort did not remain under American control. However, it helped to strengthen the United States claim to the land along the Columbia River.

Check Your Reading

1. Why did fur trappers follow the Lewis and Clark Trail?
2. Who was John Jacob Astor?
3. **GEOGRAPHY SKILL:** Why did the United States and Great Britain want to have trading posts near the mouth of the Columbia River?
4. **THINKING SKILL:** Predict what might have happened if Astor's Pacific Fur Company had not sold Fort Astoria.

4 The Hudson's Bay Company

READ TO LEARN

Key Vocabulary

Hudson's Bay Company
voyageur
fur brigade

Key People

John McLoughlin

Key Places

Fort Vancouver

Read Aloud

He was such a figure as I should not like to meet in a dark night in one of the . . . lanes in the neighborhood of London. . . . He was dressed in clothes that had once been reasonably fashionable, but [were] now covered with a thousand patches of different colors. . . .

The words above were written by the director of a large British fur company. They were used to describe John McLoughlin, about whom you will read below.

Read for Purpose

1. **WHAT YOU KNOW:** Where was Fort George, and to which country did it belong?
2. **WHAT YOU WILL LEARN:** How did John McLoughlin and the Hudson's Bay Company help bring people to the Oregon Country?

THE HUDSON'S BAY COMPANY

After the British took over Fort Astoria and renamed it Fort George, it continued to serve as an important post for fur trading. In 1821 Fort George became part of a powerful British fur company called the Hudson's Bay Company. This company had trading posts on streams and rivers that stretched from the Canadian Rocky Mountains to eastern Canada.

The Hudson's Bay Company used canoes to move furs along the streams and rivers. The difficult job of canoeing was often done by French-speaking Canadians called voyageurs. These voyageurs had to

(*above*) **Voyageurs** gathered at night and told stories. (*right*) The Hudson's Bay Company seal appears on a tea container.

be strong enough to paddle a canoe for 16 hours a day. When a voyageur had to cross land from one waterway to another, he loaded everything, including his canoe, on his back and carried it across the land.

JOHN MCLOUGHLIN

In 1824 the Hudson's Bay Company decided that it would expand its trading post at Fort George. John McLoughlin was chosen as the fort's leader because he was an able and intelligent trader.

In July 1824 McLoughlin left the Hudson's Bay Company headquarters in eastern Canada and headed west. After paddling canoes and riding horses across Canada for almost four months, he reached Fort George in November.

A NEW LOCATION

McLoughlin was not completely happy with Fort George's location. That winter, in a letter to his nephew, he wrote:

Since my arrival on the 8th of Novr [November] *we have not seen one clear sun shining day and not ten days without rain. . . .*

McLoughlin noted other problems, too. For example, huge trees had made the land around the fort hard to clear for farming.

McLoughlin found a new site on which to build a fort near the mouth of the Willamette River. A new fort was built, and it was named Fort Vancouver. In the spring of 1825, the company moved all of its equipment, trading goods, and animals to its new location.

LIFE AT FORT VANCOUVER DURING THE 1840S

Stores

Stores

Sleeping Quarters

John McLoughlin's House

Bakery

Jail

Wheat Store

Beef Stores

Kitchen

Well

Wash House

DIAGRAM SKILL: What kinds of jobs did people living at Fort Vancouver have?

EXPANDING FORT VANCOUVER

Fort Vancouver began as a little village of tents and huts made out of bark. Within three years, as a result of McLoughlin's efforts, the fort grew into a large community. It was important to McLoughlin that life at the fort be as comfortable as possible. But reaching this goal was not easy. McLoughlin's men built living quarters, a dining hall, stores, and storage houses. They planted the fields outside of the fort with potatoes, wheat, peas, oats, and Indian corn. However, life was not all work and no play at Fort Vancouver.

Music and sports were enjoyed by everyone who lived at the fort. After meals in the evening, violins

Today you can visit Fort Vancouver and imagine what life was like in 1845.

and flutes were often played for everyone to enjoy.

Life at Fort Vancouver was filled with activity. The primary business was fur trading. Animals were trapped by **fur brigades**, who were groups of company trappers who traveled on horseback. The Indians came to trade at the fort. They exchanged fur skins for muskets, knives, blankets, and beads. The Indians liked McLoughlin because he dealt with them fairly. They called him "White-Headed Eagle" because he had white hair that hung nearly to his shoulders.

Today, Fort Vancouver has been restored to the way it was during the time of John McLoughlin and the Hudson's Bay Company. You can visit the fort, which is located in the city of Vancouver in the state of Washington.

A NEW COMMUNITY

After years of service to the Hudson's Bay Company, many trappers and voyageurs wanted to settle in the Willamette Valley. John McLoughlin helped some of them begin their own farms. He provided them with seed and lent them farming equipment.

McLoughlin was the leader at Fort Vancouver for more than 20 years. Because of his kindness and strong leadership, many people from the United States and Canada were drawn to the fort and the surrounding area. Fort Vancouver had become a growing community. Today John McLoughlin is remembered as the "Father of Oregon."

 Check Your Reading

1. Which fur company did Fort George become a part of in 1821?
2. Name some of the ways in which John McLoughlin made Fort Vancouver a community.
3. **GEOGRAPHY SKILL:** What were two reasons that the Hudson's Bay Company was moved from Fort George to Fort Vancouver?
4. **THINKING SKILL:** Compare and contrast life at Fort Vancouver with life at Fort Astoria.

REVIEWING VOCABULARY

expedition   joint occupation
explorer   voyageur
frontier

Number a sheet of paper from 1 to 5. Beside each number write the word or term from the list above that best completes the sentence.

1. In 1804 St. Louis was on the ____, the edge of the settled area of the United States.
2. Meriwether Lewis was a brave ____ who traveled through the Louisiana Territory.
3. The entire ____ traveled to the South Pole, hoping to learn more about penguins.
4. The situation in which two countries share the control of an area is called ____.
5. The French-speaking Canadian fur trappers called ____ had to be very strong.

REVIEWING FACTS

1. Why was Britain able to claim the land around the Columbia River?
2. Describe how the United States bought the Louisiana Territory from France.
3. Name two ways in which Sacajawea helped the Lewis and Clark expedition.
4. Who was John McLoughlin?

5. What were two problems with the location of Fort George? To what place was the fort moved?

WRITING ABOUT MAIN IDEAS

1. **Writing a Comparing Paragraph:** Write a paragraph comparing Fort Clatsop and Fort Astoria. In what ways were they alike? Why was each fort built? By whom was each built? What became of each one?
2. **Writing a Character Sketch:** Review the section about John McLoughlin in this chapter. What kind of person do you think he was? How can you tell? Write a paragraph in which you describe some of McLoughlin's personality traits. Give several examples to support your description.

BUILDING SKILLS: READING TIME LINES

Review the time line on page 90. Then answer these questions.

1. What does a time line show?
2. What happened in 1792?
3. Copy the time line onto a sheet of paper. Then add these events.

1792   Captain George Vancouver explores the Columbia River.

1800   Thomas Jefferson is elected President.

1805   Lewis and Clark build Fort Clatsop.

REVIEWING VOCABULARY

Number a sheet of paper from 1 to 10. Beside each number write **C** if the underlined word is used correctly. If it is not, write the word or term that would correctly complete the sentence.

1. The <u>archaeologist</u> from the French part of Canada was a very strong man who trapped animals deep in the woods for their furs.
2. The Indians' <u>environment</u> included their beliefs and ways of doing things.
3. The <u>voyageur</u> traveled to unknown lands.
4. When Britain and the United States shared control of Oregon, it was known as a <u>joint occupation</u>.
5. People came to the <u>trading post</u> to buy and sell goods.
6. Many people say the moon is the final <u>frontier</u>.
7. Arrowheads, pottery, and flints are examples of <u>artifacts</u>.
8. The Lewis and Clark <u>brigade</u> explored the Louisiana Territory.
9. Native Americans built a kind of dwelling known as a <u>sandbar</u>.
10. Captain Gray was an <u>explorer</u> who named the Columbia River.

WRITING ABOUT THE UNIT

1. **Writing a Paragraph of Comparison:** Compare the arrival of the first Native Americans in Oregon with the arrival of the first white people. Consider such questions as: Why did they come? How did they get here? What did they find? How long did they stay?
2. **Writing a Description:** Review the types of homes built by Oregon Indians. Choose one type. Then write a paragraph describing the dwelling. Explain why it was a logical type of dwelling for these Indians to build.
3. **Writing from Different Points of View:** Write one or two sentences telling how each of these Indian groups might have reacted to the building of the trading post at Fort Astoria: the Chinooks, the inland valley Indians, and the high desert Indians.
4. **Writing a Letter:** Imagine that you lived at Fort George in the days after John McLoughlin became the leader there. Write a letter to a cousin back East about life at Fort George. Be sure to tell what you think is good and what you think is bad about living there.

ACTIVITIES

1. **Researching an Indian Group:** Choose one Indian group and find out more about it. Try to find out where they lived, the types of homes

they built, the types of foods they ate, what life was like for the children, and any religious ceremonies or special activities in which they took part. Write a report presenting the information you find. Illustrate your report.

2. **Writing a Book Report:** Read a book about the Lewis and Clark expedition or about Sacajawea, or read sections from the journals that Lewis and Clark kept during the expedition. Then write a book report about the qualities that made this person or these people famous.

3. **Working Together to Make a Model or Illustration:** Find out about the ships used in the late 1700s and early 1800s, such as the *Columbia* or the *Tonquin*. Work in groups to make a model or a detailed illustration of such a ship. Be prepared to tell the class about the ship.

BUILDING SKILLS: DECISION MAKING

Imagine that you are Jonathan Thorn, captain of the *Tonquin*. You have been instructed to take some men from the Pacific Fur Company to the Oregon Country to build a fort for John Jacob Astor. At the mouth of the Columbia River a dangerous sandbar stands in your way. You must decide whether to send a few sailors in a small boat to try to cross the sandbar or attempt to sail the *Tonquin* past the sandbar.

1. Your decision should help you to
   a. make up your mind.
   b. reach your goal.
   c. be popular with the crew.
2. You should first
   a. ask your first mate.
   b. think about your choices and the possible results of each one.
   c. decide what is best for the Pacific Fur Company.

 **LINKING PAST, PRESENT, AND FUTURE**

In the early 1800s fur trapping became an important part of life in the Oregon Country. What were some of the good things that resulted from fur trapping in the early 1800s? What might have been bad about it?

Fur trapping still goes on today in certain areas. Do you think that we should allow the hunting of animals for their furs in the future? Why or why not?

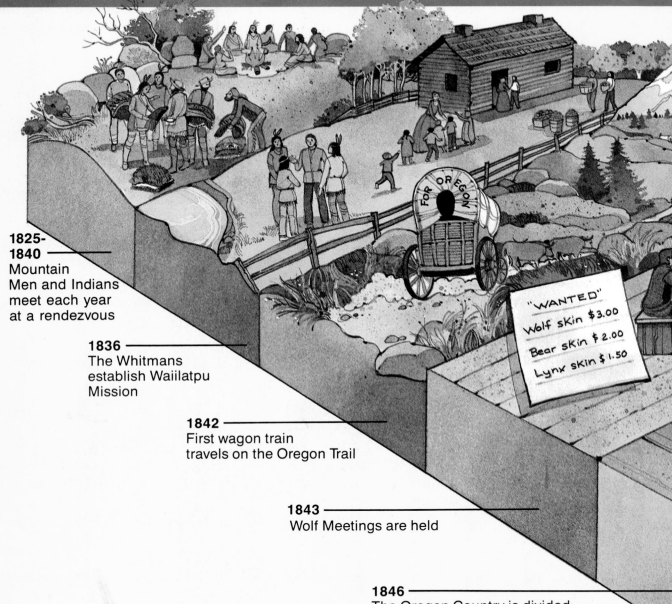

1825-1840
Mountain
Men and Indians
meet each year
at a rendezvous

1836
The Whitmans
establish Waiilatpu
Mission

1842
First wagon train
travels on the Oregon Trail

1843
Wolf Meetings are held

"WANTED"
Wolf skin $3.00
Bear skin $2.00
Lynx skin $1.50

1846
The Oregon Country is divided
between Britain and the United States
along the 49°N parallel

WHAT HAPPENED

You have read about some of
the people who helped to settle our
state, but the whole story has not yet
been told. In this unit you will read about
the pioneers and settlers that came to build
up the Oregon Country. With their help the
Oregon Country became a United States territory.

1848
President Polk signs
a law making the
Oregon Country a
United States territory.

104

UNIT 3

AMERICAN SETTLERS COME TO OREGON

CHAPTER 5

THE FIRST AMERICAN SETTLERS

FOCUS

Being an actor in a play about Captain Gray is a fun way to learn history. I liked the songs and what I learned about Tillamook.

Jacob Phillips lives in Tillamook. Each summer he acts in a musical play about Captain John Gray's exploration of the Oregon Country. In this chapter you will read about the first Americans who came to settle in the Oregon Country.

1 American Trappers and Traders

READ TO LEARN

Key Vocabulary
Rocky Mountain
  Fur Company
Mountain Men
rendezvous

Key People
William Ashley
Andrew Henry
Jedediah Smith
Nathaniel J. Wyeth

Key Places
North Platte River
Green River
South Pass
Fort Hall

Read Aloud

It was in this way that they found . . . a door to the Western Sea: the Rockies were not the impassable wall Lewis and Clark had believed them to be. . . . Wagons could roll through. . . .

In 1824 fur trappers found out about a new trail through the Rocky Mountains that made traveling easier than it had been before. In this lesson you will read about the experiences of these men who opened the way west to the Oregon Country for future American settlers.

Read for Purpose

1. **WHAT YOU KNOW:** Which country had set up a successful fur trading post in the Northwest?
2. **WHAT YOU WILL LEARN:** Who were the Mountain Men and what did they do to open the way for American settlement of the Oregon Country?

THE MOUNTAIN MEN

As you have read, the British Hudson's Bay Company was in control of the fur trading business in the Northwest. John Jacob Astor's attempt to set up an American trading post in the same area had not been successful. In 1822, two Americans, **William Ashley** and **Andrew Henry**, began American fur trading in the Northwest. Ashley placed advertisements in St. Louis, Missouri, newspapers.

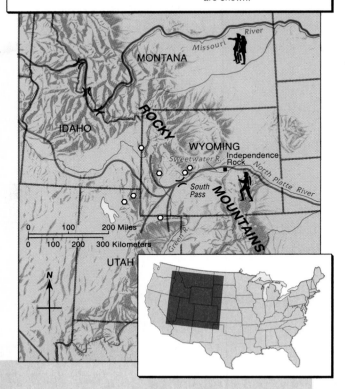

MAP SKILL: Along which important rivers did the Mountain Men travel?

YOUNG MEN
Wm. H. Ashley wishes to hire
ONE HUNDRED MEN to travel up
the Missouri River to its source,
there to work for one, two, or
three years.

Jedediah Smith was one American who answered this advertisement. Smith and other young men who signed up to work for Ashley's and Henry's Rocky Mountain Fur Company were sent out in brigades to hunt through the winter. These trappers came to be known as Mountain Men. They were called Mountain Men because they spent so much of their time in the mountains learning the secrets of nature and the ways of the wilderness.

A Mountain Man's clothing was made up entirely of animal skins. His pants, coat, and moccasins were usually made of fringed buckskin. The trapper used pieces of the fringe to repair parts of his clothing.

These brave Mountain Men often waded in icy waters to set traps for beavers. They ate little except buffalo and deer meat. Narrow escapes from large animals, such as grizzly bears, were not uncommon.

Jedediah Smith experienced the first of many brushes with death in 1823 while leading a brigade west along the North Platte River in Wyoming. One of his men later wrote the following account of Smith's experience with a grizzly bear.

He and the bear met face to face.
Grizzly did not hesitate a moment
but sprung on Smith taking him
by the head first.

A GOOD ROUTE THROUGH THE ROCKIES

Only a week and a half after Smith's wounds had been stitched, this determined man pushed his brigade westward. They asked Indians they met on the way for the best route to the Green River in Wyoming. They followed the directions the Indians had given them and in this way found South Pass. This route through the Rocky Mountains was easier to travel than the trail Lewis and Clark had found. Use the map on page 108 to trace the trappers' route west.

This South Pass trail had great importance for the future American settlement of the West. Less than 20 years after this discovery, thousands of Americans would drive their wagons across South Pass on their way west.

Smith and his men met with Ashley at the Green River in the spring of 1825. This meeting was the first rendezvous (rän′ də vü). A rendezvous was a large meeting of fur traders, trappers, and Indians from all over the Rocky Mountain region. The owners of the fur companies brought supplies to sell to the brigades and to trade with the Native Americans for furs. At this rendezvous thousands of Indians set up camp with their families.

Once the trading was done, the men took part in races, games, and contests. They feasted heartily. The Mountain Men talked for hours about the places they had seen and in this way they spread information about the West.

A WAGON JOURNEY

In the spring of 1830 Smith, who was now part owner of the Rocky Mountain Fur Company, left again

At a rendezvous Mountain Men and Indians traded, took part in contests, and exchanged information.

Nathaniel J. Wyeth's trading post at Fort Hall became a resting place for travelers heading west.

from St. Louis. He and the other partners of the company led several wagons loaded with supplies along the North Platte River. Their route took them across South Pass to the Wind River in Wyoming.

This trip was extraordinary because before this time only pack horses and mules had been led across this trail west. In 1830 Smith wrote a report about his wagon journey for the United States government. The purpose of the report was to spread the word about the "ease and safety" of traveling the route along the North Platte River to the Oregon Country.

AMERICANS WHO STAYED

In 1832 Nathaniel J. Wyeth of Boston decided to start a fur trading business in the Oregon Country.

But after two unsuccessful trips there, Wyeth gave up hope of establishing a fur business.

Wyeth, however, had made some important contributions to the further settlement of the Oregon Country. On his second trip to Oregon he built a trading post called Fort Hall. Also, some of the men who had come with him on his trips stayed and settled in the Oregon Country.

By the time Wyeth left the Oregon Country for the second time in 1836, the business of fur trading was coming to an end. There was less demand for furs since men had started wearing silk hats instead of beaver hats. There weren't many beavers left to trap anyway.

AMERICAN SETTLERS

As you have read, the Mountain Men made important discoveries that helped open the Oregon Country to settlers. After the last rendezvous in 1840, many of these men settled in the Willamette Valley and took up farming.

 Check Your Reading

1. Who were the Mountain Men?
2. Why was the discovery of South Pass important?
3. Describe a rendezvous.
4. THINKING SKILL: In what ways are today's space explorers like the Mountain Men? In what ways are they different?

110

2 The Missionaries

READ TO LEARN

Key Vocabulary
religion
missionary
mission

Key People
Jason Lee
Daniel Lee
Marcus Whitman
Narcissa Whitman
Henry H. Spalding
Eliza Spalding
Father Blanchet
Father Demers

Key Places
French Prairie
Mission Bottom
Waiilatpu
Lapwai

Read Aloud

This being a fishing post of the Indians, we easily found a canoe made of rushes and willows . . . when two Indians on horseback, each with a rope attached to the canoe, towed us over.

This is what Narcissa Whitman wrote in her journal when Native Americans helped her traveling party on their way west to the Oregon Country. Narcissa Whitman and Eliza Spalding were the first American women to cross the Rocky Mountains and settle there.

Read for Purpose

1. **WHAT YOU KNOW:** Who were the first non-Indians to settle in the Oregon Country?
2. **WHAT YOU WILL LEARN:** Why were the early missionaries important to the Oregon Country?

INDIANS PAY A VISIT

In 1831, four Nez Percé Indians visited the explorer William Clark in St. Louis. They told Clark that they wanted the white people's religion taught to their people. These Indians thought that learning about Christianity would help them

111

to understand the white people's way of life. Religion is the way people worship the God or gods they believe in. A newspaper, the *Christian Advocate*, printed the story. Afterwards missionaries began coming to the Oregon Country. Missionaries are people who teach their religion to others who have different beliefs.

MISSIONS AND MISSIONARIES

When Nathaniel J. Wyeth came to the Oregon Country for the second time in 1834, he brought along two missionaries, Jason Lee and his nephew, Daniel Lee. The Lees had been sent by their church in the East to found the first mission in the

The Nez Percés' visit to St. Louis brought missionaries to the Oregon Country.

Oregon Country. A mission was a settlement that usually included a church, houses, and farmland. At the mission Native Americans were supposed to be educated and converted to the Christian religion.

After they reached Fort Vancouver, Lee and his group decided to build their mission in the Willamette Valley. Lee finally selected a place at French Prairie, about 10 miles (16 km) from the present-day city of Salem. When Wyeth's supply ship from the East arrived, John McLoughlin, about whom you read in Chapter 4, provided a boat and crew to take the missionaries' goods to the site. He lent the missionaries seven oxen, one bull, and seven cows.

The missionaries lived in a tent at first while they cut down trees to build a small house and a barn. They also planted crops and taught the Native American children who lived at the mission. The area was called Mission Bottom. *Bottom* means "low land beside a river."

MORE MISSIONARIES

The newspaper article in the *Christian Advocate* was reprinted many times. Religious leaders made speeches at churches asking for volunteers. Marcus Whitman and his wife, Narcissa Whitman, and Henry H. Spalding and his wife, Eliza Spalding, answered the call to become missionaries in the Oregon

The Whitman and Spalding missionary party crossed South Pass on their way to the Oregon Country.

Country. They traveled by river steamer from their homes in New York State to Liberty, Missouri. For the last half of their journey they decided to travel overland. This was a trip that had never before been attempted by non-Indian women.

In late April of 1836 the party set out from Liberty with a supply of horses, mules, cattle, and wagons. The missionaries made the first part of their overland trip in the company of fur traders. The party covered about 20 miles (32 km) a day. In her journal Narcissa described a typical day.

> We are ready to start, usually at six—travel till eleven, encamp, rest and feed, start about two—travel until six . . . then encamp for the night. We encamp in a large ring—baggage and men, tents and wagons on the outside and all the animals . . . within the circle. . . .

After crossing South Pass in July, the missionaries stopped at a rendezvous at the Green River in Wyoming. They were given a warm welcome by many Mountain Men and Native Americans. Marcus Whitman, a medical doctor, was able to treat some of the trappers. In return the missionaries were fed and cared for.

ON TO THE OREGON COUNTRY

After leaving the rendezvous, the missionaries found the trip much rougher. They had new guides—trappers from the Hudson's Bay Company and 200 Nez Percé Indians. They traveled more miles each day than they had before, and the trail was more difficult. Narcissa's journal speaks of one place "so steep the wagon was upset twice." When the group was trying to cross

McLoughlin greeted the Whitmans and the Spaldings at Fort Vancouver after their long journey to the Oregon Country.

the Snake River in what is now Idaho, the wagon overturned and the horses nearly drowned.

When the horses became too tired to pull the wagons any farther, Whitman took two wheels off one wagon to make a cart. But he soon gave up that idea. He loaded as much as he could on the backs of his horses, and the two women rode sidesaddle. For the last part of the trip, the party rode down the Columbia River on Hudson's Bay Company boats, and they were greeted at Fort Vancouver by John McLoughlin.

The two women stayed at the fort for several weeks while their husbands built rough houses farther up the Columbia River. Narcissa and Eliza then traveled upriver in canoes on the way to their new homes. The Whitmans built their mission on the land of the Cayuse Indians, at Waiilatpu (Wy ēē' lăt pủ) in the Oregon Country, near what is now Walla Walla, Washington. The Spaldings built their mission at Lapwai (lap' wī) among the Nez Percé Indians.

NEW MISSIONS

Jason Lee, the Whitmans, and the Spaldings were Protestants. Protestants are one group of people who practice Christianity. Catholic missionaries came to the Oregon Country shortly after the Protestants. Catholics are another group who believe in Christianity. Most of the French-Canadians were Catholic. Their priests, **Father Blanchet** (blan shā) and **Father Demers** (də mâr), arrived in the Oregon Country in 1838. Father Blanchet founded the St. Paul's mission at French Prairie. After that other Catholic missions were started among the Indians of the coast and of the plateau.

DIFFERENT WAYS OF LIFE

In some ways the missionaries helped the Native Americans of the Oregon Country. They taught many of the Indians how to read and write. But the missionaries' attempts to teach the Native Americans to believe in the Christian religion were mostly unsuccessful. The American missionaries and the Indians of the Oregon Country lived very different ways of life. They had difficulty understanding one another's cultures. Sometimes misunderstandings arose.

The American settlers took more and more of the Indians' land. These settlers also brought many illnesses with them from which many Native Americans died.

MORE SETTLERS

Although the missionaries came to the Oregon Country to help the Indians, they ended up causing them many problems. More than anything else, the missionaries succeeded in bringing more settlers to the Oregon Country. Some of the

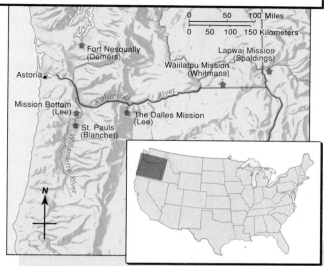

THE OREGON COUNTRY MISSIONS

⚜ Catholic mission ⚜ Protestant mission • Town

Present-day boundaries are shown.

MAP SKILL: Along which important river was the Dalles Mission located?

missionaries returned to the East to encourage others to come to the Oregon Country.

Check Your Reading

1. Who was Jason Lee and where did he settle?
2. What were some of the problems that arose between the Indians and the missionaries in the Oregon Country?
3. **GEOGRAPHY SKILL:** Along which important rivers were Lee's missions located?
4. **THINKING SKILL:** How did the missionaries encourage further American settlement of the Oregon Country?

115

Understanding Cause and Effect

Key Vocabulary

cause   effect

Wendy forgot to set her alarm clock before going to bed. The next morning she overslept. Forgetting to set her alarm clock was the **cause** of her oversleeping. A cause is something that makes something else happen. Oversleeping was the **effect** of forgetting to set the alarm. An effect is what happens as a result of something else.

Read the two sentences below.

- John won the spelling bee.
- For weeks John studied lists of spelling words every evening.

The first sentence states an event that happened. The second sentence states the cause or reason that the event happened. John won the spelling bee because he studied lists of words every evening.

Identifying cause and effect will help you to understand how events are related. You will see how one event leads to another.

Trying the Skill

Read each sentence below. Then tell which sentence states a cause and which states an effect.

- During the early 1800s the Mountain Men found trails to the West that wagons could pass through.
- Settlers soon began heading west in large numbers.

How were you able to tell which sentence was a cause and which sentence was an effect?

HELPING YOURSELF

The steps on the left can help you to identify cause and effect. The example on the right shows one way to apply these steps to the sentences on the previous page.

One Way to Find Cause and Effect	Example
1. Look at the events being described.	Mountain Men found trails, and settlers headed west.
2. In each sentence look for words that signal causes, such as *because*, *since*, *as a result of*. If you do not find any word clues, ask yourself if one event is the reason that something else happened.	Did the Mountain Men's discovery of trails that wagons could pass through cause something else to happen?
3. If the answer is yes, you have found a cause.	The discovery of trails that wagons could pass through were the reason that something else happened.
4. Look for words that signal effects, such as *so*, *therefore*, *as a result*. If you do not find any word clues, ask yourself what happened as a result of the cause. What happened is an effect.	Because the trails let wagons pass through, settlers headed west.

Applying the Skill

Now apply what you have learned. Tell which sentence below states the cause and which states the effect.

- The boat sank.
- The boat struck a reef.
- Sheep graze on the pasture.
- The grass stays short.

Now check yourself by answering the following questions.

1. What is the first thing you should do to identify cause and effect?
   a. Find the cause.
   b. Look at the events being described.
   c. Ask what happened.

2. What is one effect of the boat striking a reef?
3. What is one effect of sheep grazing on the pasture?

Reviewing the Skill

1. What is the difference between a cause and an effect?
2. What are four steps you could follow to find cause and effect?
3. Why is it important to be able to tell the difference between causes and effects?

3 Forming a Government

READ TO LEARN

Key Vocabulary

petition
The Great Reinforcement

Key People

William A. Slacum
Ewing Young

Read Aloud

The last month—what has it been? Little sleep, much fatigue, hardly time to eat, mosquitoes, cattle breaking . . . and scattering to the four winds. . . .

This is what one man wrote when he was helping to drive a herd of more than 600 wild cattle from California to present-day Oregon. In this lesson you will read about the settlers' efforts to work together to develop a strong community in the Oregon Country.

Read for Purpose

1. **WHAT YOU KNOW:** What is needed to start a community?
2. **WHAT YOU WILL LEARN:** What did American settlers do to develop a community and to begin local government?

A GROWING SETTLEMENT

Soon after the Whitmans and the Spaldings had started their missions in the Oregon Country, **William A. Slacum**, a captain in the United States Navy, came to the Oregon Country on his ship. He had been sent to find out the needs of the growing settlement. He stopped at Fort Vancouver and then went to the Willamette Valley. He talked to the farmers and the missionaries there about their needs.

Until 1838 the Hudson's Bay Company was the only place at which settlers could trade their crops and goods for supplies. But everywhere Slacum went, the people talked about the need for more cattle for milk, meat, and hides.

Slacum was on his way to California, where cattle were plentiful and cheap. He offered a free trip to anyone who wanted to buy a herd there and drive it back to the Oregon Country. The settlers chose a man named **Ewing Young** to lead a group of ten men to go with Slacum.

THE CATTLE DRIVE

When the men reached California, they bought more than 600 head of cattle. They also bought horses to use in driving the cattle back to the Oregon Country, nearly 1,000 miles (1,609 km) away.

At last, in the fall, the bawling of cows was heard in French Prairie. The men divided the cattle among those who had put up money. From then on the settlers had a good supply of milk, meat, and hides. The people of the Oregon Country had worked together to get the things that they needed to build a stronger community.

JASON LEE'S TRIP

But the community still needed laws. The settlers feared that more Americans would not come to a land thought to be lawless. "We can promise no protection but self-defense," one settler said. The people of the Oregon Country signed a **petition** asking the United States government to take "speedy possession" so that Americans would want to settle in the Oregon Country. A petition is a formal request made to a person in a position of authority.

The Granger Collection

Ewing Young and his cattle buying group led more than 600 head of cattle from California to French Prairie in the Oregon Country.

The year after the cattle drive, Jason Lee took the settlers' petition east to Washington, D.C., but nothing came of their requests. Lee, however, was successful in attracting more settlers to the Oregon Country.

Two years later Jason Lee returned to the Oregon Country with a group of 50 missionaries called **The Great Reinforcement**. To reinforce means to add strength. The settlement was growing. There were now about 150 people in French Prairie.

Soon Lee's mission came into competition with the Hudson's Bay Company over goods and land. This caused bad feeling between the Americans and the British. Once again the Americans drew up a petition, but still the United States

119

These pioneers stood in front of the tree that marks Ewing Young's grave.

government took no steps toward making the Oregon Country a part of the United States.

EWING YOUNG

Ewing Young had a large herd of cattle and a fine farm, and he had become quite wealthy. Other settlers came to him when they needed supplies or wanted to borrow money.

In 1841 Ewing Young fell ill and died. This former Mountain Man had no family, and he had not written a will. Nobody knew who owned his farm, herds, and money after his death. There were no courts to decide the question.

Right after Young's funeral, the settlers held a meeting to try to decide what to do. They elected a judge who could handle cases involving property. They also elected a sheriff and three police officers. A committee was chosen to draw up some laws. The settlers decided to meet again in a few months to vote on the laws.

The next time the settlers gathered, they found out that the committee hadn't even met. The people held a meeting to talk over the laws. Some felt that laws were needed. Others thought that the community was managing well without laws. The settlers finally went home without having decided anything, but the judge, the sheriff, and the police officers kept their titles.

WORKING TOGETHER

The settlers had worked together to get the cattle they needed. They had worked together in drawing up petitions to the United States government. Although their efforts to have the United States government take a greater interest in them had not succeeded, they had chosen local officials. This was the first step toward starting a local government.

Check Your Reading

1. Who was William Slacum and how did he help the settlers?
2. Why did Jason Lee make a trip back to the East?
3. Why did bad feelings develop between the Americans and the British?
4. **THINKING SKILL:** How did Ewing Young's death lead to the beginnings of local government?

REVIEWING VOCABULARY

Number a sheet of paper from 1 to 5. Beside each number write the letter of the definition that best matches the word or term.

1. *mission*
   a. A settlement where people of one religion try to convert other people with different beliefs
   b. A meeting of fur trappers
   c. A trail through the mountains
2. *missionary*
   a. A fur trapper
   b. An Indian religious leader
   c. A person who teaches his or her religion to people with different beliefs
3. *Mountain Men*
   a. Fur trappers who became experts in wilderness life
   b. French explorers
   c. Missionaries
4. *rendezvous*
   a. A religious ceremony
   b. A cattle drive
   c. A large meeting of fur traders, trappers, and Indians
5. *The Great Reinforcement*
   a. The addition of 50 missionaries to the Oregon Country in 1841
   b. The arrival of 600 cattle in the Oregon Country in 1838
   c. The yearly meeting of fur traders, trappers, and Indians

REVIEWING FACTS

Number a sheet of paper from 1 to 5. Beside each number write whether the statement is true or false. If the statement is false, rewrite it to make it true.

1. Jedediah Smith was a Protestant missionary in the Oregon Country.
2. A new route, the Green River Gap, was found through the mountains.
3. Fort Hall was a mission.
4. The missionaries brought American settlers to the Oregon Country.
5. William Slacum and Ewing Young led cattle to the Oregon Country.

WRITING ABOUT MAIN IDEAS

1. **Writing an Opinion Paragraph:** Which of these three men, Smith, Young, or Lee, do you think did the most to help the Oregon Country? Write a paragraph giving at least two facts to support your answer.
2. **Writing a Description:** Look closely at the pictures on pages 108 and 109. Then write a paragraph describing a typical Mountain Man.

BUILDING SKILLS: UNDERSTANDING CAUSE AND EFFECT

1. What is a cause? What is an effect?
2. List three causes of the growth of the Oregon Country.

CHAPTER 6

SETTLING OREGON

▼ FOCUS ▼

My great, great, great, great, great, great grandpa and his family came to Oregon on a wagon train in 1852. We still have an old photograph album and a Bible that came out on the Oregon Trail with him.

Nathan Aschbacher lives in Milwaukie, a town located near the end of the Oregon Trail. In this chapter you will read about the hardships that people like Nathan's relatives experienced on the Oregon Trail.

1 The Oregon Trail

READX TO LEARN

Key Vocabulary

pioneer
landmark
wagon train
self-sufficient

Key People

Elijah White
Medorem Crawford
Samuel Barlow

Key Places

Oregon Trail
Oregon City
Fort Laramie
Barlow Road

Read Aloud

Traveled all day as usual. Pressed some flowers. About seven Indians were around our wagons but did not stay long. Passed Castle Rock. Just eight weeks ago today since we left home. I think we are halfway anyhow, but if we stay in this train, we will never get there.

These words were written by 16-year-old Jane Paul Eakin in 1866. She was traveling in a wagon train with her family and many others to make a new home in Eugene, Oregon.

Read for Purpose

1. **WHAT YOU KNOW:** What does the word *pioneer* mean to you?
2. **WHAT YOU WILL LEARN:** What was life like for pioneers on the Oregon Trail?

OREGON FEVER

In the 1840s newspapers were writing about "Oregon Fever," or the desire to move to the Oregon Country. Why were so many people willing to travel to a place that they had never seen before? Some felt that farmlands in the east had become too crowded and too costly. Others wanted to start over in a new place as **pioneers**. A pioneer is a person who is among the first to settle in a region.

The United States government helped to spread Oregon Fever. It started to ask families to support

123

the growth of the United States by moving west. To encourage this move, the government offered free land to American pioneers who would make the journey.

THE OREGON TRAIL

In Chapter 5 you read about how Native Americans led Mountain Men to the South Pass through the Rocky Mountains. In the 1840s the pass became part of a long path known as the Oregon Trail. It was the main route that pioneers took to the Oregon Country.

Look at the map of the Oregon Trail below. Trace the 2,000-mile (3,218-km) route from Independence, Missouri, to Oregon City. Now find Fort Laramie and Fort Hall. Pioneers stopped at these forts for supplies and to rest before continuing on the Oregon Trail.

Numerous landmarks along the Oregon Trail helped travelers to make sure that they were going in the correct direction. A landmark is a familiar object that serves as a guide. Look again at the map of the Oregon Trail. Find these landmarks: Chimney Rock, Split Rock, and the Whitman's mission.

MAP SKILL: In which states will you find Oregon Trail landmarks?

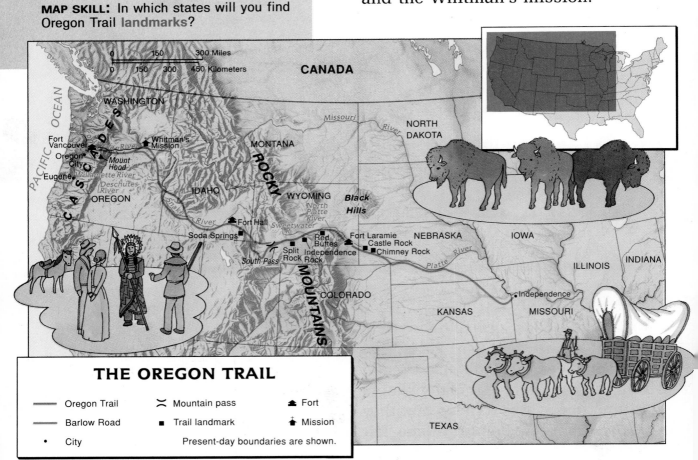

THE OREGON TRAIL

—— Oregon Trail	✕ Mountain pass	⚑ Fort
—— Barlow Road	■ Trail landmark	⚑ Mission
• City	Present-day boundaries are shown.	

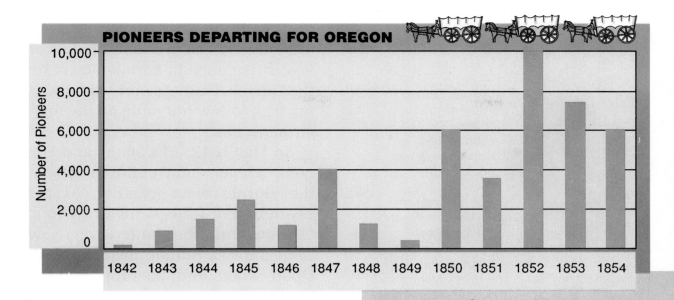

PIONEERS DEPARTING FOR OREGON

Number of Pioneers

10,000 — 8,000 — 6,000 — 4,000 — 2,000 — 0

1842 1843 1844 1845 1846 1847 1848 1849 1850 1851 1852 1853 1854

GRAPH SKILL: Susannah Bristow came to the Oregon Country with these belongings in 1848. According to the graph, how many pioneers came during that same year?

WAGONS WEST

Elijah White had been a member of Jason Lee's mission, which you read about in Chapter 5. Like Lee, White returned to the United States and encouraged people to move west with him.

In May 1842, when Elijah White arrived in Elm Grove, Missouri, more than 100 pioneers were waiting with their covered wagons to travel with him. This was the first wagon train to take the Oregon Trail to the Willamette Valley. A wagon train is a group of covered wagons that follow one another like the railroad cars of a train. Look at the graph above. It shows how many pioneers came west by wagon train during the years 1842 to 1854.

The trip to the Oregon Country took six months. On the trail, the pioneers had to be self-sufficient. Self-sufficient means that you are

125

EXCERPTS FROM THE DIARY OF JANE PAUL EAKIN

April 23, Started on our long journey. We had a sad parting. Johnnie gave me a gold ring.

May 15, Crossed the Missouri River in a ferry boat.

June 25, We camped on the prairie without any water. The Rocky Mountains are in sight covered with snow.

July 7, We came over the roughest, steepest, highest mountain roads I ever saw. . . .

August 17, We entered the Cascade Mountains. Camped in an awful lonely place. Ate supper with candle light.

August 25, Crossed the Williamette River on a ferry. We are at the end of our journey to Uncle Andrew's.

Thousands of children traveled on the Oregon Trail. Jane Paul Eakin's diary describes what it was like.

able to provide for your own needs. Each family had to carry food, water, clothing, rifles for hunting, and axes for chopping down trees.

LIFE ON THE OREGON TRAIL

What would it have been like to travel with this first wagon train? Medorem Crawford, a young pioneer traveling west, kept a journal during his six-month journey. His journal helps us to understand what it was like to be in a wagon train on the Oregon Trail. As you read about his trip, follow his route on the map on page 124.

In May 1842, 16 wagons and 105 men, women, and children, began the journey west together. At the beginning of June, Crawford wrote, "Followed up the Platte River. Saw thousands of buffalo near the trail. Good wood and pasture, but the water was poor."

After crossing the Platte River in early July, the wagon train continued along the riverbank. Soon the pioneers were within sight of the Red Buttes. This was an important trail landmark.

At the end of July they camped near a Cheyenne Indian village. Crawford wrote, "About noon the Chiefs, together with some hundreds of others, came to camp. We made them presents of ammunition and tobacco."

By the middle of August the pioneers arrived at Fort Hall, where they were able to fix their wagons and get supplies. After the group of pioneers left Fort Hall, an Indian guide helped Crawford and some other members of the wagon train to get to the Whitman's mission. Here they prepared for the final part of their journey to the Willamette Valley. This is what Crawford wrote about the last part of his trip.

September 25 . . . saw Mount Hood, passed The Dalles or rapids of the River. . . .

October 3 . . . a few of us accompanied those who were here before us to the Willamette where we found many people. . . .

October 21 . . . distance from Independence [Missouri] to Willamette Falls, according to my estimate, [is] 1,740 miles. . . .

THE END OF THE TRAIL

At the end of the Oregon Trail many pioneers traveled the rapids of the Columbia River in order to reach the Willamette Valley. You will read more about one family's dangerous journey in the Oregon Traditions lesson on page 128.

In 1846 the Barlow Road was cleared through part of the Cascade Mountains by the pioneer Samuel Barlow. This route was safer to travel than the rapids, but it was still dangerous. In order to reach this road wagons were tied to trees with rope and slowly lowered into the valley below.

A NEW LIFE

As you have read, Oregon Fever and the offer of land encouraged pioneers to move to the West. Thousands of pioneers traveled the Oregon Trail to the Willamette Valley. The trip was difficult, but the pioneers were determined to begin a new life in the Oregon Country.

Today you can retrace parts of the Oregon Trail in Wyoming by following the ruts made by covered wagons on their way west.

Check Your Reading

1. Give two reasons that Oregon Fever spread across the United States.
2. Why were Fort Laramie and Fort Hall important landmarks on the Oregon Trail?
3. **GEOGRAPHY SKILL:** In what ways did the natural features of the Oregon Trail require the pioneers to be self-sufficient?
4. **THINKING SKILL:** List three questions that you could have asked Medorem Crawford and Jane Paul Eakin to find out more specific facts about their journeys.

127

READ TO LEARN

Key Vocabulary

white water

Read for Purpose

1. **WHAT YOU KNOW:** Why did so many people emigrate to the Willamette Valley?
2. **WHAT YOU WILL LEARN:** How did one young pioneer survive the dangers of the Oregon Trail?

LISH APPLEGATE'S SWIM for LIFE

In Lesson 1 you read about the pioneers—the men, women, and children who braved the long, hard Oregon Trail. Lish Applegate and his family were among them. Eleven-year-old Lish was always ready for adventure. On hot summer days back in Missouri, he went off to the river whenever he had the chance. He taught himself to swim in the cool waters of the Osage River. Two thousand miles (3,218 km) away, on the Columbia River, the most dangerous part of the Oregon Trail, this skill would save his life.

ON THE RIVER

Lish Applegate held tightly to the side of the flat-bottomed boat as it rolled in the rough waters. The spray was so high he couldn't see his parents in the boat ahead of him. Back at Fort Walla Walla, folks had warned the travelers about the voyage down the Columbia River. It would be the most dangerous part of their

journey along the Oregon Trail. But no warning could have prepared them for these miles of white water, or churning rapids, filled with whirlpools.

It was a grand adventure for a boy like Lish. But for some passengers it was pure suffering, worse than crossing the Rocky Mountains. The boat rose and swooped, shaking loose pots and pans that had been bundled into quilts and tied down. Whole households had been packed into the flat-bottomed boats along with the passengers. For courage, Lish winked at Will Parker. Will, ten years older than Lish, wasn't afraid of anything, and he was a strong swimmer, too.

Lish looked out over the great river. Their boat was the sixth in line. He saw that the lead boat hugged the riverbank, avoiding the rougher water in the center. Their Indian guide stood tall in the bow, a red bandanna around his head so that folks could spot him. The other boats followed. Now came their turn.

"Pull!" Uncle Mack shouted. Suddenly they were drifting toward the rapids. "Harder!" he cried as he worked the steering oar at the back of the boat. "Lish, get down! Look alive, everybody! When I holler, pull on those oars for all you're worth! Rough water's coming! Everybody hold on! We'll have to ride it out!"

A sudden lurch threw everyone off balance. Boxes
came loose and tumbled forward, as if sliding downhill. Then a wall of freezing white water exploded over
the side and struck Lish like a fist. The boat turned
over and spilled him into the river. High waves crashed
over Lish's head, choking and blinding him. Kicking as
hard as he could, he fought his way to the surface. He
took a deep breath and began swimming toward a
rocky island he could see in the distance.

"Lish!"

Lish heard someone call his name. It was Will Parker, clinging to a soaked feather quilt. Lish swam
toward him and let out a sigh of relief as his fingers
closed on the feathers. Lish and Will hung on to the
quilt, steering it to the nearby island. At last their boots
touched the river bottom. They dragged themselves
ashore, too exhausted to move.

Lish recovered first. "We've got to get off this island,
Will. The other boats can't reach us here."

Will shook his head. "You go, Lish. I'm all done in.
I can't go back into that river."

"There's another way. If I follow those rocks, I think they'll take me to the riverbank. Rest here, Will. I'll try it first. If I make it, I'll come back for you."

Lish reached the riverbank over a narrow bridge of rocks that formed a pathway through the water. He did, indeed, go back for Will, and the other boats found them a short time later.

Not everyone survived the journey to the end of the Oregon Trail. Those who did finally reached the great, green Willamette Valley. Many, like the Applegate family, settled there. Lish grew up to become a lawyer. No doubt he taught his children to swim.

 Check Your Reading

1. Where did Lish learn to swim?
2. What did Lish do when the boat went over?
3. How did Lish and Will reach safety on the riverbank?
4. **THINKING SKILL:** If Lish Applegate were to travel today from Independence, Missouri, to the Willamette Valley, predict how his journey would be different.

2 The Wolf Meetings

READ TO LEARN

Key Vocabulary
population
Wolf Meetings

Key People
Joseph Meek

Key Places
Champoeg

Read Aloud

How is it, fellow citizens, with you and me, and our children and wives? I submit and move that a committee be appointed to take measures for the civil and military protection of this colony. . . .

This is how one American settler raised the question of forming a community government. He was at a meeting with American and French-Canadian settlers in the Willamette Valley in 1843.

Read for Purpose

1. **WHAT YOU KNOW:** Why is it important to have rules in your classroom?
2. **WHAT YOU WILL LEARN:** What steps were taken to form a local government in the Willamette Valley?

THE NEED FOR LAWS

You read about Ewing Young's death in Chapter 5. The concern over Young's property made the settlers realize that they needed laws. Laws were needed to settle disagreements about land ownership. The settlers also needed a leader. "As thare [there] is no laws in this country we do the best we can," one trapper wrote in his diary.

The population, or the number of people, living in the Willamette Valley was growing fast. Two main groups were settling in this area, the American pioneers and the French-Canadians who had once worked for the Hudson's Bay Company. Most Canadians did not agree that laws were needed. These Canadians relied upon John McLoughlin of Fort Vancouver as their leader.

132

They thought of him as their doctor, judge, and banker. He helped them to settle disagreements. Although John McLoughlin had been very kind to American settlers when they arrived, the settlers wanted a government of their own. They were also in favor of making laws that would unite and protect them.

THE WOLF MEETINGS

Both the American and Canadian settlers were very upset about the wolves, panthers, bears, and bobcats that were killing their cattle. The American settlers saw this problem as an opportunity to make plans to form a local government. First they would try to work together with other settlers on the common problem of wild animals. If both groups worked well together, the American settlers decided, they would try the next step in their plan. This step was to suggest writing laws for the community.

The settlers who were in favor of creating laws decided to hold public meetings with all farmers in the area. The map on this page shows where these meetings were held. The purpose of these meetings was:

to take into consideration . . . the protection of our herds against the beasts in the country.

The meetings were called Wolf Meetings because of problems with wolves and other wild animals.

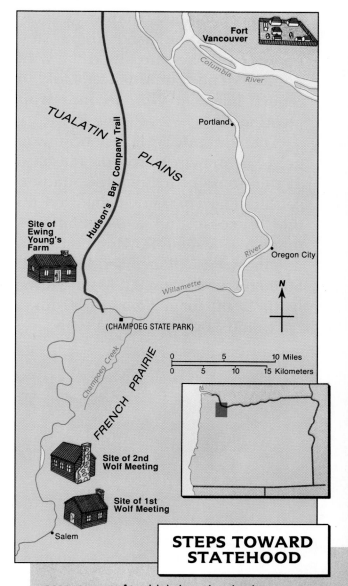

STEPS TOWARD STATEHOOD

MAP SKILL: At which location in the Willamette Valley did the first Wolf Meeting take place? Where did the second meeting take place?

A large group of American and Canadian settlers held the first Wolf Meeting on February 2, 1843. They met at the home of William H. Gray, located in present-day Salem. At the meeting a committee was appointed

133

to collect money from everyone, which would be used to pay the bounty to those who killed the wild animals. The committee was told to report back to the second Wolf Meeting.

The second Wolf Meeting was held on French Prairie on March 6 at the home of a French-Canadian settler. The committee reported on their success and a decision was made to pay the following bounty to anyone who killed a wild animal: $5.00 for a panther, $3.00 for a large wolf, $2.00 for a bear, $1.50 for a lynx, and 50¢ for a small wolf.

The vote at Champoeg was an early step toward a government for American settlers in the Willamette Valley.

The group of settlers who were in favor of forming a local government thought that the Wolf Meetings were proceeding well. They decided that they would try the second step of their plan. William H. Gray made the suggestion that they discuss writing laws. After talking it over, the settlers chose a committee of 12 men to draft some laws. They decided to meet again in two months in order to discuss the committee's report.

THE VOTE AT CHAMPOEG

On May 2, 1843, about 100 Americans and Canadians gathered at Champoeg (cham pō′ eg) in the Willamette Valley. They crowded into a Hudson's Bay Company storage building and began their meeting. The committee that was formed at the March 6 meeting proposed that the settlers use the laws that were written by the committee to form a local government. The settlers raised their voices as they agreed and disagreed with what was being said. Soon it became so noisy that the settlers couldn't hear one another. When it came time to vote, they moved outside.

But because the meeting was outside, it was difficult to count the votes. One man suggested that those in favor of a government should stand to the right, and those against a government should stand to the left. Joseph Meek, or Big Joe

Meek as the settlers called him, was an American Mountain Man. With a booming voice he called out:

Who's for a divide? All for the report of the committee and organization, follow me.

Two lines were formed and heads were counted. In a very close vote the settlers decided to form a local government. All of the American settlers voted in favor of the government. Only two French-Canadians voted with the Americans.

You can visit the site of this historic meeting in Champoeg State Park on the Willamette River. Every July the Champoeg Historic Pageant re-creates what life was like for the settlers living in the Willamette Valley during this period in history.

TOWARD SELF-GOVERNMENT

In this lesson you have read about how the increase in the population of the Willamette Valley led the settlers to realize that laws were needed. Cooperation among settlers at the Wolf Meetings led to discussions about a local government. As a result, the vote at Champoeg became a historic turning point for the American settlers who were living in the Willamette Valley.

Joe Meek was an American Mountain Man who settled in the Willamette Valley. He helped American settlers form a government there.

![checkmark] Check Your Reading

1. Why did the American settlers and the French-Canadian settlers disagree about the need for a local government?
2. What was the purpose of the Wolf Meetings and what did they accomplish?
3. What role did Big Joe Meek play during the vote at Champoeg?
4. **THINKING SKILL:** Predict what might have happened if the American settlers had not won the vote at Champoeg.

Asking Questions

Suppose that you want to buy a new bicycle. Before you go shopping, you should make a list of questions to ask the salesperson. Your list might include the following questions.

1. What special features does each bicycle have?
2. Which style of bicycle will fit your needs best?
3. What colors are available?
4. How much does each bicycle cost?

Getting answers to these questions will help you to make your choice.

Knowing what questions to ask is a useful skill in everyday life. It also helps you with your reading. When you want to learn about a topic, you should ask questions about it. Then you should read to find the answers.

Trying the Skill

Suppose you have chosen the topic of the settlers' lives on the Oregon Trail for a class report. Which two of the following questions would you ask to learn more about it?

1. What was the route of the Oregon Trail?
2. What hardships were faced by the settlers who used the Oregon Trail?
3. What were some other trails that settlers could use to travel west?

How did you know which two questions to ask?

HELPING YOURSELF

The steps on the left will help you to ask questions on any topic or subject. The example on the right shows one way to use these steps to learn more about the Oregon Trail.

One Way to Ask Questions	Example
1. Choose a topic you want to know about.	Your topic is the settlers' lives on the Oregon Trail.
2. Ask yourself what kind of information you want to know.	You want to know the route of the Oregon Trail and the hardships of passing through it.
3. List questions you can ask to get this information.	The first two questions will help you to find the information you want about the route of the Oregon Trail and about the hardships that were faced by settlers passing through it.
4. Reread your questions. Cross out any that are not related to the information you need.	The third question is not about the Oregon Trail. It would not be helpful in getting information about the topic. You should cross it out.

Applying the Skill

Now apply what you have learned. Suppose you want to know what the Oregon Trail offers tourists. Which of these questions would you ask?

1. What is the best way to travel along the Oregon Trail?
2. What is the average price of a home along the Oregon Trail?
3. Which historic sites can be found along the Oregon Trail?

Check yourself by answering the following questions.

1. Why is Question 3 useful to you?
   a. It is about the Oregon Trail.
   b. Historic sites are a tourist attraction.
   c. Few tourists visit historic sites.

2. How do you know that Question 2 is not related to the topic?
   a. Tourists often buy houses in the places they visit.
   b. The cost of housing is high along the Oregon Trail.
   c. The price of homes has nothing to do with tourism.

Reviewing the Skill

1. What is the first step in asking questions?
2. What should you do after listing your questions about a topic?
3. Why is it important to ask good questions?

3 The Provisional Government

READ TO LEARN

Key Vocabulary

provisional government
compromise

Key People

James K. Polk
George Abernethy

Read Aloud

It was at first so weak that a real government could not be said to have existed in practice until 1845 . . . [it] emerged through trial and error. . . .

One historian used these words to describe how the local government in present-day Oregon took shape.

Read for Purpose

1. **WHAT YOU KNOW:** How does your teacher help to settle student disagreements?
2. **WHAT YOU WILL LEARN:** How did the provisional government help the United States and Great Britain to settle their boundary disagreement?

A FIRST STEP

In Chapter 4 you read about the joint occupation treaty between the United States and Great Britain. Both countries continued to share the Oregon Country for nearly 20 years. A decision still had to be made about which country would own this land.

Meanwhile, the success of the Wolf Meetings helped the American settlers to gain some control of the Oregon Country. The next step was to form a local government. This government would be responsible for creating laws and making sure that everyone in the community obeyed them.

THE PROVISIONAL GOVERNMENT

The first American government was about to be formed in the Oregon Country. A committee of nine men was elected to draft some laws. On July 5, 1843, the American settlers living in the Willamette Valley gathered at Champoeg. There they voted to accept the new government. This government was called a **provisional government**. **George Abernethy** was later chosen to be the governor. The provisional, or temporary, government would serve the settlers until the United States decided whether or not the Oregon Country would become a part of the United States.

According to these new laws, the settlers were expected to donate money to pay the expenses of the provisional government. A group of men were elected to protect the set-tlers. As more American pioneers arrived in the Willamette Valley, they participated in the provisional government. Their involvement helped to strengthen the American claim to the Oregon Country.

In 1845 John McLoughlin was asked to join the provisional government. He accepted because he believed the government would be:

> . . . a union of . . . British and American subjects . . . its purpose being the protection of person and property. ⸙

The land owned by the Hudson's Bay Company would now be protected under the laws of the provisional government.

George Abernethy was chosen governor of the provisional government in the Willamette Valley.

In 1856 James K. Polk was President of the United States. How did the phrase "Fifty-four Forty or Fight" become associated with him?

"FIFTY-FOUR FORTY OR FIGHT"

In 1846 James K. Polk was President of the United States. President Polk hoped that Great Britain would give up its claim to the Oregon Country and allow it to become a part of the United States. President Polk wanted the 54°40'N line of latitude to be the northern border of the United States.

On pages 42 and 43 you read about lines of latitude and longitude. Look at the map on page 141 and find the line of latitude marked 54°40'N. The phrase "Fifty-four Forty or Fight" became associated with President Polk. If Great Britain did not accept this border, Polk wanted the United States to go to war to fight for the Oregon Country.

Great Britain disagreed with the choice of 54°40'N as the United States border. Instead they suggested the 42°N line of latitude as the border. Look again at the map and find the line marked 42°N. Both countries became angry with one another because they could not agree on a border. Would the United States and Britain go to war?

AGREEMENT IS REACHED

Neither country wanted a war. Great Britain was already at war in India. The United States was getting ready to fight against Mexico over another piece of land. Therefore, both countries looked for a peaceful compromise. A compromise is the settlement of an argument or dispute by having each side agree to give up part of its demands.

In the spring of 1846 Great Britain proposed a compromise. The British suggested that the 49°N line of latitude should be the border between the two countries. You can find this line on the map on page 141. All the land north of this parallel would belong to Great Britain, and all the land south of this parallel, including the Columbia River, would belong to the United States.

The United States decided to accept Britain's compromise. A treaty between the two countries was made. It said that the use of the Columbia River from the 49°N line of latitude west to the Pacific Ocean would remain "open to the Hudson's Bay Company and to all British people that wanted to trade with the company." However, the Hudson's Bay Company would only be allowed to use the Columbia River without charge until 1859. After 1859 the Hudson's Bay Company would have to leave the area south of the 49°N line of latitude. The Oregon Country now belonged to the United States. Each country had given up part of its original claim in order to reach a peaceful solution.

THE OREGON COUNTRY

In this lesson you have read how the provisional government helped to strengthen the American claim to the Oregon Country. You have also read how the United States and Britain settled their boundary disagreements by compromising. Although the Oregon Country now belonged to the United States, the settlers still had a lot of work to do before their area could become a state.

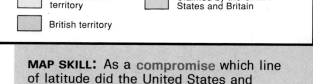

Check Your Reading

1. Why was the first government in the Oregon Country called a provisional government?

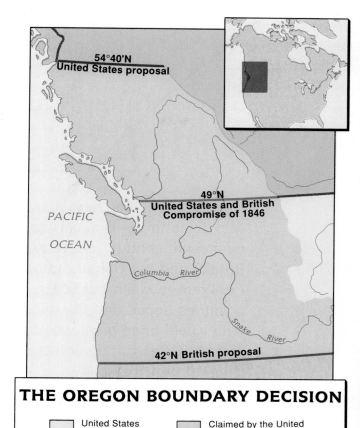

THE OREGON BOUNDARY DECISION

United States territory

British territory

Claimed by the United States and Britain

MAP SKILL: As a compromise which line of latitude did the United States and Britain agree upon?

2. What was the purpose of the provisional government?

3. **GEOGRAPHY SKILL:** Look at the Atlas map on pages 270–271. Which states of the United States have the 49°N line of latitude as their border?

4. **THINKING SKILL:** Why did the United States' acceptance of Great Britain's boundary compromise seem to be the best choice for the United States to make at the time?

Should Oregon Be a Part of Great Britain or the United States?

In Chapter 4 you read about some of the early explorers who came to the Oregon Country during the last part of the nineteenth century. These explorers came from Spain, Great Britain, and the United States. Each country wanted its own explorers to claim the Oregon Country. The leaders of these countries hoped that the natural resources found in the new land would bring great wealth to their countries. From 1792 to 1846 Great Britain and the United States both claimed ownership of this land.

You have read how the British Hudson's Bay Company had developed Fort Vancouver into a growing fur-trading community. However, in 1843 the first wagon train brought 100 American pioneers to the Oregon Country. And by 1846 thousands of American settlers had come to live in the area. It was now clear that a decision had to be made about which country would control this land.

Did Great Britain or the United States have the stronger claim to the Oregon Country?

POINT ☆\☞

Great Britain Should Own Oregon

The British claimed the Oregon Country in 1792 when Captain Vancouver sailed up the Columbia River. During the next 50 years they worked to develop a trading community in this area. But by 1846 American citizens threatened to take control of the Oregon Country because they outnumbered the British population there.

In an address to the public in 1845, John McLoughlin stated why he thought that the Oregon Country rightfully belonged to Great Britain.

> The Hudson's Bay Company has opened roads and has made other advances at a great outlay of money. They have carried on business that has helped the country.

- According to John McLoughlin, how did the Hudson's Bay Company help to improve the Oregon Country before the Americans arrived?

COUNTERPOINT ☜/☆

The United States Should Own Oregon

The United States claimed the Oregon Country because Captain Gray sailed the Columbia River in 1792. As the United States was expanding westward, its leaders sent expeditions to the Oregon Country. By 1845 hundreds of American pioneers began to settle there and soon outnumbered the British population. They wanted the area to become part of the United States.

Peter H. Burnett, a pioneer, told why he felt that Americans should control the Oregon Country.

> The moment we brought our families, cattle, and loaded wagons to the Columbia River in 1843, the question was decided in our favor. Of course Britain would not want a colony settled by American citizens.

- According to Peter Burnett, why would Britain not have wanted to control the Oregon Country?

UNDERSTANDING THE POINT/COUNTERPOINT

1. What reasons did the British have for wanting to possess the Oregon Country?
2. What reasons did the United States have for wanting to possess the Oregon Country?
3. Which side had the stronger case? Why?

4 The Oregon Territory

Key Vocabulary

territory
Congress

Key People

Peter Skene Ogden
Joseph Lane

Read Aloud

We have been among you for 30 years without shedding blood. If the Americans begin war it will not end until every man of you is cut off from the face of the earth!

A fur trapper spoke these words of warning to a Cayuse chief as tensions built between the settlers and the Indians. These tensions caused the American settlers to take steps to make the Oregon Country a territory.

Read for Purpose

1. **WHAT YOU KNOW:** What kind of government did the Oregon Country have?
2. **WHAT YOU WILL LEARN:** Why did the United States make the Oregon Country a territory?

MASSACRE AT THE WHITMAN'S MISSION

During the fall and winter of 1847 a terrible misunderstanding occurred between the American settlers at the Whitman's mission and the Cayuse Indians. Measles swept through many settlements and Indian villages. This sickness was brought by settlers who came west, and it left hundreds of Indians dead. Marcus Whitman tried to help the Cayuse by giving them medicine, but the medicine did not work. The Cayuse who took the medicine died anyway. This led some of the Cayuse to think that Whitman was poisoning them.

In late November a group of Cayuse attacked the mission. They killed Marcus and Narcissa Whitman, along with 12 other people. More than 50 people, including children, were taken as prisoners.

The attack on the mission became known as the Whitman Massacre. A massacre is the killing of many people at the same time.

When news of the Whitman Massacre reached Fort Vancouver, a Canadian fur trapper named **Peter Skene Ogden** took a small group of men to talk to the chief of the Cayuse. He told the chief that if the captured settlers were not set free, the Americans might start a war. The Cayuse chief released the prisoners. Then the American settlers gathered a group of 500 men who went to the Cayuse Indians. They asked the Cayuse to hand over those Indians who had attacked the mission. The Cayuse did not surrender these men until the following year. In the fall of 1848, five Cayuse were brought to Oregon City, where they were hanged.

After the Whitman Massacre the settlers wanted greater protection than the provisional government could give them. They turned to the United States government for help.

BIG JOE MEEK IN WASHINGTON

In March 1848 the settlers sent Big Joe Meek to Washington, D.C., to ask the national government for help. When Meek arrived he was dirty, and his whiskers were long. His deerskin jacket and trousers were ragged. He told newspaper reporters about the Whitman Mas-

Today Marcus Whitman is remembered as a brave pioneer who paved the way for future settlers.

sacre and the reason for his journey. Meek went to the White House and spoke to President Polk about making Oregon a **territory** of the United States. A territory is an area of land

145

Joseph Lane became the first governor of the Oregon Territory.

Country was now a United States territory. President Polk appointed Joseph Lane as governor of the territory. When Lane arrived in the Oregon Territory he said, "I declare the laws of the United States to be in force of said [Oregon] territory." Big Joe Meek was appointed United States marshal. Meek's job was to help protect the settlers in the Oregon Territory.

THE OREGON TERRITORY

As you have read, the American settlers turned to the United States government for help after the Whitman Massacre. They wanted their area to become a United States territory. In August 1848 the Territory of Oregon was established. At last the settlers were protected by the laws of the United States.

that is protected by the national government but does not have the rights of a state. However, the government would help the territory to build roads and government buildings. It would also provide mail service and an army if necessary.

After the President listened to Meek, Polk spoke with the men in Congress about the Oregon Country. Congress is the branch of the United States government that makes laws. On August 14, 1848, Congress passed the Act to Establish the Territorial Government of Oregon. President Polk signed this act and it became a law. The Oregon

Check Your Reading

1. How did a misunderstanding between Marcus Whitman and the Cayuse Indians lead to the Whitman Massacre?
2. How did Peter Skene Ogden help with the release of the prisoners held captive by the Cayuse Indians?
3. Why did the settlers want Oregon to become a territory?
4. **THINKING SKILL:** Beginning with the Whitman Massacre, list all the events in this lesson in the order in which they occurred.

REVIEWING VOCABULARY

compromise   self-sufficient
pioneer   territory
population

Number a sheet of paper from 1 to 5. Beside each number write the word or term from the list above that best matches the definition.

1. A person who is among the first to settle in a region
2. A settlement of a dispute in which each side gives up some demands
3. Able to take care of one's needs
4. The number of people living in a place
5. An area of land that is protected by the national government but has none of the rights of a state

REVIEWING FACTS

Number a sheet of paper from 1 to 5. Beside each number write whether the statement is true or false. If the statement is false, rewrite it to make it true.

1. Many Cayuse near the Whitman Mission died of Oregon Fever.
2. The settlers decided to form a government so they could pass laws about how to deal with the problem of wild animals killing their cattle.
3. The northern boundary of the Oregon Country was decided through a compromise.
4. Joe Meek tried to convince President Polk to make Oregon a United States territory.
5. The Whitman Massacre was caused by a misunderstanding between the United States government and Marcus Whitman.

WRITING ABOUT MAIN IDEAS

Writing a Debate: Imagine that you witnessed the meeting at Champoeg at which the Oregon settlers voted to set up a government. Before the vote people spoke for and against the government. Choose one side and write what you would have said to convince others of your opinion.

BUILDING SKILLS: ASKING QUESTIONS

1. Which steps should you follow in asking good questions?
2. Suppose that you were doing a report on the career of Joe Meek. Which of these questions would help you in your research?
   a. Where was he born?
   b. How did he become a Mountain Man?
   c. Did he attend the Wolf Meetings?
   d. Was he married?
   e. How was he chosen to go to President Polk?

REVIEWING VOCABULARY

compromise	population
mission	rendezvous
missionary	self-sufficient
Mountain	territory
Men	The Great
pioneer	Reinforcement

Number a sheet of paper from 1 to 10. Beside each number write the word or term from the list above that best completes the sentence.

1. When the Oregon Country became a ____ of the United States, it did not have all the rights of a state.
2. The ____ tried to convert the Indians to Christianity.
3. The ____ of the area grew larger after The Great Reinforcement.
4. Because Jack and José had different ideas about what to do, they had to reach a ____.
5. The pioneers who traveled west had to be ____.
6. A ____ is one of the first people to settle in a new area.
7. Jedediah Smith and the other fur trappers met at the ____.
8. ____ were fur trappers who knew the secrets of the wilderness.
9. The ____ included farmland.
10. The 50 missionaries that Jason Lee brought to the Oregon Country were called ____.

WRITING ABOUT THE UNIT

1. **Writing a Paragraph:** Many changes came to the Oregon Country after the American settlers moved in. Changes affected the Indians, the wild animals, the landscape, and other aspects of the country. Write a paragraph describing at least two of these changes.

2. **Exploring Sources of Information:** How do we know about the lives of the pioneers who traveled west? Much of our information comes from people's journals. Write a composition in which you answer these questions: Do you think that journals are a good source of information about historical events? What can you learn from such journals? What would you probably not learn from them? What other sources might also be useful for learning about pioneers' lives?

3. **Writing a Speech:** What do you think Joe Meek said to President Polk when he tried to convince him to make the Oregon Country a territory of the United States? Write a speech that he could have made. Mention how the change would help the Oregon Country and how it would help the United States. Read your speech to your classmates.

ACTIVITIES

1. **Making a Travel Brochure:** Find out what you can see along the Oregon Trail today. Then make a travel brochure that includes pictures of and words about the sights along the trail.

2. **Researching Women Pioneers:** Use encyclopedias or other books to find out what life was like for women pioneers. Try to answer such questions as: How many women pioneers were there? How did they spend their time in their new homes? Which dangers did they face? Were they generally happy?

3. **Working Together to Make a Diagram or Model:** Work in groups to make a diagram or model of a mission. Include the buildings, the farmland, and the people at work and at play. Be sure to label the parts of the diagram or model.

BUILDING SKILLS: UNDERSTANDING CAUSE AND EFFECT

Read the paragraph below and answer the questions that follow.

> Oregon Fever spread through the East. Stories about the Oregon Country grew wilder and wilder. One story claimed that wheat in Oregon grew as tall as men. When eastern farmers heard such stories, they flocked to the Oregon Country.

1. What is the difference between a cause and an effect?
2. Name a cause in the paragraph. Name an effect.
3. What word or words might help you to recognize the difference between cause and effect?
4. Explain why it is important to be able to tell the difference between causes and effects?

 **LINKING PAST, PRESENT, AND FUTURE**

In the 1800s the population of Oregon was made up mainly of Indians and settlers who traveled here from the East. Today our population is much more varied. Try to find out about the groups of people that make up Oregon's population today. In what way do you think our population might change in the future?

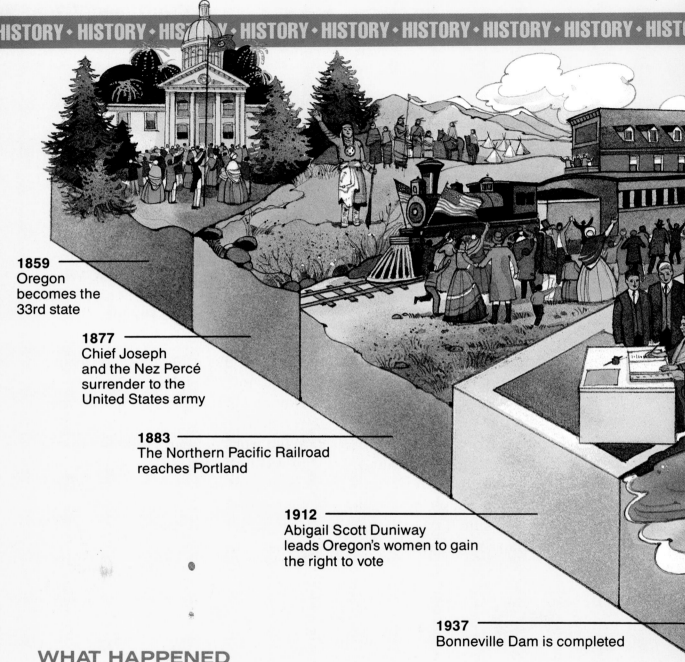

1859
Oregon
becomes the
33rd state

1877
Chief Joseph
and the Nez Percé
surrender to the
United States army

1883
The Northern Pacific Railroad
reaches Portland

1912
Abigail Scott Duniway
leads Oregon's women to gain
the right to vote

1937
Bonneville Dam is completed

1938-1990s
Oregon leads
the nation with
laws protecting
the environment

WHAT HAPPENED

After Oregon became a state,
many changes took place. Wars between
the settlers and the Indians ended in bitter
disagreement. New forms of transportation helped
make life easier and new ideas in government gave
citizens more power. Oregonians are still working hard
to build our state and to protect its air, land, and water.

150

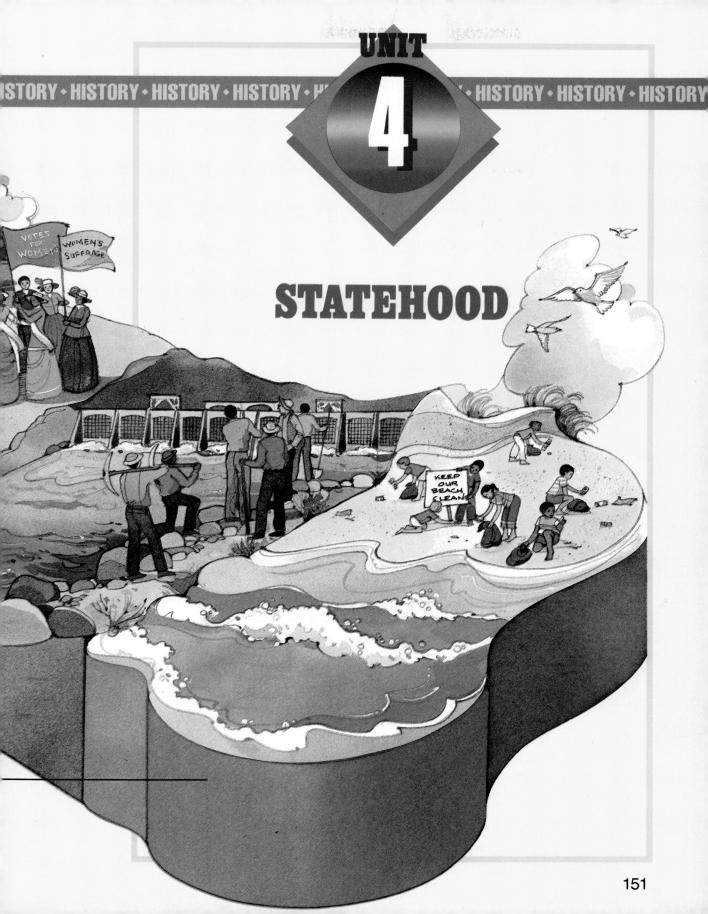

UNIT
4

STATEHOOD

VOTES FOR WOMEN

WOMEN'S SUFFRAGE

KEEP OUR BEACH CLEAN

CHAPTER 7

STATEHOOD

FOCUS

My family has lived on our farm since 1853 before Oregon was a state. I've always wanted to know what it was like here before they built our house.

Jodi Chastain's family farmed this land near Maupin when Oregon was still a territory. In this chapter you will read about the process by which Oregon became a state.

1 Oregon Becomes a State

READ TO LEARN

📑 Key Vocabulary

Donation Land Act
ghost town

constitution
constitutional
    convention

Key Places

Jacksonville
Washington
    Territory

📑 Read Aloud

But now the people were called upon to lay the foundation of a state; to decide upon matters affecting their interests for all time.

It was not easy for a territory to become a state during the years between 1855 and 1865. There were problems in Oregon and in other parts of the nation.

📑 Read for Purpose

1. **WHAT YOU KNOW:** How many states make up the United States today?
2. **WHAT YOU WILL LEARN:** Why did the settlers want the Oregon Territory to become a state?

A GROWING TERRITORY

Settlers kept coming to the Oregon Territory. By 1848, 13,000 people lived in Oregon. Most of them settled in the more than 30 towns in the Willamette Valley.

In 1850 the Donation Land Act was passed by Congress. This act allowed each white male settler to claim 320 acres (130 ha) of land if he had lived on that land for at least four years. If he had lived there for less than four years, he could claim only half as much. The Donation Land Act also said that a married couple could claim twice as much land as a single man. However, a single woman was not allowed to claim any land at all.

GOLD RUSH

In 1848 gold was discovered in California. There were more than

70,000 pioneers who rushed there hoping to become rich. The gold rush brought cash into the Oregon Territory. Oregon settlers sold lumber, beef, and salmon to the miners in California. The miners paid for these goods in cash or gold dust, which was used instead of cash.

In 1850 gold was discovered in the southwestern part of Oregon along the Rogue River. This discovery led to the founding of many mining towns, such as Jacksonville. Many settlers stayed in some of these towns even when the gold was gone. Other mining towns, such as Granite, in northeast Oregon, became ghost towns. A ghost town is a town that became deserted when its mines closed down and people moved away. All that remains are crumbling buildings.

Can you imagine what living in the ghost town of Granite must have been like during mining times?

BECOMING A STATE

Many settlers in Oregon felt that the territory was ready to become a state. A state has more power than a territory does. If Oregon were a state, the people would be allowed to choose their own governor and to take part in voting for President of the United States.

But before Oregon could become a state, its people had to solve several problems. One was that the Oregon Territory was too large to be governed easily as one state. Some settlers asked Congress to divide the territory into two territories. In March 1853 a law was passed that created the Washington Territory.

A second problem arose because settlers could not agree on a constitution, or a plan for the new state government. Because some of the settlers wanted to allow slavery and others did not, they voted three times not to hold a constitutional convention This was a meeting where a constitution would be written.

DISAGREEING ABOUT SLAVERY

Slavery was not an issue only in Oregon; the entire nation was divided over this issue. Because the states in the north did not allow slavery, they were called "free states." The states in the south were called "slave states" because they permitted slavery. The ancestors of slaves had been brought from Africa and forced to work on large farms. The settlers in Oregon and lawmakers in Congress argued about whether Oregon should become a slave state or a free state.

THE CONVENTION OF 1857

In 1857 Oregon finally held a constitutional convention. The settlers agreed that they would vote separately on the constitution and the slavery issues. This decision allowed them to vote in favor of the constitution. Then they passed a law that said that slavery would be illegal. However, they also passed a law that said that freed slaves and other African-Americans could not live in Oregon.

Congress now had to approve the constitution. But it was still divided over the slavery issue. Two more years passed before it agreed that Oregon should be a free state. At last, on February 14, 1859, President James Buchanan signed the law that made Oregon a state.

Within a short time, however, the northern and the southern states were no longer able to resolve their differences peacefully. The North and South fought each other in the Civil War from 1861 to 1865. Oregon supported the North. The victory of the North ended the practice of slavery throughout the United States.

THE STATE OF OREGON

As you have read, the process of making Oregon a state took nearly

Citizens in every town of Oregon celebrated statehood day.

ten years. Decisions about the size of Oregon's territory, the state constitution, and the issue of slavery played important roles in this process. Oregon also tried to become a state during a difficult time in our nation's history. However, the people of Oregon did not give up. They worked hard to reach their goal.

 Check Your Reading

1. How did the gold rush help people in the Oregon Territory?
2. What were some of the problems that the settlers faced in trying to make the Oregon Territory a state?
3. **THINKING SKILL:** Beginning with the gold rush, list the events in this lesson that led to statehood.

2 Indian Wars

Key Vocabulary
reservation
treaty

Key People
Sarah Winnemucca
Captain Jack
Chief Joseph

Read Aloud

You promise us good things, but your promises are very forked. They branch out in many different directions.

This is how Chief Winnemucca reacted when the United States government promised him a new home and a better way of life. For hundreds of years Native Americans had lived freely on Oregon's land. Now the government was forcing them to move.

Read for Purpose

1. **WHAT YOU KNOW:** How did the way of life of the Native Americans depend on Oregon's natural resources?
2. **WHAT YOU WILL LEARN:** Why did some Native Americans go to war with the settlers?

LAND PROBLEMS IN OREGON

In Chapter 3 you read that the groups of Native Americans in Oregon shared a deep love for their land. It was their source of food, shelter, and clothing. For hundreds of years the Indians had roamed freely over the land they called "mother earth."

When missionaries came to Oregon in the 1830s, they faced some conflicts with the Indians. Once the Oregon Territory had become a state, new conflicts arose. By 1860, 50,000 white settlers had already claimed land in Oregon. New settlers kept coming and they, too, wanted the Indians' land. But Indians did not want to give up land that had belonged to them.

The United States government came up with a plan that would end the conflict between the settlers and the Indians. Each group of Native Americans was told to move to a reservation. A reservation is a piece of public land set aside for Indians to live on. They were told that there they would learn to build houses and to farm the way settlers did.

A WAY OF LIFE COMES TO AN END

The government encouraged the Indians to give up their land. If they signed a formal agreement called a treaty, the government promised to provide them with food, clothing, tools, and money. But few Indians wanted to live on reservations. For some, one piece of land seemed too small and limiting. When one Nez Percé Indian was told to leave his homeland, he said:

The earth is part of my body. I belong to the land out of which I came. The earth is my mother.

Some groups of Indians did move to reservations. But they found their new way of life difficult. Often the food that was promised to the Indians was sold to other people by government officials. Many reservations had poor soil in which crops would not easily grow. Hungry and unhappy, many Native Americans left the reservations. When this happened, United States soldiers would track them down. Often there would be fighting between the soldiers and the Indians.

COOPERATION WITH THE GOVERNMENT

Many Indians thought it was wiser not to fight with the United States government. Some tried to help the government and the Indians cooperate with each other. One Paiute Indian who did this was Sarah Winnemucca. She lived on

Native Americans were told to move to reservations, like Warm Springs. There, Indian children would have to be taught by American teachers.

the Malheur Reservation in eastern Oregon and worked for the United States Army as a scout. One of Winnemucca's jobs was to translate Indian languages for army officers. She also started the first Indian school in Nevada, which was run solely by Native Americans. Winnemucca became the first Native American to publish a book in English, called *Life Among the Piutes*.

WAR WITH THE MODOC INDIANS

In 1864 the Modoc Indians were forced to sign a treaty and to leave their homeland, which was along Lost River near the California border. The Modocs were told to move north and to share a reservation with the Klamath and Paiute peoples. However, the Modoc Indians did not get along with the Klamath Indians. Captain Jack, a leader of the Modocs, decided to break the treaty agreement. He returned with some of his people to their old homeland.

In 1872 the United States Army was sent to convince Captain Jack to return peacefully to the reservation. In case he refused, 1,000 soldiers were prepared to take the Modocs back to the reservation by force. Captain Jack and his people hid from the army in nearby caves. They refused to surrender peacefully unless they were allowed to live near Lost River. The soldiers

Sarah Winnemucca, a Paiute Indian, was a translator, a teacher, and an author of a book about her people.

158

refused to make any agreements until the Modocs surrendered.

The Modoc Indians had only 60 warriors to protect their families against capture by the soldiers. The warriors fought off the army for six months. Finally they became tired, and Captain Jack surrendered. He was taken prisoner and given an army trial for killing American soldiers. After the trial Captain Jack and other Modocs were hanged.

CHIEF JOSEPH AND THE NEZ PERCÉ

Some groups of Nez Percé had agreed to move to a reservation in Idaho. But one leader, Chief Joseph, refused to sign a treaty. He wanted to stay with his people on their homeland in the Wallowa Valley, in northeastern Oregon. In the summer of 1877 the United States Army convinced Chief Joseph and the Nez Percé to move to Idaho. But as the Nez Percé were getting ready to leave, three young warriors killed four settlers. This act led to war.

The Nez Percé fled their homeland and headed for Canada, where they thought that they would be safe. The United States Army followed and chased them down. For three months Chief Joseph's warriors managed to defend themselves and their families against the army, which outnumbered them. However, many Nez Percé, including women and children, were killed.

Chief Joseph wanted the Nez Percé to stay on their homeland. They refused to move to a **reservation**.

In the fall of 1877 the Nez Percé were just south of the Canadian border. Thinking that they were safe Chief Joseph set up camp. However,

159

a group of soldiers surprised the Nez Percé with a sudden attack. Chief Joseph realized that the time had come to surrender. He said:

I am tired of fighting. Our chiefs are killed. It is cold and we have no blankets. The little children are freezing to death. My people, some of them have run away to the hills, and have no blankets, no food; no one knows where they are. . . . Hear me, my chiefs! My heart is sick and sad. From where the sun now stands, I will fight no more forever.

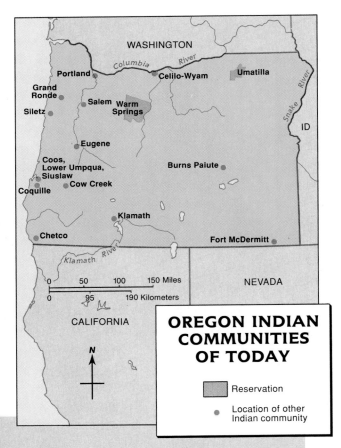

OREGON INDIAN COMMUNITIES OF TODAY

Reservation

Location of other Indian community

MAP SKILL: How many Indian reservations and communities are in Oregon today?

THE END OF THE INDIAN WARS

After the war was over, the government promised to send Chief Joseph and his people to Idaho. However, they were sent to Oklahoma instead, where many became sick and died. Seven years later Chief Joseph moved to the state of Washington, where he died in 1904.

By the end of 1878 the wars with the Native Americans had come to an end. All the Native American groups were now living on different reservations throughout the state of Oregon. Today many Native Americans still live on reservations. The Oregon Indian Communities of Today map, on this page, shows where in Oregon these reservations are located.

 Check Your Reading

1. Why was there a struggle for land in Oregon?
2. Name two Native American leaders and describe why they were important.
3. **GEOGRAPHY SKILL:** Look at the map on this page. What are the names of the two largest Indian reservations in Oregon today?
4. **THINKING SKILL:** Predict what life would be like today for the Native Americans of Oregon if they had not been forced to move to reservations.

3 Transportation Changes Lives

READ TO LEARN

Key Vocabulary

stagecoach
steamboat
technology

immigrant
portage railroad
transcontinental
  railroad

Key People

Henry Villard

Read Aloud

Give us a railroad! Though it be a rawhide one with open passenger cars and a sheet iron boiler . . . anything on wheels drawn by an iron horse! But give us a railroad.

Oregon was a long way from the eastern United States. The state needed better and faster ways to move people than the wagon trains of the pioneers. The words above are from a Pacific Northwest newspaper of 1880.

Read for Purpose

1. **WHAT YOU KNOW:** What kinds of transportation did explorers and pioneers use to come to Oregon?
2. **WHAT YOU WILL LEARN:** How did new forms of transportation change life in the state of Oregon?

EARLY TRANSPORTATION IN OREGON

You know that early explorers and pioneers came to Oregon by ship, by canoe, on horseback, and by covered wagon. But as towns gradually developed, so did new forms of transportation. These new forms made it easier for the settlers to travel and to transport goods.

The first stagecoach came to Oregon in 1846. A stagecoach was a closed carriage pulled by teams of horses. Twice a week the stagecoach carried passengers to and from Oregon City and the Tualatin settlement. The fare was expensive, and the journey over unpaved roads was rough and sometimes very dangerous.

161

Though the ride was not smooth, the **stagecoach** helped to improve the methods of transportation for people living in Oregon.

Stagecoach drivers had to be skilled and strong. They sat on a seat on top of the coach and guided the animals through a difficult journey over rough roads. When the roads became wet, the stagecoach often got stuck in the mud. Then the passengers had to get out and push, while mud and water ran into their boots. Other stagecoach lines soon followed with better coaches and the promise of smoother rides. Instead of bumping up and down, the new stagecoaches were built so that they would swing from side to side.

STEAMBOATS

River travel across Oregon was important to settlers. It was often faster and cheaper than traveling by land. Rivers were like highways. Many towns developed near them because they made travel and communication easier.

The **steamboat** was already an important means of transportation along the Mississippi and Ohio rivers. It had a large paddle wheel and was powered by a steam engine. The advantage of the steamboat over other large boats was that it could travel against the flow of a river's current.

Steamboats were used by companies to ship their goods along the

Columbia and Willamette rivers. In 1850 the first steamboat to be used by the public began to operate in Oregon. Its name was *Columbia*, and it took people from Astoria to Portland and Oregon City, along the Columbia and Willamette rivers.

THE OREGON STEAM NAVIGATION COMPANY

Steamboat companies soon began to compete with one another to move passengers and goods along the Columbia and Willamette rivers. The competition became too great for some companies, and they began to lose money. In 1860 several steamboat companies joined together to form the Oregon Steam Navigation Company. The company transported passengers, mail, gold, and many other goods. By 1880 it owned 26 riverboats and controlled most of the business along the Columbia River.

RAILROADS

Oregon was changing quickly. Although American settlers could still remember their rugged journey west, technology was now helping to make their lives easier. Technology is the use of new ideas and tools to meet people's needs. The railroad was a new form of technology. It could travel farther in a single morning than a covered wagon could travel in one week.

Many railroad companies, like the Union Pacific, often hired people from other countries to work on the railroad.

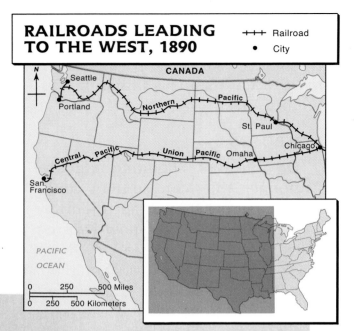

RAILROADS LEADING TO THE WEST, 1890

+++ Railroad
• City

CANADA

N

Seattle
Portland
Northern   Pacific
St. Paul
Chicago
Central Pacific   Union Pacific Omaha
San Francisco

PACIFIC OCEAN

0   250   500 Miles
0   250   500 Kilometers

MAP SKILL: In which cities did the Northern Pacific Railroad stop?

Railroads were already running along the eastern part of the United States by 1860. They moved passengers from city to city and from state to state. Railroads were important because they made journeys faster and they created jobs for people.

Some railroad workers lived on work trains that followed them as they built railroad lines across the country. The workers made smooth roads on which to lay down logs called railroad ties. Iron rails were placed on top of the ties and fastened into place with spikes. Much of the work of laying down railroad tracks was done by immigrants. Immigrants are people who come to a country in which they were not born in order to settle there.

Many Chinese immigrants were hired to work on the railroads in Oregon. A special type of railroad built in Oregon was called a portage railroad. These railroads often had only one or two railroad cars and transported people and goods short distances around river rapids. Portage railroads improved the system of transportation within Oregon. But the people of our state were still isolated from the rest of the United States.

THE TRANSCONTINENTAL RAILROAD

The most important development in transportation came after the Civil War ended in 1865. Congress asked the Union Pacific and the Central Pacific railroad companies to build a railroad across the United States. It would be called a transcontinental railroad because it would stretch across the continent from the East Coast to the West Coast. People would soon be able to make the journey west using the fastest, safest, and cheapest form of transportation ever developed. The Union Pacific Railroad worked its way west from the East Coast, while the Central Pacific Railroad worked its way east from the West Coast. Look at the map above and locate these two lines.

HENRY VILLARD

A second transcontinental railroad was being built by the Northern Pacific Railroad. It started in Minnesota in the early 1870s and moved west. Ten years later, in the early 1880s, workers began laying railroad tracks east from Portland along the Columbia River. Look again at the map and find this railroad line. The man who helped to bring the two ends of this line together was Henry Villard. He was a wealthy immigrant from Germany. Villard had been a newspaper reporter, but he was also an expert on railroads.

In 1881 Henry Villard borrowed money and bought the Northern Pacific Railroad. Many railroad crews worked hard to connect rail lines. Tunnels were dug, and bridges were built. In some places whole mountainsides were blasted away in order to lay track.

At last, on September 8, 1883, the two crews met in Montana. A golden spike was hammered into the track to connect the two ends. When the first train traveled along the tracks, town after town celebrated its arrival.

EAST MEETS WEST

As you have read, different forms of transportation made it possible to travel greater distances in shorter amounts of time. People were now able to cross the continent in five days on the transcontinental railroad instead of the six months it had taken by wagon train. Eventu-

Through the work of Henry Villard the people of Oregon could now travel to the East Coast by train.

ally more railroads were built connecting Oregon with California, Washington, and the East Coast. To people in Oregon, the rest of the United States now seemed much closer than ever before.

Check Your Reading

1. How did the different types of transportation mentioned in this lesson help to improve travel in Oregon?
2. **GEOGRAPHY SKILL:** Look at the map on page 164. Where did the Central Pacific and the Union Pacific railroads meet?
3. **THINKING SKILL:** Describe two effects that were made by the transcontinental railroad.

Reading Maps at Different Scales

In this chapter you have read about how the transcontinental railroad helped to link our state with the rest of the United States in 1890. The map on page 164 shows that the transcontinental railroad went from Chicago, Illinois, to Portland. On a railroad map of Oregon you can find other railroad routes that exist in our state today. But, as you know, Oregon covers a large area. How can a small map of the state show a long distance such as that between Salem and Portland?

Map Scale

No map is as large as the part of the earth that it shows. All maps are drawn to scale. You read on page 11 that a scale compares the distance on a map with the real distance on the earth. On the maps in this book, scale is shown by a double line.

Map A below shows the state of Oregon and its many railroads. Find the map scale on **Map A**. The top line on the map scale shows how many miles of Oregon are shown by 1 inch on the map. The bottom line shows how many kilometers of Oregon are shown by 2 centimeters on the map. How many miles does 1 inch stand for on this map? How many kilometers do 2 centimeters stand for?

Making a Map Scale

To find distance on a map easily, you can make a scale strip. You read how to do this on page 11. For **Map A** your strip should look like this.

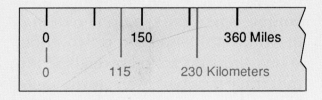

Suppose that you wanted to find the distance between The Dalles and Hermiston. Place the straight edge of your scale strip below the dots for the two places. You should place the zero on your scale strip below the dot for The Dalles. Now read the numbered marks on your scale strip below the dot for Hermiston. What is the distance in miles and in kilometers?

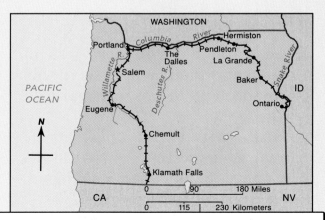

MAP A: Railroads

★ State capital   • Other city   +++ Railroad

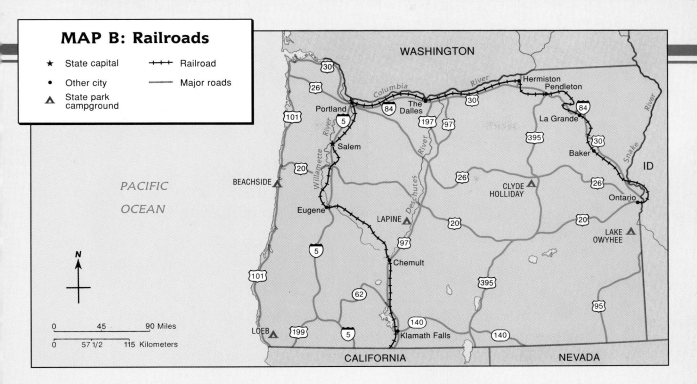

MAP B: Railroads

★ State capital
● Other city
▲ State park campground
+‒+‒+ Railroad
— Major roads

WASHINGTON

PACIFIC

OCEAN

Portland
Salem
BEACHSIDE
Eugene
The Dalles
Hermiston
Pendleton
La Grande
Baker
CLYDE HOLLIDAY
Ontario
LAPINE
Chemult
LOEB
Klamath Falls
LAKE OWYHEE
ID
CALIFORNIA
NEVADA

N

0   45   90 Miles
0   57 1/2   115 Kilometers

Comparing Map Scales

Now look at **Map B** above. This map shows exactly the same area as **Map A**. But each map is drawn to a different scale. Make a scale strip for **Map B** as you did for **Map A**. Use the scale strip to find the distance between The Dalles and Hermiston in miles and kilometers. What did you notice about the distances on **Map A** compared with the distances on **Map B**?

Even though maps are often drawn to different scales, real distances do not change. On **Map A** the distance between Chemult and Klamath Falls is about 0.5 inches (about 1 cm). On **Map B** it is about 1 inch (about 2 cm). One inch stands for a greater distance on **Map A** than it does on **Map B**. We say that **Map B** has a larger scale than **Map A**.

Scale on a map depends on the amount of information shown. More information can be shown on a large-scale map than on a small-scale map. **Map A** would be very crowded and hard to read if it had all of the information shown on **Map B**.

Compare the information shown on **Map A** with that shown on **Map B**. Notice that many more places are shown on **Map B** than on **Map A**.

Reviewing the Skill

1. What is a map scale?
2. How does **Map B** differ from **Map A**?
3. Which map would you use to find the distance between Salem and LaPine Campground? What is this distance in miles? In kilometers?
4. Why is it useful to draw maps to different scales?

167

READE TO LEARN

Key Vocabulary

legislature   recall
amendment   progressive
initiative   suffrage
referendum

Key People

William U'Ren
Abigail Scott Duniway

Read Aloud

*The important thing was to restore the lawmaking power
where it belonged—into the hands of the people. . . .
Once given that, we could get anything we wanted.*

These are the words of William U'Ren, a young lawyer
who worked to change Oregon's system of government. As
a result Oregon became the first state to give its citizens
a direct role in developing laws.

Read for Purpose

1. **WHAT YOU KNOW:** How did Oregon adopt its state
   constitution?
2. **WHAT YOU WILL LEARN:** How did the Oregon System
   help the people of Oregon?

PROGRESS AS A STATE

When Oregon adopted its constitution in 1857, there were 52,000
people living in the state. The constitution gave voters the right to
elect a legislature. A legislature is a
group of elected leaders who make
laws. Until the year 1900 the legislature passed laws using the same
lawmaking procedures.

By 1890 there were more than
300,000 people living in Oregon.
This growth in population was
causing many problems in the state.
The owners of large companies had
gained a lot of power and wealth.
They often pressured lawmakers to
pass laws that would help only
them. For example, the legislature
let the railroad companies charge

168

high rates for the shipping of cattle and wheat. But the farmers were not able to pay such high rates. Many citizens wanted these unfair laws to change.

THE OREGON SYSTEM

During the late 1890s William U'Ren (ûr en'), a member of Oregon's legislature, proposed making an amendment to the state constitution. An amendment is a change in or an addition to a constitution. U'Ren was in favor of laws that would give the voters more direct control over the state government. In 1899 U'Ren introduced the initiative (i nish' ə tiv) amendment to the state legislature. An initiative is the right of citizens to introduce a new law. The initiative amendment gave voters the right to create new laws directly, without involving the state legislature. This was an important step for citizens. If the state legislature did not make laws that the citizens wanted, the citizens themselves could create them.

Citizens who supported a new law were required to have a specific number of voters sign a petition. If enough people signed the petition, the proposed law would be voted on. If a majority of citizens voted for the proposed law, or initiative, it would become law.

Another part of the initiative amendment that William U'Ren introduced at this time was called the referendum. The referendum gave voters the right to change laws that already existed. If enough voters signed a petition that said they wanted to change a law, their proposal would appear on the ballot at the next election. In 1902 the initiative and referendum amendment became law and were added to the state constitution.

In 1908 the recall amendment was added to Oregon's constitution. It gave people the power to remove leaders from government office. The initiative and referendum, and recall amendments became known as the "Oregon System." Many states followed Oregon's lead and adopted similar changes.

William U'Ren helped the citizens of Oregon participate directly in the making of state laws.

Abigail Scott Duniway used this typewriter to type articles about the women's **suffrage** movement which she published in her newspaper.

RIGHTS FOR WOMEN

The adoption of the Oregon System helped Oregon to become known as a **progressive** state. A progressive state is one that allows its citizens to participate in the making of laws. However, many people thought that other laws still needed to be changed because women did not yet have the right to vote. At the turn of the century, women across the United States were fighting for **suffrage**, or the right to vote. **Abigail Scott Duniway** became the leader of the women's suffrage movement in Oregon.

When Duniway was 17 years old, she came to Oregon in a covered wagon. After her arrival she married a farmer and opened a hat store. Many of Duniway's women custom-

ers told her about their troubles. Some husbands had sold property that had belonged to their wives. Other husbands had sold furniture that had been bought with money their wives had earned. There were no laws to protect the rights of women. And because women were not allowed to vote, they could not change the laws.

Abigail Scott Duniway became so angry because of the stories she heard that she vowed to spend the rest of her life fighting to help women get their rights. In 1871 she started a newspaper called *The New Northwest*. In this newspaper she wrote and published articles about the injustices that women faced in Oregon. Pleading the cause of women's rights, Duniway traveled all over Oregon by stagecoach, by steamboat, and on horseback. But many people did not want to listen to her. "Take that crazy woman out of the house and take care of her," the leader of a meeting once said, refusing to let her speak.

In other parts of the United States, women like Abigail Scott Duniway also devoted their lives to gaining rights for women. They fought for these rights in state legislatures. They marched in suffrage parades. They carried signs in front of the White House in Washington, D.C., asking, "How Long Must Women Wait for Liberty?"

In 1912 Oregon became one of the first states in the United States to give American women the right to vote. The women of Oregon now had a voice in their government. Abigail Scott Duniway had fought hard to make this important change happen.

But it took many more years of struggle before women all over the United States finally won the right to vote. In 1920 the United States Congress approved an amendment to the nation's Constitution that finally gave American women the right to vote.

In 1912, when women gained the right to vote in Oregon, Abigail Scott Duniway, center, was the first woman to vote.

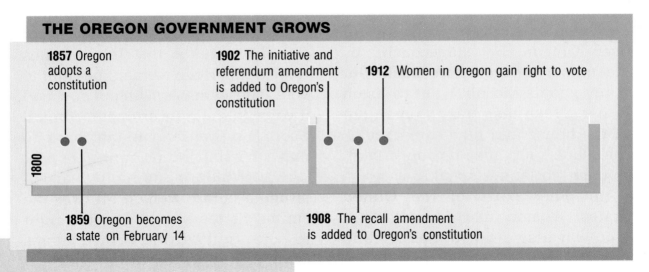

THE OREGON GOVERNMENT GROWS

1857 Oregon adopts a constitution

1902 The initiative and referendum amendment is added to Oregon's constitution

1912 Women in Oregon gain right to vote

1800

1859 Oregon becomes a state on February 14

1908 The recall amendment is added to Oregon's constitution

TIME LINE SKILL: How many years passed between the adoption of the constitution and women voting?

OTHER LAWS

Oregon passed many progressive laws during the early 1900s. Some of these laws helped to protect the rights of prisoners, children, and workers. Another law, which you read about in Chapter 2, opened the Oregon coast to all citizens. This means that no one is allowed to own a private beach along the ocean. In some states landowners can own beach property right up to the water's edge. But in Oregon, citizens are free to use all of the beaches along the coast.

A PROGRESSIVE STATE

In this lesson you have read about how the Oregon System, women's rights, and progressive laws brought some important changes to Oregon. The time line above shows you how much Oregon's government has grown between the year 1857, when the constitution was adopted, and the year 1912, when women began to vote. These same changes still benefit us as citizens of Oregon today.

Check Your Reading

1. Explain how citizens could make or change laws using the initiative and referendum processes.
2. Why did Oregon become known as a progressive state?
3. Why did Abigail Scott Duniway devote her life to the cause of women's rights?
4. **THINKING SKILL:** If you had been a member of the state legislature at the time when the initiative and referendum amendment was introduced, would you have voted for or against making it a law? Explain the reasons for your decision.

REVIEWING VOCABULARY

Number a sheet of paper from 1 to 10. Beside each number write **C** if the underlined word or term is used correctly. If it is not, write the word that would correctly complete the sentence.

1. Oregon's Native Americans were sent to live in <u>ghost towns</u>.
2. By means of a <u>referendum</u>, people can make their own laws.
3. In the early 1900s some women worked for the right to vote, called the <u>initiative amendment</u>.
4. In 1854 Oregonians began trying to write a plan of government, or an <u>amendment</u>.
5. The <u>constitutional convention</u> had passed a law about owning land.
6. The <u>stagecoach</u> traveled across the nation on rails.
7. Steamboats and stagecoaches are kinds of <u>transportation</u>.
8. A person who moves to a new land to live is called a <u>progressive</u>.
9. The <u>technology</u>, or agreement, between the Indians and the United States provided for the Indians to move to certain lands.
10. The people used a <u>recall</u> to remove the mayor from office.

REVIEWING FACTS

1. How did slavery make it hard to write an Oregon state constitution?
2. Why were Native Americans told to move to reservations?
3. Name three accomplishments of Sarah Winnemucca.
4. In what way did Henry Villard help Oregon?
5. Who was Abigail Scott Duniway?

WRITING ABOUT MAIN IDEAS

1. **Writing an Interview:** Write an imaginary interview with Abigail Scott Duniway. Write at least five questions and five answers.
2. **Writing a Speech:** In 1883 Sarah Winnemucca told Congress about the wrongs done to American Indians. Write the speech that Winnemucca might have given.

BUILDING SKILLS: READING MAPS AT DIFFERENT SCALES

Use the maps on pages 166–167 to answer these questions.

1. What is the difference between a large-scale and a small-scale map?
2. Which map—Map A or Map B— would you use to find the distance between Salem and the LaPine campground? Why?
3. For what reason might you use a large-scale map? When might you use a small-scale map?

173

CHAPTER 8

OREGON GROWS

FOCUS

It was interesting to see all the ships and how they unload the steel. I am very interested in ships and where they come from.

This is how Gabe Branch described his visit to the Port of Portland, where hundreds of large ships load and unload products from all over the world. In this chapter you will read how Oregon grew and changed in the 1900s.

1 Oregon Faces New Challenges

READ TO LEARN

Key Vocabulary

World War I
conservation
Great Depression
New Deal
hydroelectric

Key People

Julius Meier
Franklin D.
    Roosevelt

Key Places

Timberline Lodge

Read Aloud

The only thing we have to fear is fear itself.

This is a famous remark made by Franklin D. Roosevelt when he became President of the United States in 1932. The United States was suffering through a difficult time. Living conditions were so bad that people feared for the future. Roosevelt was trying to give Americans hope.

Read for Purpose

1. **WHAT YOU KNOW:** How does your family provide for its daily needs, such as food, clothing, and shelter?
2. **WHAT YOU WILL LEARN:** What was the Great Depression, and for what purpose was the New Deal set up?

WORLD WAR I

The beginning of the twentieth century brought great changes to the United States and to Oregon. Important events in other parts of the country and the world caused these changes. One of these important events was a world war.

World War I started in 1914 among European countries. The war divided Europe into two enemy forces. Germany, Austria-Hungary, and Turkey led the fight on one side. Great Britain, France, and Russia led the fight on the other side.

The United States government did not want to be involved. But when German submarines began attacking American ships in 1917, the United States went to war.

OVER THE TOP
FOR YOU

Buy U.S.Gov't Bonds
THIRD LIBERTY LOAN

Oregonians bought more war bonds than people of any other state. By buying bonds, people at home could join in the war effort.

Oregon enthusiastically joined the war effort both overseas and at home. Many Oregonians volunteered to serve in the army or navy and went overseas to fight. Because of the large number of Oregonians who volunteered to help in the war effort, Oregon was nicknamed "the volunteer state." Oregonians were among the first American soldiers to fight in Europe. Many were honored for their bravery in some of the most important battles of the war.

Oregonians at home pitched in as well. They helped in other ways. They had "wheatless" or "meatless" days. On those days they ate no bread or meat, which saved food that could be sent to the soldiers.

Women knitted caps and sweaters for soldiers. Teachers and students also helped. While teachers read aloud to their students for a short time every day, the students knitted squares for blankets to send to the soldiers. An Oregonian, Claudia Lewis, wrote a poem about her memories of school during this time.

> In the sixth grade
> we knitted squares
> for blankets for the soldiers,
> and the school asked me
> to play the piano in the hall
> in the morning,
> when everyone marched in.

Americans also bought Victory Bonds and Liberty Bonds to help pay for the war. People from Oregon bought more bonds than the people of any other state in our country.

Oregon's many natural resources played an important part in helping to support the war effort. Oregon farmers plowed more than 1 million acres (404,700 ha) of new land for wheat. The forests in Oregon provided wood for building army camps, ships, and small airplanes.

The war brought a business boom, too. Oregon's factories were busy making many goods. Some factories canned salmon, others made butter and cheese—all products that could be sent to the soldiers overseas.

Many ships were needed to carry troops and supplies to Europe. Some Oregon shipyards turned out wooden ships, while others made ships from steel.

AFTER THE WAR

In 1918 Germany surrendered and the war ended. When the soldiers came home, they found a changing world. New inventions and machinery were changing the lives of many Americans. During the next few years more and more Americans drove automobiles. This created a need for better roads.

The state highway department of Oregon built many new roads. The Columbia River Highway was built along the south side of the Columbia Gorge. The steep slopes of the gorge made this highway difficult to build. But the effort was worthwhile because the Columbia River Highway made it easy for people to drive from Portland to Eastern Oregon.

As more Oregonians began to travel around their state, many became interested in conservation. Conservation is the protection of natural resources. While the war was raging, lumber companies had been cutting down trees at a furious pace. After the war new machinery made it possible to cut down trees even faster. Also, many fish had been caught and canned during the war, and this natural resource of Oregon was also decreasing.

Oregonians started to realize that they must find ways to conserve their valuable natural resources. National and state forests were increased in size. Oregon's government began to limit by law the number of fish that could be caught and the times of the year in which they could be caught.

The Columbia River Highway made it easy for people to visit parts of Oregon that they had never seen.

THE GREAT DEPRESSION

During the war and for a few years afterward, business in Oregon was booming. When the fighting stopped, however, there was less need for goods such as wheat, beef, fish, and lumber. Some lumber mills closed. Farmers and ranchers found it difficult to sell their wheat and cattle. Fishing boats were tied up at their docks.

In 1929 the Great Depression started. This was a time when businesses failed all over the country. Men and women who didn't have enough money to buy food for their children stood in lines waiting for free bowls of soup. Banks closed and people lost their savings. Stores were boarded up. By 1934 many of Oregon's businesses had collapsed. Many people were out of work. In the words of the state's governor, Julius Meier, "Oregon is dead broke."

THE NEW DEAL

In 1932, when the Great Depression was at its worst, Franklin D. Roosevelt became President of the United States. Roosevelt came up with a plan called the New Deal for helping people hurt by the Great Depression. This plan was meant to get businesses started again and to create jobs for people. As part of the New Deal, work projects would be started all over the nation.

Some of the biggest projects in the Northwest were dams. The first of these to be built was the Bonneville Dam on the Columbia River near Portland. This project provided jobs for thousands of Oregonians.

Some of these dams provided water for irrigation. Others, like the Bonneville Dam, helped to prevent floods and provided large amounts of hydroelectric power. *Hydro* means "water," so *hydroelectric power* means "electricity that is created by water power."

Another United States government project in Oregon was the construction of Timberline Lodge on Mount Hood. The government decided to put many Oregonians to work building a lodge that would be used for recreation. In 1937 Presi-

During the Great Depression many Oregonians were out of work. Businesses had closed and jobs were hard to find.

Since President Roosevelt dedicated Timberline Lodge in 1937, over 30 million people have passed through its doors.

dent Roosevelt visited beautiful Timberline Lodge. He dedicated the building "as a monument to the skill and faithful performance" of the many Oregon workers employed by his New Deal program.

ANOTHER WORLD WAR

The New Deal put many people to work, but it did not end the Great Depression. Unfortunately, the depression did not end until the United States entered another world war. In the next lesson you will read about the part that Oregon played in this war.

Check Your Reading

1. What did Oregon produce during World War I?
2. What changes did Oregon soldiers find when they returned from the war?
3. What hardships did the people of Oregon experience during the Great Depression?
4. **THINKING SKILL:** What effect did the New Deal have on the lives of Oregonians?

1933: Should Dams Be Built on the Columbia River?

For centuries before American settlers came to the northwest coast of the United States, Native Americans were using the Columbia River as a source of much of their food. This natural resource has continued to be important to Oregonians.

In 1933, however, the Columbia River was looked upon not only as a source of food and transportation. As you have just read, many people thought that by building dams along the Columbia River, the river could also be used to provide hydroelectric power. President Roosevelt thought that the building of dams on the Columbia River would make an excellent New Deal project. It would provide jobs for people who were out of work during the Great Depression.

But the problem with building the dams was that they would block the river, which would prevent the salmon from swimming upriver to lay their eggs. If this happened, there would be fewer salmon. Those who earned their living from the fishing industry would be hurt. Should dams have been built on the Columbia River?

POINT ☆\☞

Dams Should Be Built on the Columbia River

In 1933, during the Great Depression, thousands of people were out of work. Senator Charles McNary of Oregon wrote to President Roosevelt about building a dam on the Columbia River at Bonneville. He said that this project would create many jobs. It would also provide Oregonians with many other benefits. McNary wrote:

> This . . . would mark the first step in the . . . use of this great river for flood control . . . and electrical power.

President Roosevelt supported the idea of building the Bonneville Dam. He believed that it would open the way to building other dams on the Columbia River. Roosevelt said:

> It means cheap manufacturing . . . economy and comfort on the farm and in the household.

- What, in McNary's and Roosevelt's opinions, would be the major advantages of building dams?

COUNTERPOINT ☜/☆

Dams Should Not Be Built on the Columbia River

So many fishermen lived in cities like Astoria, that it could be said the entire city depended on the Columbia River for its livelihood. Many people believed that dams would ruin the fishing business. Mayor Eaton stated the Astoria city council's point of view.

> The fishing industry should not be . . . lost to dams . . . . If salmon runs are reduced, the city might face economic difficulties.

Fishing on the Columbia River was also a way of life for many Native Americans. Chief Thompson of the Wyam Indians expressed why many people did not want dams built.

> I don't know how I would live if you would put up a dam which will flood my fishing places . . . . It is the only food I depend on to live.

- According to Mayor Eaton and Chief Thompson, how would the building of dams affect the fishing industry and the lives of fishermen?

UNDERSTANDING THE POINT/COUNTERPOINT

1. Why did some people want dams on the Columbia River?
2. Why did some people oppose the dams?
3. Which side do you think made the stronger case? Why?

2 World War II

READ TO LEARN

Key Vocabulary

Liberty Ship
Liberty Train
segregation
discrimination
bracero

Key People

Henry Kaiser

Key Places

Vanport City

Read Aloud

What's going to happen when the fighting stops? Can the Northwest go back to fish, fruit, and sawmills, or have these changes come to stay?

This is what a writer named Frederick Simpich wrote in the 1940s when the United States became involved in another world war. Being at war caused so many changes in Oregon that people wondered whether the state would ever be the same again.

Read for Purpose

1. **WHAT YOU KNOW:** In which ways did Oregon grow during the first part of the twentieth century?
2. **WHAT YOU WILL LEARN:** How was Oregon changed by World War II?

WAR COMES AGAIN

In 1939 another world war began in Europe and Asia, with Germany, Austria, Italy, and Japan on one side and France, England, the Soviet Union, and China on the other side. On December 7, 1941, Japanese aircraft attacked American ships that were docked in Pearl Harbor, Hawaii. This act brought the United States into World War II.

Once again the people of Oregon helped their country to fight a world war. Some Oregon soldiers were the first to go overseas and to become involved in active duty. Almost

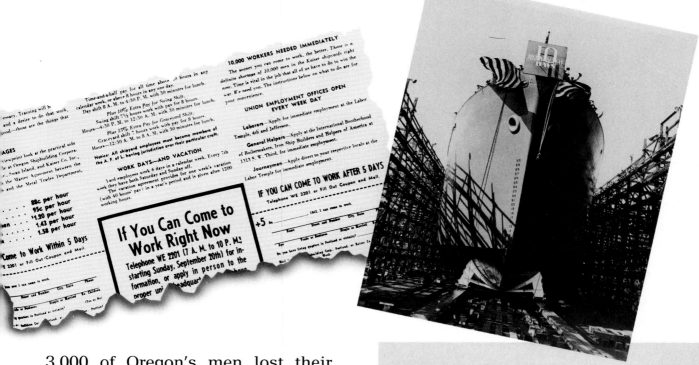

The **Liberty Ship** the Joseph N. Teal, was built in less than two weeks with the help of many workers.

3,000 of Oregon's men lost their lives in battle.

At home in Oregon, people planted "victory gardens" to raise food. In Oregon, as well as throughout the country, each family had booklets of coupons that it used when buying its share of items such as meat, sugar, and gasoline that were in short supply.

In Oregon the shipbuilding business grew. By 1942 Portland had become one of the major shipbuilding centers in the United States. A man named **Henry Kaiser** built three huge shipyards in the Portland area. The Kaiser shipyards turned out ships faster than they had ever been built before. These ships were called **Liberty Ships**. They carried supplies to soldiers overseas. The Kaiser shipyards produced more ships than any other shipyard in the United States. The

other large wartime business in Oregon was the making of aluminum, a strong but lightweight metal used to build aircraft. Because making aluminum requires electricity, Oregon's location near the hydroelectric power produced by the Bonneville Dam made it an ideal spot for aluminum production.

WORKING IN WARTIME

Many extra workers were needed to fill all the jobs offered by these businesses. The Kaiser Company ran newspaper advertisements to attract workers. This company also ran special **Liberty Trains**, which brought thousands of workers from other parts of the country. Port-

chicken coops, sheds, and empty service stations. They slept in the backseats of cars or they took turns sleeping in available beds.

To provide housing for his workers, Kaiser built Vanport City near the shipyards in the Portland area. One magazine described Vanport City as the "nation's newest, most unusual city."

SEGREGATION

In Vanport City segregation was practiced. Segregation is the separation of one group from another. African-Americans were forced to live in separate neighborhoods. Vanport City was not the only place where African-Americans met with discrimination. Discrimination is an unfair difference in treatment. In Portland, too, segregation existed. For example, African-Americans could use Portland's swimming pools only one day a week.

Vanport City was built to house Kaiser shipyard workers. Many residents planted victory gardens to help raise food during wartime shortages.

land's population grew by 90,000 people in 1942.

This great increase in population created some problems. There weren't enough houses for all these people. People made their homes in

Another group of newcomers were Hispanics (hi span' iks), or people from Mexico and other Spanish-speaking countries. The United States worked out a plan with Mexico under which Mexico would provide temporary workers called **braceros** (brä ser' ōs). These workers would return home when the war was over. The braceros harvested the extra crops that Oregon farmers grew for the war effort. Like African-Americans, Hispanics were also discriminated against.

JAPANESE-AMERICAN REMOVAL

Some Americans became afraid that Japanese-Americans would cooperate with Japan against the United States war effort. The United States government ordered all the Japanese living on the West Coast to leave their homes and move to "relocation" camps. "Relocation" camps were government camps set up in the inland western states, such as Idaho and Utah. The Japanese were forced to stay at these centers until the war was over.

Many of the Japanese-Americans were loyal citizens. Many were soldiers in the armed services and were fighting overseas. But hardly anyone protested against their removal.

AFTER THE WAR

After the war Oregon no longer needed all of its workers, so thousands returned to their former

Japanese-Americans living on the West Coast were forced to move to guarded camps such as this one in Wyoming.

homes. Those who stayed needed houses, cars, and furniture, and they had saved enough money to buy them. Business was better than expected. There was no depression as people had feared. Oregon was still a growing, thriving state.

Check Your Reading

1. Which businesses became important in Oregon during World War II?
2. Why was Vanport City built?
3. **GEOGRAPHY SKILL:** Find Japan on the map on page 256. Why did most Japanese-Americans live along the Pacific Coast of the United States?
4. **THINKING SKILL:** Look at the photograph on this page and describe what you see.

185

READ TO LEARN

Key Vocabulary
pollution
greenway

Key People
Tom McCall

Read Aloud

There is still an America that is wild, and clean, and free. But there is also a dying dream of America where the waters are poisoned by the wastes of man.

Tom McCall, one of the most important governors of Oregon, used these words to introduce a television program about the pollution of the Willamette River. He was determined not to allow the state to lose its natural beauty. In this lesson you will find out what McCall and others did to protect Oregon's environment.

Read for Purpose

1. **WHAT YOU KNOW:** What changes did World War II bring to Oregon?
2. **WHAT YOU WILL LEARN:** What has Oregon done since 1945 to help protect its natural resources?

MORE AND MORE PEOPLE

We have seen that the war brought many people to live in Oregon. Others came as tourists to see Oregon's beautiful mountains, desert, and beaches.

To provide for the needs of these new people, many more businesses were started. Shopping centers and hotels were built on what was once farmland. More waste materials from Oregon's factories poured into the streams and were released into the air. These waste materials caused **pollution** (pə lü' shən) of Oregon's environment. Pollution is what makes the air, soil, or water dirty. Unless something was done, pollution was going to seriously damage Oregon's environment.

Pollution from Oregon's factories harms our state's environment.

THE STORY OF A RIVER

When settlers first came to Oregon, the Willamette River was so clean that it was safe to drink. Countless fish swam in its waters. But more and more towns began to dump waste materials into the river. Businesses, such as paper mills, used this river to carry off the chemical wastes from their factories. The Willamette River became extremely polluted. Fish could no longer live in it, and it was "too filthy" for people to swim in.

Tom McCall, who was a television broadcaster in Portland, loved Oregon and wanted to keep it beautiful. He became so alarmed at the condition of the Willamette that he called it "a stinking mess." In 1961 he prepared a TV program about it, called *Pollution in Paradise*. The program won a national award and made people want to clean up the Willamette River.

In 1967 McCall became the governor of Oregon. He worked to pass a new law that would require a state permit before any city or business could release polluting materials into the river. Although towns and paper companies fought the law, McCall worked hard for the law and it was passed. Within a few years

187

the fish returned, and people could catch salmon right from the Portland waterfront. The Willamette River was clear and beautiful again and clean enough for swimmers. Tom McCall had shown that strict laws can bring about important changes.

THE BANKS OF THE WILLAMETTE

The banks of the Willamette were still green with farmland and trees. Many citizens wanted to keep them that way. Under McCall's leadership more laws were passed to protect Oregon's land. The first of these laws established parks on the riverbanks, while the second made plans for a greenway along the river. A greenway is a strip of land set aside in fields and forests where the building of homes and busines-

ses is not allowed. Most of the riverbank is now part of the greenway.

Oregon led the nation in planning how to use its land thoughtfully. The state started by passing a law that required cities and counties to make plans for their growth. The law required that housing be built in certain places and businesses in others, while some areas were kept as farmland and some as forests.

THE BOTTLE LAW

Oregon was the first state to pass a bottle law. Have you ever taken empty bottles or cans to the store and received some money for them? You can do this because of the bottle law. This law requires beer and soft drinks to be sold in cans or bottles that can be returned to the store. A fee called a deposit is added to the price of each bottle or

Tom McCall led Oregon's fight to preserve its natural resources.

can. When the container is taken back to the store, the fee is returned. Again, Tom McCall took the lead in getting this law passed.

Today we know that the bottle law keeps the roadsides much cleaner because most cans and bottles are returned for their deposits. Most people are in favor of the law, and a number of other states have adopted similar laws.

OTHER PLANS

Oregon has been the leader with other plans, too. It passed a wild rivers act to protect certain scenic rivers from being spoiled by dams. It bans aerosol (âr′ ə sôl) cans, which release a spray that is harmful to the air. It limits the times of the year when farmers may burn their fields. It also limits the pollution that automobiles and trucks in cities may release into the air. Oregon is known all over the nation as a leading state in the move to con-

Today, salmon are caught on Portland's waterfront. The Willamette River is once again a source of recreation for boaters.

serve natural resources and to protect the environment.

✔ Check Your Reading

1. Why did Oregon need laws to protect its environment?
2. What was done to save the Willamette River?
3. Name and describe some laws that Oregon was the first state to pass.
4. **THINKING SKILL:** Which law do you think Oregon will pass next to improve its environment?

Comparing Maps

Key Vocabulary

population map
precipitation map
land-use map

Throughout this book you have been using maps to help you understand how the history and geography of Oregon fit together. Each of these different maps has helped you to look at Oregon in a different way. What have you learned about our state from the maps in this book?

By comparing maps that show different kinds of information, you can learn even more about a place. The maps on page 191 all show different kinds of information about Oregon. Read the title of each map. What kind of information is shown on each of these maps?

Different Kinds of Maps

Map A is a population map. It shows the number of people per square mile (per sq km) in different areas of our state. You can use it to find in which areas of Oregon many people live and in which areas few people live.

Map B is a precipitation map. It shows the average amount of rain, snow, hail, or other moisture that falls each year in different parts of Oregon.

Map C is a land-use map. It shows how Oregonians use the land in different areas to earn their livings.

Study the key for each map to make sure that you understand what the colors used on the map stand for. Find the key on **Map A**. It uses different colors to show how many people live in different areas. Which color is used to show areas in which there are fewer than 10 people per square mile (less than 4 people per sq km)?

Map B uses colors to show four different ranges of precipitation. Which color is used to show 20–40 inches (50–100 cm) of precipitation?

You can now use all three maps to make comparisons. You can look at how population, precipitation, and land use affect each other. For example, do areas with little precipitation appear to be good for dry-land farming?

Reviewing the Skill

Compare the maps on page 191 and answer the questions below.

1. Look at the land-use map and the population map. Do more people live in farming areas or in forests?
2. Do areas with low precipitation usually have high, low, or average populations?
3. Why is it helpful to compare different kinds of maps of the same place?

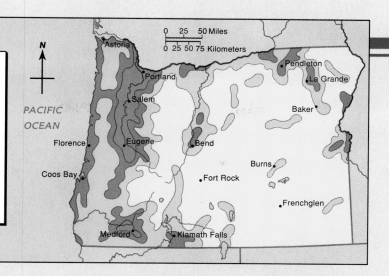

MAP A
OREGON:
Population

People per
square mile

People per
square kilometer

Fewer than 10 — Fewer than 4

10–25 — 4–10

25–50 — 10–20

More than 50 — More than 20

MAP B
OREGON:
Precipitation

Inches — Centimeters

Less than 20 — Less than 50

20–40 — 50–100

40–60 — 100–150

More than 60 — More than 150

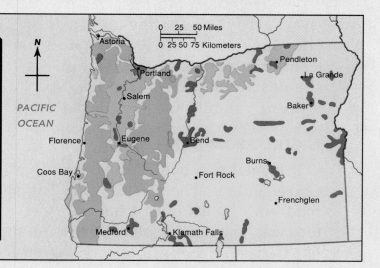

MAP C
OREGON:
Land-Use

Dry-land farming

Irrigated farming

Livestock raising

Forestry

Manufacturing

Little or no economic
activity

191

READ TO LEARN

Key Places

Yamhill

Read for Purpose

1. **WHAT YOU KNOW:** How did Oregon change after World War I?
2. **WHAT YOU WILL LEARN:** How did Beverly Cleary's mother help to open a library in a small Oregon town?

YOUNG *Beverly Cleary*

    In this chapter you have read about the challenges that Oregon has faced in the twentieth century. Tom McCall is one of many Oregonians who has worked hard to meet these challenges. In this lesson you will read about Beverly Cleary's mother and how she made a positive change in the lives of her fellow Oregonians.

    Beverly Cleary is the author of the "Henry Huggins" and "Ramona" books, which are set in Portland. Here, in a part of her own story, *A Girl from Yamhill*, she describes what it was like to grow up in the small town of Yamhill, Oregon during the 1920s.

A GIRL FROM YAMHILL

    I owned two books: the Volland edition of *Mother Goose* and . . . *The Story of the Three Bears.* . . . Mother read both books until I had memorized them. Mother, too, was starved for books, perhaps to take her mind off her worries. "Yamhill needs a library," she said. "There is entirely too much gossip. People would be better off reading books."

Somehow, in spite of all her work on the farm, Mother summoned enough energy to start a campaign for a library. She asked for donations of books and a bookcase or cupboard that could be locked. A glass china cupboard was carried upstairs to the Commercial Clubrooms over the Yamhill Bank. The community donated books, boring grown-up books with dull pictures that were a disappointment to me. . . .

With this small beginning, Mother opened the library every Saturday afternoon, when country people came to town to shop. . . . I looked forward to the walk uptown to the library, where, even if there were no books for children, I could sit in a leather chair with its stuffing coming out and be seen and not heard. I listened to talk with big words I did not understand, but I did understand when women spoke angrily about the high price of sugar and cost of canning fruit and making jam when summer came.

Mother persisted. She arranged a silver tea to raise money for the library, and someone gave a luncheon at which a woman played a saxophone solo. The library now had $16! Mother called a meeting for the purpose of securing a traveling state library for Yamhill. . . .

Mother wrote that the library had 64 permanent volumes . . . and that 100 people had asked for books. Men wanted adventure, a boy asked for forestry, an old lady who was ill sent in for cheerful stories, women who lived in lonely places asked for books. She concluded this article by saying, "Our children need and are entitled to the use of a library just as much as city children are."

Crates of books began to arrive from the Oregon State Library in Salem. At last Yamhill had books for children—and what good books they were! Books by Beatrix Potter were among the many that came out of those state library crates. My favorite was *The Tailor of Gloucester,* not only because I loved the story, but because of the picture of the waistcoat so beautifully embroidered by mice. I studied that picture and knew that someday I wanted to sew beautifully, too. . . .

That brave little library brightened the lives of many of us that winter, and in the spring, when flowers bloomed again, the library had 142 books in addition to 62 state books.

Check Your Reading

1. What imaginary characters has Beverly Cleary made famous?
2. Why was the library open on Saturday afternoons?
3. What sort of books did Yamhill readers request?
4. **THINKING SKILL:** Which three questions would you ask Beverly Cleary about growing up in Yamhill during the 1920s?

REVIEWING VOCABULARY

conservation   New Deal
discrimination   pollution
Great Depression

Number a sheet of paper from 1 to 5. Beside each number write the word or term from the list above that best completes the sentence.

1. If we do not practice _____ of forests, we may run out of trees.
2. When factories let their wastes go into the river, they are causing water _____.
3. During the _____ many businesses closed and people lost their jobs.
4. President Roosevelt's plan to help people during the Great Depression was called the _____.
5. When people are treated unfairly because of their race, they are victims of _____.

REVIEWING FACTS

Number a sheet of paper from 1 to 5. Beside each number write the letter of the phrase that is most closely associated with the name or term listed below.

1. Franklin D. Roosevelt
2. Vanport
3. braceros
4. Tom McCall
5. Liberty Trains

a. Tried to help people with the New Deal
b. The Oregon governor who led the fight against pollution
c. The community built for new workers during World War II
d. Run by the Kaiser Company to bring in workers from other parts of the country
e. One group that faced discrimination in Oregon during World War II

WRITING ABOUT MAIN IDEAS

Writing a Journal Entry: Imagine that you are in the fourth grade during World War II. Write a journal entry about three ways in which the war effort is affecting your life. For example, certain kinds of food are scarce. Try to include a few sentences about how you feel about these changes.

BUILDING SKILLS: COMPARING MAPS

Use the maps on pages 186–187 to answer these questions.

1. How many people per square mile live in Eugene?
2. About how much precipitation falls along most of the coast of Oregon?
3. Why is it helpful to compare different kinds of maps of the same place?

REVIEWING VOCABULARY

amendment	immigrant
conservation	pollution
constitution	progressive
discrimination	suffrage
hydroelectric	transportation

Number a sheet of paper from 1 to 10. Beside each number write the word from the list above that best matches the definition.

1. The right to vote
2. A plan of government
3. A means of moving goods and people
4. Something that is added on
5. A person who moves to a new country to live
6. Things that make the soil, air, or water dirty
7. The protection of natural resources
8. The unfair difference in the treatment of people
9. Having to do with electricity made by the force of water
10. Favoring improvements that help the people of a place

WRITING ABOUT THE UNIT

1. **Making a Chart:** Make a chart about advances in transportation. Include advances such as the use of stagecoaches, steamboats, railroads, the Columbia Highway, and airplanes. In the chart name each advance, tell when it was developed, and explain how it helped or changed life for people in Oregon.

2. **Writing a Comparing Paragraph:** Consider the way in which Indians were treated in Oregon in the 1800s and the way in which Japanese-Americans were treated in this country during World War II. Then write a paragraph telling how the methods of treatment were the same and how they were different.

ACTIVITIES

1. **Preparing a Biographical Report:** Read about one of the following people: Sarah Winnemucca, Chief Joseph, Captain Jack, Abigail Scott Duniway, or Tom McCall. Prepare a short biography of the person. Include information about his or her personal and public life.

2. **Working in a Group to Improve the Environment:** Work with others in a small group to reach agreement about a new law that could be passed to help the environment. Then design posters or flyers that tell people about the new law and will convince them to support it. Discuss the law with the rest of the class. After the discussion, ask the class to vote for or against the law.

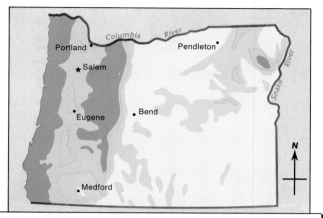

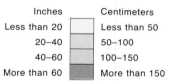

OREGON: Yearly Precipitation

Inches		Centimeters
Less than 20		Less than 50
20–40		50–100
40–60		100–150
More than 60		More than 150

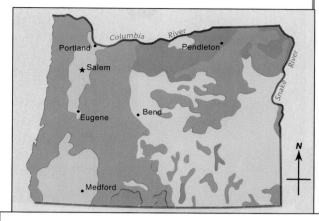

OREGON: Natural Vegetation

- Desert vegetation
- Shrub and grass
- Grass
- Mixed forest
- Needleleaf forest

BUILDING SKILLS: COMPARING MAPS

Study the two maps on this page. Then answer these questions.

1. What different kinds of information are shown on the two maps?
2. Which color is used to show needleleaf forest?
3. Find the areas with the greatest amount of precipitation. What type of vegetation grows there?
4. What kind of natural vegetation is found in Pendleton? How much precipitation does Pendleton get?
5. What is one conclusion that you can draw from reading these two maps?

LINKING PAST, PRESENT, AND FUTURE

You have read about the fight for women's rights that took place in the early 1900s. At that time one of the most important issues for women was suffrage. Today women are still working for equal rights. Which issues most concern women today? In what ways have women already achieved some equal rights? Which issues need to be resolved in the future?

State Bird:
Western
Meadowlark

State Nut: Hazelnut

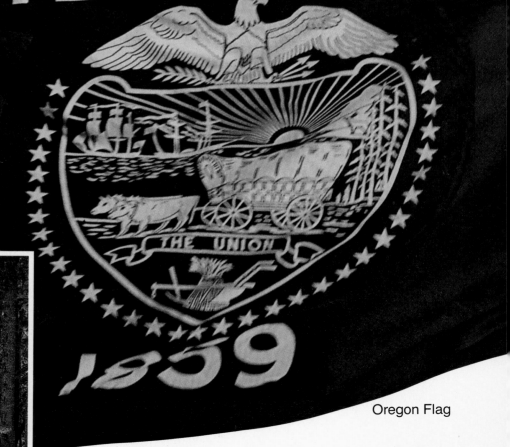
Oregon Flag

State Tree: Douglas fir

UNIT 5

OREGON TODAY

LIFE IN OUR STATE

On these pages you will see some of the symbols of our state. These are all things found in our state that make it different from any other state. In the last units you read the story about Oregon's past. Now let's find out what our state is like today.

State Animal:
Beaver

State Flower:
Oregon grape

State Seal

199

CHAPTER 9

LIFE IN OREGON

FOCUS

I live in Hood River only a half an hour away from Mount Hood. Hood River has lots of sports—wind surfing, hiking, swimming, and snow skiing. I'm on the swim team. I ski and I play soccer, basketball, and baseball, too.

This is the way that Forest Kuykendall explained why he likes living in Hood River. In this chapter you will read about the many people who live in Oregon and about some of the things they like to do.

1 A Pioneer People

READ TO LEARN

📋 Key Vocabulary

powwow   heritage

📋 Read Aloud

Oregon is a varied state, and our citizens represent many cultures and values.

Governor Neil Goldschmidt spoke these words about the people of Oregon. In this lesson you will read about the different types of people who live in our state.

📋 Read for Purpose

1. WHAT YOU KNOW: What do you feel is special about your community?
2. WHAT YOU WILL LEARN: What is special about the people of Oregon?

OREGON'S POPULATION

Today more than 2.5 million people live in Oregon. Our state is the thirtieth-largest state in population in the United States. However, only nine states have more land. Most of Oregon, therefore, is not very populated. This is not true of the Willamette Valley, which is home to many of Oregon's people.

Most Oregonians—about six out of ten—live in cities. Later in this chapter you will read more about Portland, Oregon's largest city.

OREGON SPIRIT

Are you enthusiastic about taking part in school activities? If so, people might say that you have school spirit. Many Oregonians have this kind of feeling about their state. J. A. Buchanan expressed his Oregon spirit in our state song, "Oregon, My Oregon." He wrote:

Onward and upward ever,
Forward and on, and on. . . .

These words mean that the people of Oregon look to the future.

201

From earliest times Oregonians have been trailblazers, or pathfinders. From the pioneers who found their way west across the Oregon Trail, to the Oregonians who passed the first laws protecting the environment, the people of our state have been leading the way. No wonder Oregon's professional basketball team is called the Portland Trail Blazers.

WHO WE ARE

Just as Oregon's land has many faces, so do its people. Indians were the first people to live in Oregon. As you know, they settled the land of our state thousands of years ago.

The almost 30,000 Native Americans who now live in Oregon make their homes throughout the state. Some Oregon Indians, like Michael Tailfeathers, about whom you read

What are some ways that you show your Oregon spirit?

at the beginning of Chapter 3, live on reservations. Michael and his family live on the Warm Springs Reservation in the central part of Oregon. Michael shows his spirit by competing in traditional Native American dancing contests at **pow-wows** in Oregon and other states around the country. A powwow is a gathering of Indians at which they take part in activities that celebrate their **heritage**. Heritage is the ways and beliefs that are handed down from one generation to another.

Michael likes the countryside where he lives. He especially enjoys walking through the woods and the smell of the forest in the morning when the air is crisp and cold. One of Michael's favorite activities is finding the tracks left by such animals as bear, deer, and elk.

At the beginning of the last chapter, you met Gabe Branch from Portland. Gabe enjoys life in the city. He is proud to live in the biggest city in Oregon. Gabe is particularly interested in ships. Luckily for him, he lives near the Port of Portland, where there is plenty of ship activity.

As you read in the beginning of Chapter 6, Nathan Aschbacher's ancestors were pioneers who came to the Oregon Country by wagon train on the Oregon Trail. Six generations ago, a direct ancestor of Nathan's was a member of Oregon's first Constitutional Convention. He helped to make Oregon a state.

Nathan's family, along with other people who are descendants of Oregon's first non-Indian settlers, keeps their pioneer heritage alive. Each year they show their Oregon spirit by taking part in a pioneer picnic. They eat foods like those that their ancestors ate and take part in old-fashioned activities such as making ice cream.

Other Oregonians, like Chase Shank, about whom you will read in the next chapter, are newcomers to Oregon. Chase was born in the Asian country of Korea, which is one of our Pacific Rim neighbors. He and his brothers and sisters are the first members of their family to live in Oregon. One reason Chase likes living in Oregon is that he loves our state's forests. He thinks he is lucky to live in a house that is surrounded by trees.

A VARIED STATE

As you can see, the people of Oregon are as different from one another as the Cascade Mountains are from the Columbia River. No matter which part of the state people from Oregon live in, or when they came to settle here, they help to make Oregon a special place to live.

These pictures by Gabe, Chase, and Nathan show what they like about living in Oregon.

Check Your Reading

1. Where does Oregon rank among the other states according to its size and population?
2. For what reasons can the people of our state be considered "trailblazers"?
3. In what ways do Michael Tailfeathers and Nathan Aschbacher each keep his heritage alive?
4. **THINKING SKILL:** List three questions you could ask to find out more about the heritage of one of the children in this lesson.

2 The Arts in Oregon

READ TO LEARN

Key Vocabulary

folk art

Key People

Walt Morey
Ursula Le Guin

Key Places

Ashland

Read Aloud

Artists . . . are found throughout the state . . . as well as [in] nooks and crannies where city, valley, coast, mountains, or desert inspire artistic expression.

These words mean that no matter where in Oregon you may travel, you can always find art.

Read for Purpose

1. **WHAT YOU KNOW:** Where can you go in your community to enjoy art?
2. **WHAT YOU WILL LEARN:** What kinds of art do people in Oregon enjoy today?

ART IN OUR STATE

Mrs. Barlow asked her class what kinds of art they liked.

"I like oil painting," said Tim Morehouse.

"I like watching plays," said William Gilmore.

"Music is one of my favorites," said Molly Hall. "My sister enjoys playing the harp with the Portland Youth Philharmonic."

"I like to read books," said Judith Stark. "My favorite stories are by Beverly Cleary."

Each of these students is talking about a different art form that is found in Oregon. When you think of art, you might think of painting and sculpture. But acting, music, and writing are also among the many forms of art. Which art form do you like best?

THEATER IN OREGON

Many actors like to perform at the Oregon Shakespearean Festival in **Ashland**. The festival is famous for its yearly productions of William

Shakespeare's plays. William Shakespeare lived about 400 years ago in England. But the plays he wrote are still popular today.

One theater at Ashland was built in the style of the theaters of Shakespeare's time. It is round and has no roof, so the audience can watch a play while sitting under the stars.

OREGON WRITERS

Judith's favorite writer, Beverly Cleary, grew up in Oregon. She lived in Portland and has described many of its places in her books. You read a part of one of her many books, *The Girl from Yamhill*, in the Oregon Traditions lesson on page 192. What are the titles of some of your favorite Beverly Cleary books?

Other well-known writers from Oregon include **Walt Morey** and **Ursula Le Guin**. Morey wrote books about the outdoors, like *Gentle Ben*. Le Guin wrote the Earthsea series of science-fiction books.

MUSIC IN OREGON

The harp, the instrument played by Molly's sister, is often found in orchestras. The Portland Youth Philharmonic was founded in 1924. It was the first orchestra in the United States to be made up of young people under the age of 21.

Music is celebrated at many of Oregon's festivals. At the Peter Britt Music and Arts Festival that takes place in Jacksonville you can hear

(*above*) One of Shakespeare's plays is performed in Ashland. (*below*) Beverly Cleary recalls her childhood in *A Girl from Yamhill*.

Beverly Cleary

A Girl from Yamhill
A Memoir

Isaac Shamsud-Din painted this mural about Oregon's African-American history. It hangs in Portland's Justice Center.

many different kinds of music. Each year during the month of August, musicians gather there to play music that ranges from classical to country. Where can you go in your community to listen to the kind of music that you like?

OTHER ART FORMS

Folk art is a type of creative art that has been passed down from generation to generation. Folk artists are usually taught by members of their families or communities.

Today the northwest coastal Indians still use cedar for weaving baskets and for carving figures. One Indian artist, Lillian Pitt, enjoys making decorative masks out of clay, beads and feathers.

Another type of creative art is mural painting. In this art form a large picture is painted on a wall. Isaac Shamsud-Din is an artist who paints murals that show the history of African-Americans in Oregon.

ART FOR EVERYONE

As you have read, art is not limited to just painting and sculpture. Acting, writing, music, and folk art are also forms of art that can be found everywhere in our state.

 Check Your Reading

1. Name four forms of art.
2. What is folk art?
3. Name two art festivals that you can visit in Oregon.
4. **THINKING SKILL:** Look at the photograph above. How would you describe this mural to someone who has not seen it?

206

Oregon Traditions

READ TO LEARN

■ **Key People**

James DePreist

■ **Read for Purpose**

1. **WHAT YOU KNOW:** What role do the arts play in the life of our state?
2. **WHAT YOU WILL LEARN:** How did James DePreist struggle to reach his goal?

Oregon's James DePreist

It is opening night of the new season. Every seat in the concert hall is filled. The audience applauds as a tall, strong-looking man walks stiffly across the stage. He climbs the steps to a small platform, then puts down his crutch and seats himself on a tall stool. When he lifts his baton, music sweeps through the auditorium. The audience catches its breath. This will be another great season for the Oregon Symphony Orchestra. A symphony orchestra is a large group of musicians who play different instruments.

James DePreist, conductor of the Oregon Symphony Orchestra, is one of our state's treasures, like Mount Hood. He wasn't born in Oregon, but his life story reminds us of the courage and strength of our pioneers.

JAMES DEPREIST'S EARLY LIFE

James DePreist grew up in Philadelphia. The famous comedian Bill Cosby was his high-school classmate. When James was six, his father died. He was raised by

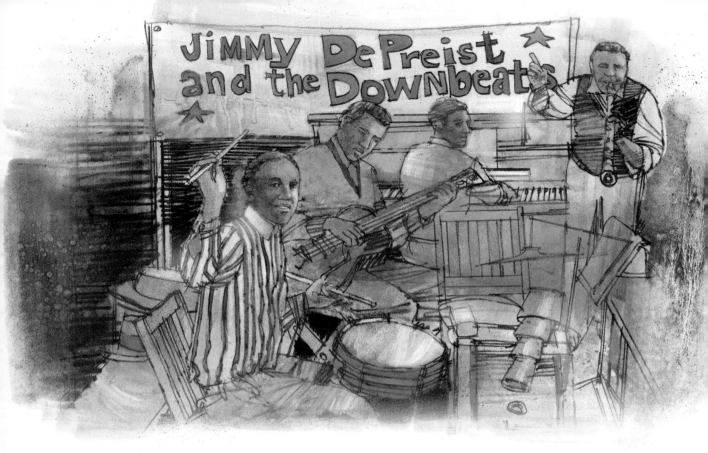

his mother, grandmother, and aunts. They taught him that there was nothing he couldn't do if he really tried.

Music always played an important role in James's life. His aunt, the famous singer, Marian Anderson, took him to many concerts. He studied the piano and learned to play the drums. He even formed his own combo—Jimmy DePreist and the Downbeats. In college his jazz group won a national music award.

James worked hard in college and thought about going to law school. Then, in 1962, he was invited to visit Asia. He had a very exciting time. In Bangkok, the capital of Thailand, he played at the palace with the king, another jazz fan. Later that evening he went to a rehearsal of the Bangkok Symphony, and the conductor invited him to lead the orchestra.

That experience changed James's life. Now he knew what he wanted to be—a symphony orchestra conductor. But his dream almost never came true. A few weeks later he caught polio (pō′ lē ō).

DEPREIST FIGHTS BACK

Polio is a disease that attacks the nervous system. People who fall sick from polio usually lose their ability to walk. Medicines have been developed to prevent people from catching polio. Unfortunately, the medicine didn't work for James. He lost his ability to walk and had to be flown home from Asia, lying helpless on a stretcher.

Then, instead of having a chance to begin his career, he had to enter a hospital in Philadelphia. There, slowly and painfully, he learned to walk again, with crutches and metal braces. James worked on both his body and his mind. He had lost the ability to walk as freely as before, but he still had the ability to think— and to dream.

James began to study music seriously. He even entered a contest for young conductors. But when he arrived at the studio where the contest was to take place, he found that there was no elevator. He struggled on crutches, step by painful step, up the stairs to the second floor. James lost that contest, but a year later he tried again, and this time he won.

He continued to work and study. Soon success followed. He was invited to lead orchestras in major cities all around the world. Itzhak Perlman, a famous violinist who had also suffered polio, saw James conduct. After the concert he asked James why he struggled to stand up straight in front of the orchestra. "You need strength and control in your upper body. Why don't you just sit down?"

Itzhak Perlman's suggestion made sense. From then on James DePreist conducted while seated on a high stool. In 1980 he became music director of the Oregon Symphony Orchestra. The courage with which James DePreist always faced life helped him to become one of Oregon's finest artists.

Check Your Reading

1. What did James's family teach him when he was very young?
2. Which two events changed James's life?
3. How did James struggle to achieve his dream?
4. **THINKING SKILL:** Predict how James's career might have turned out if he hadn't caught polio.

3 Sports and Recreation

READE TO LEARN

Key Vocabulary

recreation

Key People

Dale Murphy
Dick Fosberry
Don Scholander
Mary Decker
   Slaney

Key Places

Willamette
   National Forest
Mount Hood
   National Forest
Owyhee River

Read Aloud

Oregon is for the active of heart, body, and soul. People here fish . . . in mountain streams or dig for clams on coastal beaches. Thanks to Mount Hood . . . you can ski all year-round. . . . In the Columbia Gorge, there's a spot that's earned the title "Wind Surfing Capital of the World."

This is how one writer described some of the ways in which people in Oregon have fun. The natural beauty of our state provides the background for many activities.

Read for Purpose

1. **WHAT YOU KNOW:** What are your favorite ways of spending free time?
2. **WHAT YOU WILL LEARN:** What kinds of recreational activities do people in Oregon enjoy?

ENJOYING OUR STATE

If you could spend this day in any way you choose, what would you do? Head for the coast? Pick up your fishing pole or your camping equipment? Go to watch a basketball game or a track meet? These activities are all different kinds of **recreation**. Recreation includes the many ways that people relax and enjoy themselves.

Almost everywhere you go in Oregon, you can enjoy the natural beauty of our state. Oregon provides the perfect setting for many types of outdoor recreation.

FUN OUTDOORS

Imagine going for a thrilling ride in a rubber raft on the Rogue River with some of your friends. Everyone wears a life jacket and helps to paddle toward the curling whitewater waves. All of a sudden the raft begins to bob up and down like a cork. Water splashes into the raft as everyone laughs and gets wet.

Almost half of our state is covered with lakes, mountains, rivers, and forests that you can explore and enjoy. Many of these areas are part of our state's 13 national forests. There are countless places to enjoy mountain climbing, hiking, and camping. Willamette National Forest is Oregon's largest forest. Mount Hood National Forest is outstanding for winter sports like skiing and snowmobiling.

For people who like wind surfing, bicycling, and swimming, Oregon has much to offer. There are more than 223 state parks in our state where you can enjoy these activities. If you like to fish, the Columbia and Umpqua rivers and the Owyhee (ō wī' hē) River in Eastern Oregon are just some of the fine places where you can relax with your fishing pole.

SPORTS IN OREGON

The crowd cheers as Lori Dale dribbles the ball down the court. Her team is 1 point behind with only 5 seconds left in the game. Quickly Lori aims and shoots for the basket. The buzzer sounds just as the ball goes through the hoop. Lori's team has won.

For many Oregonians sports are a favorite form of recreation. Those who like to watch basketball have many opportunities to do so. They can watch the Portland Trail Blazers, the Ducks, or the Beavers play. The Ducks are the University of Oregon's basketball team. The Beavers are Oregon State University's basketball team.

Baseball fans cheer for Dale Murphy, who grew up in Portland. He plays outfield for the Atlanta Braves. He has won the Most Valuable Player Award two times.

White water rafting on the Rogue River is one of the many different forms of recreation that Oregonians enjoy.

Some other famous athletes who came from Oregon are **Dick Fosberry**, **Don Scholander**, and **Mary Decker Slaney**. They have all participated in the Olympics. Mary Decker Slaney has set many track records. Dick Fosberry won a gold medal in the high-jump event. Don Scholander made history in 1964 by becoming the first swimmer to win four gold medals during a single Olympic Games.

Do you like to fly kites? Every September a kite festival and competition takes place in the town of Yachats on the coast. The air is filled with hundreds of colorful kites. Prizes are awarded for the largest, the smallest, and the most unusual kites.

ENJOYING LIFE

As you have read, there are many places in our state where you can enjoy recreation. Whether you like

(*above, left*) Runner Mary Decker Slaney wears number 596 in a track race.
(*above*) Trail Blazer Jerome Kersey aims for the basket.

to go hiking or swimming, watching sports or taking part in them, it is easy to enjoy life in Oregon.

Check Your Reading

1. Name three kinds of recreational activities that people can enjoy in our state.
2. What kinds of sports do people like to watch or play in our state?
3. **GEOGRAPHY SKILL:** How might the geography of the area in which you live determine the kinds of recreation or sports you take part in?
4. **THINKING SKILL:** Predict what life would be like if people did not take time for recreation.

213

Recognizing Point of View

Key Vocabulary

point of view

Read what Liza and Danny have to say about skiing.

Liza: Skiing is fun for both skiers and spectators.

Danny: Skiing is a dangerous sport. Skiers can get hurt.

Liza and Danny have different **points of view**. A point of view is the way in which a person looks at something. People often look at the same subject from different points of view. Being able to identify a person's point of view allows you to make up your own mind about the subject.

Trying the Skill

Below, Gabe Branch and Michael Tailfeathers give two different points of view about the best place to live in Oregon.

Gabe: I think that there is no better place to live than in the city of Portland. I can enjoy many activities in the city. I can also watch the ships at the Port of Portland.

Michael: I think that the best place to live is in the country. Only in the country can I walk through the woods and find animal tracks.

How would you describe the two points of view?

HELPING YOURSELF

The steps on the left will help you to recognize a person's point of view. The example on the right shows how to apply these steps to Gabe's statements on the previous page.

One Way to Determine Point of View	Example
1. Identify the subject.	The subject is the place in Oregon in which Gabe likes to live.
2. Identify the information given.	Gabe likes living in Portland. He enjoys activities in the city and watching the ships.
3. Identify words that are expressions of opinion. They tell how a person feels about something.	Gabe uses the words *I think that there is no better*. These words tell you that he is giving his opinion.
4. Tell the point of view expressed.	Gabe thinks that Portland is the best place to live.

Applying the Skill

Now apply what you have learned. Identify the points of view expressed by Laura and Mary.

Laura: Dams on the Columbia River will force Indians and people in the fishing industry to give up their way of life.

Mary: Oregonians will benefit from dams on the Columbia River because they will provide water power for low-cost manufacturing.

To check yourself, answer the following questions.

1. Which subject are Laura and Mary talking about?
   a. how dams will affect people's lives
   b. the people who live along the Columbia River
   c. how the Great Depression affected people's lives

2. Which words help you to determine Laura's point of view?
   a. *dams on the Columbia River*
   b. *will provide water power*
   c. *will force Indians and people in the fishing industry to give up*

3. Mary's point of view is shown by:
   a. the subject that she identified
   b. the facts that she included
   c. her use of the words *will benefit*

Reviewing the Skill

1. Define *point of view.*
2. What are some steps that you should take to identify a person's point of view?
3. When have you used this skill?
4. Why is it important to understand a person's point of view?

215

4 City Life

READspace TO LEARN

Key Vocabulary

Portland Rose
    Festival
architecture

Key People

Asa L. Lovejoy
Francis W.
    Pettygrove
Pietro Belluschi

Read Aloud

No one lived there and the place had no name; there was nothing to show that the place had ever been visited except a small log hut. . . . We were then actually encamped on the site of the city of Portland, but there was no prophet with us to tell of the beautiful city that was to take the place of the gloomy forest.

These words were spoken by a pioneer describing the site of Portland, which he had visited as a boy in 1843. In this lesson you will read about this beautiful city today.

Read for Purpose

1. **WHAT YOU KNOW:** What has helped Portland to grow?
2. **WHAT YOU WILL LEARN:** What is life like in Portland today?

STUMPTOWN

The small log hut and the land around it that you read about in the Read Aloud on this page were claimed by **Asa L. Lovejoy** and **Francis W. Pettygrove**. Each owned half of the land of what is now Portland. Lovejoy wanted to name the town "Boston" for his hometown in Massachusetts. Pettygrove liked the name "Portland" better because it was the name of his hometown in Maine. These two men couldn't settle their argument so they decided to toss a coin. Pettygrove won the coin toss. When Portland was first settled, it had so many tree stumps that it was nicknamed "Stumptown."

From this beginning Portland grew to become our state's largest city. Portland's excellent location near important waterways attracts ships and businesses from all over the world.

A LIVABLE CITY

Many Portlanders talk about how livable their city is. They describe its miles of parkland and jogging paths. With Mount Hood in the distance and the Willamette River running through Portland's center, natural beauty is never very far away.

Portland offers a great deal more than beautiful scenery. It has a mild climate. It is also known as a center for education since it is home to many excellent colleges and universities. Portland State University is located right in the heart of the city.

In the last two lessons you read about some of the arts and recreational activities that Oregonians enjoy. Portland is a major center for culture in Oregon. The theater, the ballet, and the symphony can all be enjoyed in Portland.

Each year thousands of visitors attend the second-largest rose parade in the nation—the Portland Rose Festival. This parade has marching bands, show horses, and colorful floats covered with flowers. There are bicycling, boating, skiing, and tennis competitions, too.

With more than 106 parks, Portland is never very far from nature.

The largest children's parade in the United States takes place at this festival. More than 10,000 children dress up in costumes and march or ride their decorated bikes in this parade. Visitors can also attend shows, concerts, and art exhibits.

A WELL-DESIGNED CITY

Portland's varied architecture makes it an interesting city. Architecture is the art of designing buildings. The Pioneer Courthouse Square forms Portland's main plaza, or public square. Almost 50,000 Oregonians helped to pay for building costs by purchasing bricks at $15 apiece. These bricks, bearing the names of the buyers, were used to build the plaza's surface.

This float (*right*) from the Rose Parade is one of Portland's beautiful attractions.

GRAPH SKILL: About how many people lived in Portland in 1920?

WE'VE GOT IT ALL
OREGON

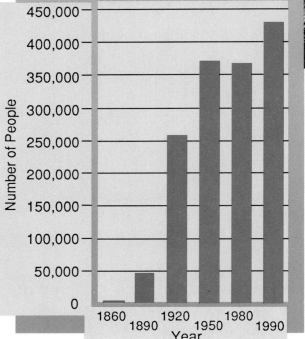

PORTLAND'S POPULATION

Number of People (vertical axis)

450,000
400,000
350,000
300,000
250,000
200,000
150,000
100,000
50,000
0

Year: 1860 1890 1920 1950 1980 1990

Pietro Belluschi, one of Oregon's famous architects, designed the Oregon Art Institute. This museum is known for its collection of Northwest Coast Indian art.

A GROWING CITY

Portland looks very different today than it did when it was called Stumptown. It has grown from a single log hut to a large, modern city. Look at the graph on this page that shows Portland's population growth since 1843. During which time period did Portland grow the most? Today around 430,000 people live in and around Portland. Although it has had its share of problems as any growing city would, Portland remains beautiful.

PORTLAND TODAY

As you have read, Portland is a beautiful city that has continued to grow and improve over time. Its excellent location along important waterways has helped it to become a major business center. Its beautiful scenery and many opportunities for work, learning, and recreation have helped it to become our state's largest city.

 Check Your Reading

1. How did Portland get its name?
2. Describe three things you could do for recreation in Portland.
3. Name two buildings that are examples of Portland's interesting architecture.
4. **THINKING SKILL:** Compare and contrast the Portland of 1843 with today's Portland.

218

REVIEWING VOCABULARY

Number a sheet of paper from 1 to 5. Beside each number write **C** if the underlined word is used correctly. If it is not, rewrite the sentence using the word correctly.

1. *Architecture* is a type of wall painting.
2. *Folk art* is art created by old folks.
3. *Heritage* is a word meaning ways and beliefs handed down from one generation to the next.
4. A *powwow* is a gathering of Native Americans
5. *Recreation* is the art of designing buildings.

REVIEWING FACTS

1. What happens at the yearly Shakespeare Festival?
2. Where in Oregon could you go to hear classical music?
3. What are three outdoor activities that are enjoyed by Oregonians?
4. How did Portland's location help it to grow into a large city?
5. How did Oregon's citizens help to build Pioneer Courthouse Square?

((≡►WRITING ABOUT MAIN IDEAS

1. **Writing a News Story:** Imagine that you are a reporter for your local newspaper. You have been sent to cover this year's Portland Rose Festival. Write a news story about the festival.
2. **Writing a Paragraph:** Which sport do you most enjoy watching or participating in? Write a paragraph telling why you like this sport and identify where someone could play or watch it.

BUILDING SKILLS: RECOGNIZING POINT OF VIEW

Read this conversation. Then answer the following questions.

Amos: I think we should name this town Boston. Some day it will be a great city, like the one I come from in Massachusetts.

Francis: No, let's name it Portland. Then it will always remind me of my hometown in Maine. Portland is a name we all can be proud of.

1. What is point of view?
2. What are some steps that you could follow to identify a person's point of view?
3. What is Amos's point of view on the subject? What is Francis's point of view?
4. For what reasons is it important to recognize a person's point of view?

CHAPTER 10

OREGONIANS AT WORK

FOCUS

This log is 4 feet across. But I've seen logs that are bigger around than my whole height!

Chase Shank lives in Sweet Home, where many people earn a living from trees. In this chapter you will find out more about the lumber business and also about other ways in which Oregonians can earn a living.

1 Logging and Lumbering

READ TO LEARN

🗔 Key Vocabulary

logging   economy
lumbering   timber
industry

🗔 Read Aloud

Chop, chop go the men with their great double-headed axes. Then the teeth of a long crosscut saw tear through the wood, and the tree begins to tremble . . . and the choppers raise their warning cry of "Timber!"

These words describe early logging in Oregon. In this lesson you will learn more about the lumber business.

🗔 Read for Purpose

1. **WHAT YOU KNOW:** What are some important natural resources that are found in our state?
2. **WHAT YOU WILL LEARN:** Why is the lumber industry important to Oregon?

MANY TREASURES

As you have read, Oregon is rich in natural resources. Forests are Oregon's most abundant natural resource. When people think of Oregon, they often think of trees. Our state has nearly 30 million acres (21 million ha) of trees, covering nearly one half of Oregon's land.

Many Oregonians earn their living from logging and lumbering. Logging is the business of cutting down trees, cutting them into logs, and transporting the logs to a mill. Lumbering is the business of cutting and preparing logs.

Lumbering is an important industry in Oregon. An industry is all of the businesses that make one kind of product or provide one kind of service. The lumber industry is one important part of Oregon's economy. The economy is the use of resources, money, and goods to

Early loggers cut down trees with axes. The logs were then dragged by oxen over skid roads to mills.

Oregon. Oregon is the leading **timber** state in the entire nation. Timber is a "stand" of trees. A stand is a group of plants growing in a continuous area.

Most of Oregon's forests are in the mountains or on lower land in the western half of the state. The most common tree in the western part of the state is the Douglas fir, and the most common tree in the eastern part is the ponderosa pine.

EARLY LOGGING

You have learned that forests were important to our earliest people. The Indians used cedar for making canoes, lodges, and bark clothing. The Hudson's Bay Company chopped down trees to provide the lumber with which to build Fort Vancouver and other structures.

The trees were a nuisance to the first farmers because they made clearing the land difficult. But as more settlers came, they needed large amounts of wood for housing and fuel. Lumbering soon became an industry.

THE GROWTH OF LOGGING

In the 1800s many early loggers lived harsh lives in isolated lumber camps. They slept in bunkhouses and ate hearty meals in dining halls.

At first loggers had to cut down trees with axes and saws. It often took a whole day for two men to cut down a single tree. The cut logs

meet people's needs and wants. Many people in Oregon depend on Oregon's forests for jobs, lumber, forest products, and recreation.

THE LUMBER INDUSTRY

The industry of lumber and wood products is the largest one in were then floated down a stream or dragged by oxen over a skid road. A skid road was a road with logs lying crosswise like railroad ties. The logs, called skids, were half-buried in the ground about 5 feet (152 m) apart from one another. Several logs were hooked together and pulled along the skid road by oxen.

A "skid greaser" was usually a teenager who ran along the road between the last ox and the logs. He dipped a stick into a can of grease and smeared it onto each skid. This made the road slippery so that the logs could be pulled along easily to the mill.

LOGGING TODAY

Today the lumber industry has changed greatly. One Oregonian has written:

> The logging camps are gone from the woods; now the lumberjacks live in modern towns . . . and travel daily in their automobiles over good roads to the timber operations.

Loggers now cut logs with chain saws and load them by bulldozers onto large trucks. If the ground is very rough, sometimes helicopters lift the logs out of the woods.

MANY KINDS OF JOBS

Mr. Jerome's fourth-grade class in Sweet Home was discussing a newspaper article about Oregon's lumber industry.

"Raise your hand if someone in your family works in the lumber business," said Mr. Jerome.

Almost half of the students in his class raised their hands.

"What does your Mom or Dad do, Bob?" said Mr. Jerome.

"My dad is a tree farmer," said Bob. "He went to college to learn about soil nutrition and fertilizers. He learned about how to control insects that harm trees. He even learned about plant breeding and how to grow 'special trees' that never get diseases. This year my dad's farm planted more than 1 billion seedlings! In 60 to 90 years these trees will be fully grown."

Today the **logging industry** must think carefully about which trees to cut down.

"My mother is a logging engineer," said Steve. "She had to go to college for five years to learn how to do her job. My mom takes measurements of the land from which roads are built so that loggers can get in and out of the forest. She has to make sure that the loggers are able to remove the logs without hurting themselves or the environment."

"My father learned what he knows from his father, and my grandfather learned from his father," said Mary Beth. "My relatives have been loggers ever since they came to Oregon over 100 years ago! My grandfather was a logroller. We still have his logrolling boots with the steel spikes. When my family gets together, they sure have some great stories to tell about their logging experiences."

Lumberjacks sort logs as they float downriver to a lumber mill.

DIFFERENT NEEDS

You have just read about three students in Oregon whose families depend on the lumber industry for earning a living. As you will read later in this chapter, many other people in our state earn their livings by making products out of lumber.

People from other states, as well as from other countries, also depend on Oregon's most important natural resource. Japan, one of our Pacific Rim neighbors, buys 20 percent of Oregon's wood. Perhaps you have seen logs being loaded onto ships at the Port of Portland, headed for Japan.

FOREST CONSERVATION

It's not just people who depend on Oregon's trees. Many birds and other animals depend on Oregon's forests for their homes. Because so much depends on our forests, conservation is a very important issue. The early loggers "cut and moved on" as fast as they could, but the people of Oregon soon began to realize that they must protect their forests.

Our state has been among the first states to pass laws concerning logging and the protection of the environment. Some of these conservation laws control how the forests may be used—which areas may be cut down, and which areas will remain as homes for wildlife or as places for recreation. Other Oregon

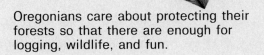
Oregonians care about protecting their forests so that there are enough for logging, wildlife, and fun.

conservation laws require loggers to plant trees in areas in which they have been cut down.

People don't always agree about forest practices, as you will read in the Point/Counterpoint that follows this lesson. They ask questions such as: If trees are removed from the banks of streams, won't that damage the public water supply? Have we the right to disturb the forest's birds and animals?

Oregonians and lawmakers are trying to find the answers. One professor at Oregon State University has written:

People in Oregon want to balance all of the uses of our forests. We want plenty of lumber. We also want a place to go camping, we want clean water, and we want a place for all the animals to live.

Check Your Reading

1. What is the largest industry in our state?
2. Why are forests important to Oregonians?
3. What are some of the jobs in the lumber industry?
4. **THINKING SKILL:** Compare and contrast the lumber industry of today with the first days of logging in the middle 1800s.

225

How Should Oregon Make Use of Its Forests?

Forests are one of Oregon's most valuable natural resources. As you have read, the logging industry provides many jobs for Oregonians. Some of the oldest forests in the United States are found in our state. They are called "old-growth" forests because they have been standing for hundreds of years without being cut down.

Many people are concerned about losing old-growth forests to the logging industry. An old-growth forest takes hundreds of years to replace. These people believe that the logging industry will destroy the forestland and the plants and animals that can survive only in this type of environment. But the logging industry believes that there are enough trees in Oregon for everyone. To make sure that there will always be trees for logging, as well as for people's recreation, they intend to plant new trees in places where old ones have been cut down.

Should the old-growth forests be preserved?

POINT ☆⟍👉

Our Forests Should Be Preserved

Many people believe that the old-growth forests in Oregon are in danger of being lost forever to the logging industry. Environmental groups like the Sierra Club are trying to protect old-growth forests. The club's president, Fredric Sutherland, said:

> . . . The ancient forests are almost gone, and whether they are saved or not won't make much difference for the future of logging jobs in Oregon. It will, however, make all the difference in the world to the Northern Spotted Owl and other creatures that need old-growth forests for their survival. We should save what we can now, while there's still time.

- According to Fredric Sutherland, what effect will cutting down the old-growth forests have on the environment?

COUNTERPOINT 👈⟋☆

Our Forests Should Be Harvested

People who defend logging say that it provides many jobs and strengthens our economy. Many towns in Oregon depend on logging. Karen Robertson from Sheridan, a logging town, said:

> Imagine New York City without Wall Street. That is what Oregon would be like without the wood industry. . . . In the early 1980s . . . many mills closed. Environmentalists cannot know how fearful of repeating that suffering the families in my back-woods town are. Many of us believe that the more than 2 million acres already set aside by the government to be left in their natural state is enough.

- In Karen Robertson's opinion, why would it be wrong for the government to set aside more land to be left in its natural state?

UNDERSTANDING THE POINT/COUNTERPOINT

1. Why do some people think that old-growth forests should be preserved?
2. Why do some people think that old-growth forests should be harvested?
3. Which side do you think makes the stronger case? Why?

2 Fishing and Agriculture

READING TO LEARN

Key Vocabulary

livestock   hatchery
agriculture

Read Aloud

Oregon agriculture is perhaps the most diverse of any comparable [similar] geographic area on earth. No fewer than 172 [crops] are produced within the state.

Read for Purpose

1. **WHAT YOU KNOW:** Which kinds of foods do you like to eat?
2. **WHAT YOU WILL LEARN:** How are fishing and agriculture important to Oregon's economy?

NEW WAYS OF LIFE

A long time has passed since the early days of Oregon when people lived by fishing in nearby rivers and by eating food grown on their own land. Now most people buy their food in supermarkets or in corner grocery stores. Still, farming and fishing are a way of life for many Oregonians today.

MANY KINDS OF PRODUCE

In Chapter 1 you read about how our state is divided into regions. Because each region has different landforms, types of soil, and amounts of precipitation, our state is able to grow many different kinds of produce.

Farms throughout Oregon also raise **livestock**. Livestock are animals that are raised on a farm or ranch to be sold at a market. Look at the product map on the next page. It shows that sheep are raised in the southwestern and eastern parts of our state, and that poultry is raised in the west. It also shows that fruits are grown along the lower part of the Columbia River and in and around Medford. Which kinds of

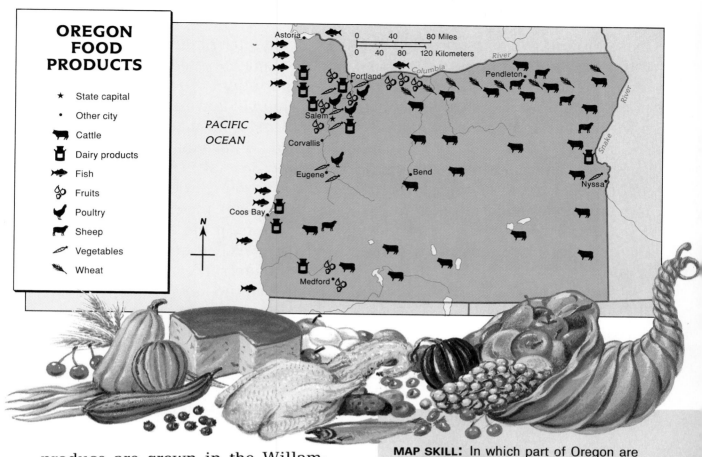

OREGON FOOD PRODUCTS

★ State capital
• Other city
🐄 Cattle
Dairy products
🐟 Fish
Fruits
🐓 Poultry
🐑 Sheep
Vegetables
Wheat

PACIFIC OCEAN

Astoria
Portland
Columbia River
Pendleton
Salem
Corvallis
Eugene
Bend
Nyssa
Snake River
Coos Bay
Medford

0   40   80 Miles
0 40 80 120 Kilometers

N

MAP SKILL: In which part of Oregon are most crops grown?

produce are grown in the Willamette Valley? Which kinds of produce are grown in the region where you and your family live?

FISHING

Fishing, like farming, is another important source of food. People who fish haul in about 100 million pounds (45 million kg) of fish each year. Salmon is one of Oregon's most valuable fish, but shrimp, tuna, flounder, oysters, and rockfish are also important. Salmon are caught in nets or by trolling. Trolling is a type of fishing in which a fishing line that trails behind the boat is used. The line is baited with shiny hooks that attract salmon.

Large machinery is used to lower these fishing lines and to raise them when they are loaded with fish.

The crew on a trolling boat spends one or two weeks at a time on the ocean. Everyone sleeps and eats on the boat. The fish that are caught are stored on the boat in several large freezers that keep the fish fresh until they are brought to port.

THE FARMING AND FISHING MARKET

You might think that only the people who grow crops, raise cattle, or catch fish earn their living from

229

these products. But the people who transport products around the state and around the country also earn their living from them. Other people make food products from crops, cattle, or fish.

Still others earn their living by selling food in stores or by preparing and serving food in restaurants. As you can see, farming and fishing are very important to Oregon's economy.

A WAY OF LIFE

Look at the photographs on this page. You can see how people harvested wheat long ago and how they do so today. How do farming methods appear to have changed?

In Chapter 7 you read about how technology has changed our state's transportation. Today, technology has made farming and fishing much easier for many people. Land that would have taken days to plow by hand now takes only a few hours with a modern tractor. A combine harvester can pick grain, separate the grain from the stalk, and throw out the stalk, all at once.

Computers are also helping to make farming and fishing easier. Some combine harvesters and tractors have computers that help the operator. Other machines with computers can milk and feed cows.

FARMING AND FISHING TODAY

Today **agriculture** is more than just farming. Agriculture is the science and business of raising crops and farm animals. Some people in agriculture work in laboratories. One of their jobs is to produce better

Early harvesting methods took many days, but today combines make harvesting faster and easier.

kinds of plants. For example, by working with cells from apple trees, scientists have produced some apples that grow more easily and others that taste better.

Likewise, scientists have learned how to raise fish in a **hatchery**. A hatchery is a place in which fish eggs are hatched. Scientists are able to hatch fish eggs by creating the same conditions that exist in an ocean or in a river. The fish are raised in the hatchery until they are almost grown. Then they are taken to the ocean or a river. Hatcheries, like the one at Trask River near Tillamook, are important for stocking the ocean and the rivers with fish.

Now that farming and fishing are done with large equipment, engineers and mechanics are needed to build and fix these machines. In Eastern Oregon, where the soil is dry, engineers also find ways to irrigate, or bring water to, the soil.

A CAREER IN AGRICULTURE AND FISHING

As you have just read, farming and fishing are an important part of Oregon's economy. They provide many people with jobs. You might enjoy a visit to a local farm or fishing port to learn more about these kinds of jobs. Even if you never live on a farm or fish in the ocean, there are other jobs that you might someday have in the agriculture or fishing industries.

A fisherman on a trolling ship off the coast of Oregon hauls in a large net filled with perch, sole, and codfish.

Check Your Reading

1. Name three types of fish that are found in Oregon.
2. In what ways has recent technology made changes in farming and fishing methods?
3. What are some kinds of jobs available in the business of agriculture? What are some kinds of jobs available in the fishing industry?
4. **GEOGRAPHY SKILL:** Look at the map on page 229. In which part of our state are most of the fruit farms located? Where are most of the fishing ports located?
5. **THINKING SKILL:** Look at the pictures of farm equipment on page 230. In what ways does technology contribute to farming?

231

Reading Circle and Line Graphs

Key Vocabulary

graph
circle graph
line graph

Graphs are special kinds of diagrams that show information in a form that is easy to understand. Graphs are used to present a set of facts and to compare them.

In this chapter you have read about the land and resources of Oregon. You read that Oregonians can grow many kinds of produce because of the different landforms, amounts of precipitation, and types of soil in the different areas of our state. A graph can show the different kinds of fruit that are produced in Oregon. It can also show the fruit production in one area over a number of years. Graphs give a lot of information without using many words.

Reading a Circle Graph

One kind of graph is a **circle graph**. This kind of graph shows at a glance how the parts of something are related to the whole.

A circle graph is a circle that is divided into parts. Because the parts of a circle graph look like the slices of a pie, a circle graph is also called a pie graph.

Large amounts of five kinds of fruit and one kind of nut are grown in Oregon. Suppose that you wanted to compare the amounts of the different fruit and nut crops grown in our state. The circle graph below can help you.

First read the title of the graph. The circle represents the total amount of

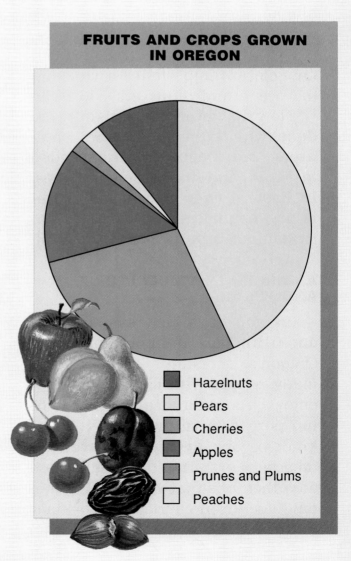

FRUITS AND CROPS GROWN IN OREGON

■ Hazelnuts
□ Pears
▨ Cherries
▨ Apples
▨ Prunes and Plums
□ Peaches

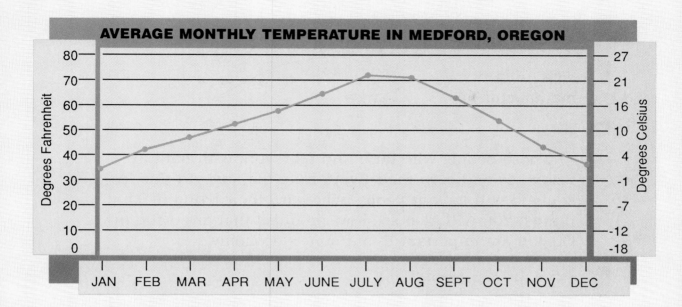

AVERAGE MONTHLY TEMPERATURE IN MEDFORD, OREGON

Degrees Fahrenheit: 80, 70, 60, 50, 40, 30, 20, 10, 0

Degrees Celsius: 27, 21, 16, 10, 4, -1, -7, -12, -18

JAN FEB MAR APR MAY JUNE JULY AUG SEPT OCT NOV DEC

fruit and nuts grown in Oregon. Each part of the circle represents a different kind of fruit or nut. Look at the graph and its key. Which of the five fruits is produced in the largest amounts?

Reading a Line Graph

Another kind of graph is a **line graph**. A line graph shows changes over time. The line graph on this page shows the average temperature in Medford, Oregon, for one year.

To read a line graph, first look at its title. Next read the labels across the bottom of the graph. What information do these labels give? Find the label on the left side of the graph. What information does this label give?

Notice that for each month on the graph, a dot shows the average temperature in Medford. The dots are joined to make a line. The line rises or falls on the graph as the temperature increases or decreases. Trace the line with your finger. When does the temperature in Medford go up? When does the temperature in Medford go down?

Reviewing the Skill

Use the information and the graphs in this lesson to answer the following questions.

1. What is a circle graph used for?
2. Which fruit is produced the most after pears?
3. What is a line graph used for?
4. Is the average monthly temperature in Medford higher in June or July?
5. When is the average temperature in Medford in the low 40s?
6. Why are graphs useful?

233

3 Manufacturing

READ TO LEARN

Key Vocabulary

manufacturing

Key Places

Nyssa

Read Aloud

Those people who farm and fish work with natural resources and earn their living from the land. In this lesson you will look at people who earn their living making things. You will also see how products that are made in Oregon are important to our state's economy.

Read for Purpose

1. **WHAT YOU KNOW:** In what ways are logging, farming, and fishing important to Oregon?
2. **WHAT YOU WILL LEARN:** What are some of the important manufacturing industries in Oregon?

JOBS IN MANUFACTURING

What do a paper bag, a computer chip, and canned fruit have in common? All these products are manufactured in Oregon. **Manufacturing**, or the making of goods, is another major source of employment in Oregon. In recent years the number of people who work in manufacturing industries has been increasing.

LUMBER AND WOOD MANUFACTURING

Have you ever passed a truck filled with logs and wondered where those logs were going? Raw logs are not of much use to people unless they are manufactured into products. How many products can you name in your classroom that are made from wood?

The manufacturing of wood products is one of the most important industries of our state. After leaving the forest, some logs are brought to mills. There the logs are carried on a moving belt toward the teeth of whirling saws that cut them into boards. These boards can be used for building houses or for

Manufacturing turns lumber into wood chips and plywood. These products in turn are made into paper and furniture.

making furniture. Oregon mills produce lumber for construction businesses all around our country.

Other logs are brought to a paper mill where they are shredded into wood chips. Next the wood chips are mixed with chemicals and cooked to a brown, pulpy mass, which is then bleached and thinned with water. After the pulp is spread out, pressed, and dried, you can easily recognize it as paper.

How many different kinds of paper do you use each day? One kind of paper is used for newspapers. Another kind, called kraft, is used to manufacture paper bags. Still another kind can be found in your notebook. Each year the wood

manufacturing industry in our state produces tons of paper and many paper products.

HIGH TECHNOLOGY

Have you ever played a video game? Do you know how to use a computer? Have you ever flown in an airplane? The high-technology industry, or "high-tech" industry as it is called, manufactures some of the parts that are needed to make this equipment work.

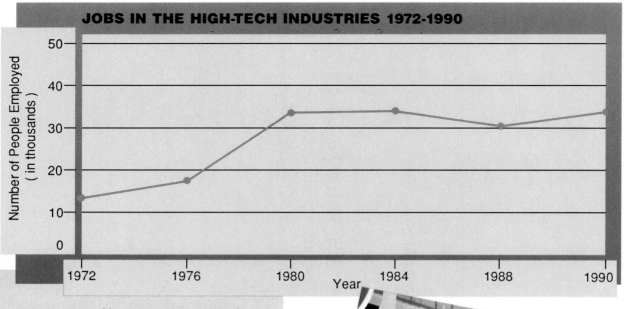

JOBS IN THE HIGH-TECH INDUSTRIES 1972-1990

Number of People Employed (in thousands)

50
40
30
20
10
0

1972   1976   1980   Year   1984   1988   1990

GRAPH SKILL: How many more people were employed in high-tech industries in 1990 than in 1976?

Video screens, irrigation equipment, and aircraft equipment are just a few of the high-tech products that are manufactured in our state. The high-tech industry is Oregon's fastest growing industry. During the 1980s more than 33,000 workers were employed by high-tech firms in our state. In the early 1990s employment by high-tech firms is expected to double. This type of industry does not depend upon natural resources in its process of manufacturing. Therefore, high-tech equipment can be manufactured almost anywhere in our state.

OTHER MANUFACTURED GOODS

The Willamette Valley has one of the largest canning and freezing industries in the United States. Each year millions of pounds of fruits and vegetables that are grown in our state are canned or frozen. Then these products are shipped to places in our state or to other parts of the nation.

Wine making is a new industry in the Willamette Valley, where grapes are grown in vineyards on the hillsides. On the coast, factories in Tillamook County produce

236

Jobs in the manufacturing industries have increased to produce more products made in Oregon.

cheese, and factories in Nyssa, which is along the eastern border of our state, make sugar from sugar beets.

WORKING TOGETHER

So far in this chapter you have read about the industries of logging, farming, fishing, and manufacturing. These industries are not completely separate. For example, irrigation equipment is manufactured by some factories. Farmers buy this equipment to irrigate their crops. The crops are then sold to factories where they can be canned or frozen. Oregonians work together to help build our state's economy.

 Check Your Reading

1. What does the word *manufacturing* mean?
2. Name three different kinds of products that are manufactured in Oregon.
3. Why can high-technology equipment be manufactured almost anywhere in our state?
4. **THINKING SKILL:** In what ways do Oregon's industries contribute to its economy?

237

4 Tourism

READU TO LEARN

Key Vocabulary
tourist
service industry

Key Places
Washington Park Zoo
Wallowa Lake

Read Aloud

We will cash in, year after year, on our crop of scenic beauty.

Samuel Hill, an Oregon businessman and lawyer, spoke these words to persuade the state of Oregon to build a highway through the rugged Columbia River Gorge. Completed in 1915, this highway helped business and encouraged people to visit our state. It has became famous as one of the most beautiful routes in the nation.

Read for Purpose

1. **WHAT YOU KNOW:** What are some reasons that people might have for wanting to visit our state?
2. **WHAT YOU WILL LEARN:** How has the tourist industry helped Oregon's economy?

VISITORS FROM OTHER STATES

"There's one from Connecticut!"

"I see one from Alaska!"

As they rode along the Columbia River Highway, Peter and Marisa looked for license plates on automobiles from other states.

"Why do so many people come to Oregon?" Marisa asked their mother.

"For the same reasons that you like to live here," she answered. "Because we have beautiful land and many interesting sights to see."

A GREAT PLACE TO VISIT

Whether it's a trip to Portland's Washington Park Zoo or a family camping vacation at Wallowa Lake, near Joseph, many tourists spend their vacations in Oregon. A tourist

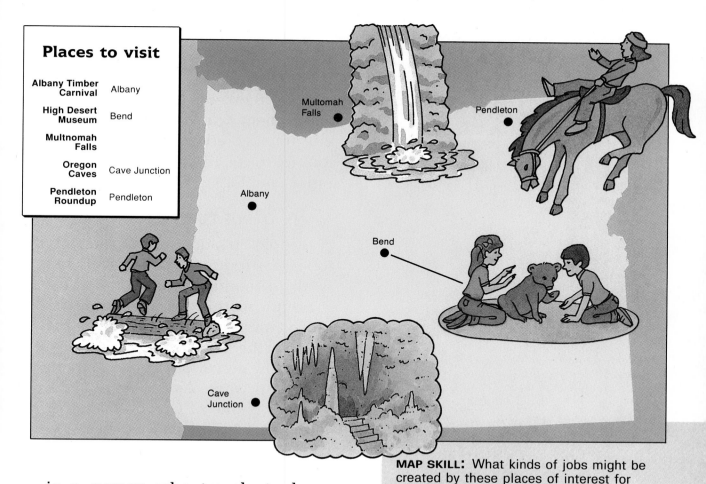

Places to visit

Albany Timber Carnival	Albany
High Desert Museum	Bend
Multnomah Falls	
Oregon Caves	Cave Junction
Pendleton Roundup	Pendleton

Multomah Falls

Pendleton

Albany

Bend

Cave Junction

MAP SKILL: What kinds of jobs might be created by these places of interest for people in the **tourist** industry?

is a person who travels to learn about and enjoy other places.

Where do tourists in Oregon like to go? They like to take trips to see the desert and the forests. They like to fish for salmon, to go skiing or sailboating, to attend fairs and rodeos, and much more.

The map on this page shows some of the places that people find interesting and fun to visit in Oregon. You can see why many Oregonians spend their vacations right in their own state. How many of these places have you visited?

In recent years over 6 million visitors from across the United States

and from other countries have come to Oregon. The number continues to rise every year.

TOURISTS AND JOBS

People whose jobs are created by tourism work in the tourist industry. Tourism is one of Oregon's largest industries. Tourists buy from our stores, stay at our hotels and campgrounds, eat in our restaurants, and go to our museums, concert halls, and many other places of interest. Shopkeepers, waiters,

239

Service industry workers, like the beach patrol officer and the guide at Fort Clatsop, earn a living by helping people.

guides, hotel and campground workers are among the many people who depend on the tourist industry for earning a living.

Tourists use our roads, bridges, and highways to travel around Oregon. The workers who keep the roads in good condition also earn their livings, in part, from the tourist industry.

OREGON'S SERVICE INDUSTRIES

Tourist workers make up part of Oregon's **service industry**. Service industries are different from manufacturing industries. Service workers do not make things. Instead, they do useful work that people need and want.

Your teacher is a service worker. He or she teaches you and is paid for it. Education is a very important service. Bankers, lawyers, doctors, government workers, and truck drivers are all service workers. They, too, earn a living from helping other people.

MANY OPPORTUNITIES

People in our state have many job opportunities. Some Oregonians work in manufacturing industries, making anything from paper to video equipment. Other Oregonians work in the service industries, providing the services that people both need and want. As you have read, tourism is one of Oregon's leading industries. It creates jobs for many people in our state and contributes to Oregon's economy.

 Check Your Reading

1. Why is tourism considered a service industry?
2. Name some jobs that the tourism industry creates in Oregon.
3. How does tourism help Oregon's economy?
4. **GEOGRAPHY SKILL:** Look at the map on page 239. Name one popular tourist attraction along Oregon's coast. Name one along the Columbia River.
5. **THINKING SKILL:** How are service and manufacturing industries alike and different?

REVIEWING VOCABULARY

agriculture   manufacturing
economy   service industry
lumbering

Number a sheet of paper from 1 to 5. Beside each number write the word or term from the list above that best completes the sentence.

1. The person who drives the truck that carries logs to the mill works in the _____ industry.
2. Bankers, teachers, and doctors are examples of people who work in a _____.
3. The science and business of raising crops and farm animals is called _____.
4. Tourism and lumbering are important parts of Oregon's _____.
5. Making skateboards in a factory is an example of _____.

REVIEWING FACTS

1. Name three jobs that are a part of the service industry.
2. What is logging? Why is it important to Oregon?
3. Why is it important to conserve our forests?
4. How are salmon caught?
5. Why do you think canning is an important industry in the Willamette Valley?

WRITING ABOUT MAIN IDEAS

1. **Writing About a Driving Tour:** Plan a driving tour of Oregon. Include five sights that you would stop to see. Write a few paragraphs describing the route of the tour and the sights along the route.
2. **Writing a Children's Story:** Write a story for children about the Oregon logging industry in the 1800s. The main character should be a tree. The story should teach its readers about the early days of logging, as well as be entertaining.
3. **Planning a Menu:** Study the product map on page 229. Make a meal plan for one day that uses only foods produced in Oregon. Write the menu for each meal. Beside each item, list one place from which that food might have come.

BUILDING SKILLS: READING CIRCLE AND LINE GRAPHS

1. What is a graph?
2. Which kind of graph—circle graph or line graph—would be better to show the amount of pears that were produced in Oregon in 1980, 1985, and 1990? Why?
3. Why is it useful to know how to read graphs?

CHAPTER 11

OREGON'S GOVERNMENT

FOCUS

It's fun being on the Student Council because I get to work on school problems and raise money for different school projects.

Renata Smith is a Student Council Representative at her school in Troutdale. She enjoys being involved in her school government. In this chapter you will learn about our nation's government and about Oregon's state and local governments.

1 State Government

READ TO LEARN

Key Vocabulary

taxes   executive branch
legislative   veto
   branch   judicial branch
bill

Key People

Neil Goldschmidt

Read Aloud

As fourth-grade students . . . we are just beginning to be aware of state government and the abilities of its citizens to draft bills . . . and to support their beliefs. We ask that we be allowed to present to you, in person, a list . . . of the reasons we feel the hazelnut should be named the state nut.

A Camp Fire group wrote these words in a letter to the governor of our state. In this lesson you will read about how state government works by following the process that this group used to help make the hazelnut the state nut.

Read for Purpose

1. **WHAT YOU KNOW:** What are some rules that students at your school must follow?
2. **WHAT YOU WILL LEARN:** How does the government of Oregon work?

WHAT IS GOVERNMENT?

Have you ever taken a trip to one of Oregon's beaches? You probably enjoyed the cool ocean and warm, sandy beaches that were there for you. But who paved the roads that you used to get there? Who paid for the trash cans and who emptied them? Who kept the beach clean?

To pay for the services that you have just read about as well as for many others, the state collects money from the people. This money is called taxes. Look at the circle graph on the next page. It shows how each dollar of taxes in Oregon is spent. Which service gets the most tax money?

How is the decision made about where to spend the money? The people of our state elect leaders to the state government. These men and women follow a process in order to make decisions and laws for the state. Let's read about how our state government works.

THE LEGISLATIVE BRANCH

In 1989, when the Camp Fire group about whom you read at the beginning of this lesson was in the fourth grade, the members had seen a television program about hazelnuts. They learned that Oregon produces 98 percent of all American hazelnuts. The program suggested that the hazelnut should be Oregon's state nut.

This Camp Fire group from the town of Clackamas thought that this was a fine idea, and they decided to do something about it. You read part of the letter that they wrote to Governor Neil Goldschmidt. After reading the letter, Goldschmidt invited the group to the State Capitol Building in Salem.

In order to begin the process of making the hazelnut the state nut, the governor told the Camp Fire group that they would first be working with Oregon's state legislature, the legislative (lej' is lā tiv) branch of Oregon's government. A branch is a part of government. The members of the legislative branch meet and make laws. Oregon's state legislature has two parts, the House of Representatives and the Senate.

Governor Goldschmidt met with the Clackamas Camp Fire group in his office in Salem.

244

Senator Joyce Cohen wrote a **bill** about making the hazelnut the state nut. A bill is a plan for a law. This bill was called Bill SCR5.

The governor asked the Camp Fire group to present reasons for supporting Bill SCR5 to two committees, one from the Senate and one from the House. Each member wrote out her reasons. Some of the reasons were:

> *As the beaver was important to the settlement of the state, the hazelnut should be allowed to shine along with the Douglas fir in its importance to the economy of Oregon. The hazelnut . . . was important to Indians and pioneers. . . . It is in keeping with the spirit of the state.*

The girls went to Salem twice to meet with the two committees. At both meetings each girl read what she had written. The committees liked the bill. However, the full Senate and the House both had to pass the bill in order for it to be passed on to the governor. The committee members recommended Bill SCR5 to the House and the Senate. The House and the Senate then voted in favor of the bill.

THE EXECUTIVE BRANCH

But the Camp Fire group wasn't finished yet. The bill had to be signed by the governor in order for it to become a law. The governor of Oregon is the head of a second part

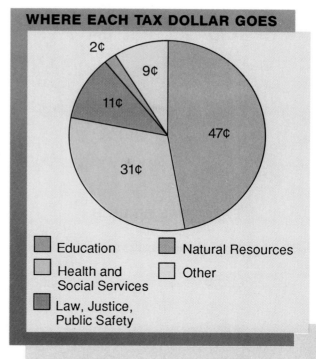

WHERE EACH TAX DOLLAR GOES

2¢
9¢
11¢
47¢
31¢

- Education
- Health and Social Services
- Law, Justice, Public Safety
- Natural Resources
- Other

GRAPH SKILL: How much of each tax dollar in our state goes to Health and Social Services?

of the government, the **executive** (eg zek′ yə tiv) **branch**. The executive branch makes sure that the state's laws are carried out. After both houses of Oregon's state legislature have passed the bill, it goes to the governor. If the governor does not like the bill, he or she can **veto** it, or refuse to sign it. If the governor signs the bill, it will become a state law. If the governor vetos the bill, it goes back to the state legislature. If two thirds of the House and the Senate vote in favor of the bill, it becomes a law.

So the Camp Fire group went to Salem again to discuss the bill with the governor. After talking it over he decided to sign, and the hazelnut

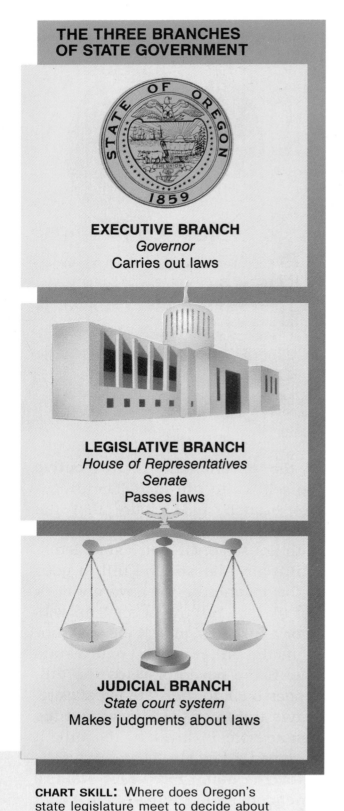

THE THREE BRANCHES OF STATE GOVERNMENT

EXECUTIVE BRANCH
Governor
Carries out laws

LEGISLATIVE BRANCH
House of Representatives
Senate
Passes laws

JUDICIAL BRANCH
State court system
Makes judgments about laws

CHART SKILL: Where does Oregon's state legislature meet to decide about laws?

became Oregon's state nut. The chart on page 247 reviews the steps a bill goes through to become a law.

THE JUDICIAL BRANCH

Bill SCR5 had become a law. But a third branch of government—the **judicial** (jü dish′ əl) **branch**—still had the power to remove it. The judicial branch is the state's court system. The chart on this page illustrates the three branches of Oregon's state government.

Oregon's judicial branch has many different judges and courts. These judges and courts decide the cases of people who are accused of breaking the laws. They also make sure that no laws in our state go against the Oregon constitution.

Suppose that someone thought that Law SCR5 went against the Oregon constitution. The judicial branch would then look at the law. If the judges thought it agreed with the Oregon constitution, they would decide to keep the law. But if it did not agree, the law would be removed. Nobody has challenged SCR5 and the law still stands.

WHAT OUR GOVERNMENT NEEDS

Not every bill that is suggested by citizens becomes a law. But in only a few years you will be old enough to take an active part in the government. When you are 18 years old, you will be able to vote. This

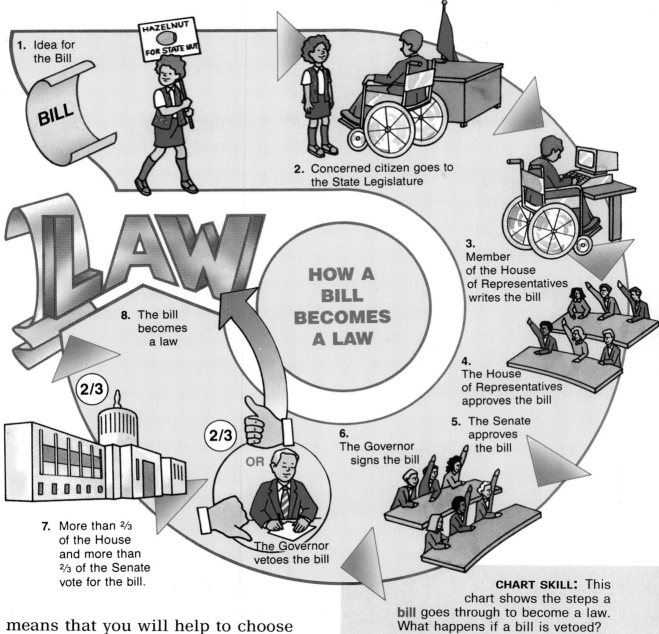

1. Idea for the Bill

BILL

HAZELNUT FOR STATE NUT

2. Concerned citizen goes to the State Legislature

3. Member of the House of Representatives writes the bill

4. The House of Representatives approves the bill

5. The Senate approves the bill

6. The Governor signs the bill

HOW A BILL BECOMES A LAW

8. The bill becomes a law

LAW

2/3

7. More than 2/3 of the House and more than 2/3 of the Senate vote for the bill.

2/3

OR

The Governor vetoes the bill

CHART SKILL: This chart shows the steps a **bill** goes through to become a law. What happens if a bill is vetoed?

means that you will help to choose the people who will make our laws and those who will enforce them.

 Check Your Reading

1. How does the government get the money to pay for government services?

2. What are the three branches of state government?

3. What can you do to help our government, and why is your help important?

4. **THINKING SKILL:** Think about the things that you wish were different in your community. Then decide on an idea that you would like to see become a law.

Reading Newspapers

Key Vocabulary

headline   dateline

byline   lead

How do people across the United States learn about what is happening in their own area or in other areas? One way is through newspapers. Almost every American city and town has its own newspaper. These newspapers print important information about events that have recently taken place.

The Parts of a News Article

A news article has several parts. The first is the **headline**. The headline is printed in large type across the top of the story. It catches your attention. The next part is the **byline**, which tells who wrote the article. Some articles also have a **dateline**, which tells where and when the article was written.

An Oregon News Article

The first paragraph of a news article is called the **lead**. In the lead the reporter aims to catch your interest. Look at the news article on this page. How does Melissa Smith get you interested in her story?

A good news article answers four questions: (1) *Who* was involved in the story? (2) *What* happened?

Students Try to Ban Paper Milk Cartons

By Melissa Smith

EUGENE, January 18—On Wednesday high school students in Portland and Eugene called for paper milk cartons to be outlawed in Oregon school lunches. Students say that the cartons contain chemicals that are harmful to the milk.

During an interview the students claimed that milk picks up harmful chemicals, called dioxins, that are used during the manufacturing process of milk cartons. The dioxins are in the chemicals that are used to bleach, or whiten, paper and cardboard made from brown-colored pulp.

"We, as consumers, must decide whether we want these harmful chemicals to be part of our lives," Michelle Brundage, a junior at South Eugene High School, told *The Oregonian*, a local newspaper. We want unbleached paper for our milk cartons," said Sean Sheldrake, president of Lincoln High School's environmental protection club.

(3) *When* did the event take place? (4) *Where* did it occur? These are called the *Who*, *What*, *When*, and *Where* of the story. Can you find these parts in the article on this page?

Reviewing the Skill

1. What is the headline of the article on this page? What is the byline?
2. Does the story have a dateline?
3. Answer the *Who*, *What*, *When*, and *Where* questions by referring to the news article.
4. What kinds of things can you learn from reading news articles?

2 Local Government

READE TO LEARN

Key Vocabulary

county   commissioner   city manager
county seat   city council   mayor

Read Aloud

Especially in local government, one person can make a difference. One person's vote can give us a new school or a park. When you don't vote, your future is in someone else's hands.

This was said by Bonnie L. Hays who has been working in her local government for many years and has the highest government office in Washington County. She knows how much more effectively local government works if everyone takes part.

Read for Purpose

1. **WHAT YOU KNOW:** In which city or town, and in which county, do you live?
2. **WHAT YOU WILL LEARN:** How do the governments of Oregon's towns, cities, and counties work?

LOCAL GOVERNMENT

In the last lesson you read about how our state government makes decisions. Some decisions, however, are left to the governments of smaller areas.

Suppose that you live in Antelope, Oregon, a small city of only 39 people. There have been some disagreements about where people may hunt in and around Antelope. Does Oregon's state legislature meet to decide this issue? The answer is no. This decision is made by the various leaders of the local government.

The people in Roseburg may want large police and fire departments. Gresham, a growing town, may want to add more teachers to the school system. Bicyclists in Eugene may want to build another bike path in one of their parks. Small towns and big cities have different needs. Local government is there to meet those needs.

COUNTIES

All of the hundreds of towns and cities in Oregon are grouped into various counties. Our state has 36 counties. As you can see from the map on this page, they are different shapes and sizes.

Can you find the county in which you live? Each has a county seat, the town in which the county government is located. Most counties are run by a board of commissioners. Commissioners are officials who are elected by the people of the county.

These county boards make laws. They also make plans for using and caring for land, and they provide many services such as health clinics. Another important official is the sheriff, who heads a department that helps to enforce the laws. There is also a system of county courts and county judges. Counties pay for all of these services with tax money.

THE CITIES

Oregon has many cities of different sizes, which cooperate with

MAP SKILL: Which three counties make up Oregon's eastern border?

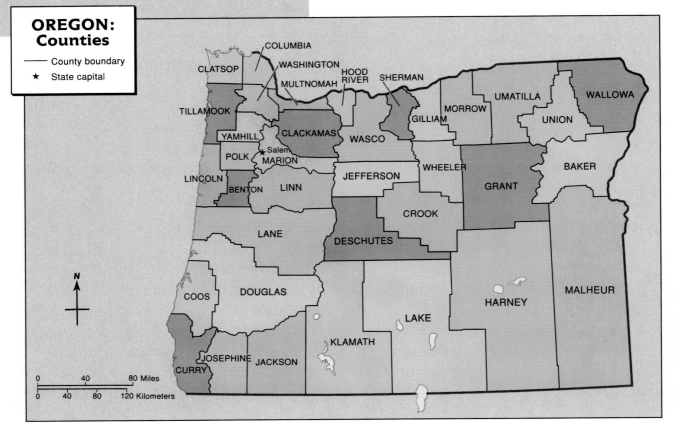

OREGON: Counties

— County boundary
★ State capital

county governments in providing services. For example, Roseburg, the county seat of Douglas County, has a city government. The city government maintains its own streets, while the county government maintains the roads outside of the city.

Oregon's city governments are not exactly alike. Most cities in Oregon have a legislature called a **city council**. The city council is elected by the people and makes laws for the city. In some cities the council appoints a **city manager**. A city manager takes care of the city's daily business. In other cities a **mayor** is elected by the people. The mayor serves as the executive officer of the city in the same way that our governor serves as the executive officer of the state. Our largest city, Portland, is run by a board of commissioners and a mayor.

SPECIAL DISTRICTS

Have you heard or read the terms *school district*, *fire district*, and *Metro*? These are the names of special districts that overlap city lines and may include towns and other nearby areas of a county. These districts may provide many services, such as schools, fire protection, sewage disposal, water, irrigation, and parks and recreation.

WORKING TOGETHER

The local governments are not completely separate from the state

Firefighters provide important public services.

government. They work together on some things, such as providing education and protecting the environment. As you will read in the next lesson, Oregon's government also works with other state governments and with the national government.

Check Your Reading

1. What are some of the services provided by local government?
2. How are the needs of a small town different from those of a large city?
3. **THINKING SKILL:** How is the government of Portland different from other city governments?

251

3 Oregon and the National Government

READ TO LEARN

Key Vocabulary

House of Representatives
Senate

Key People

Mark Hatfield
Bob Packwood

Read Aloud

Ask not what your country can do for you—ask what you can do for your country.

When John F. Kennedy became President in 1961, these words were part of a famous speech he delivered to all Americans. Government serves us, but it depends on us, too, for it works best when we give it support.

Read for Purpose

1. **WHAT YOU KNOW:** In what ways have you made a difference in a group such as the Boy Scouts, the Girl Scouts, or the Four-H clubs?
2. **WHAT YOU WILL LEARN:** How does our national government work, and why is it so important?

THE UNITED STATES GOVERNMENT

In this lesson you will read about Oregon and the national government. Like our state government, the national government has three branches. The legislative branch is called Congress and is made up of the House of Representatives and the Senate. The executive branch is led by the President. The judicial branch is made up of our national, or federal, courts.

The number of people that a state sends to the House of Representatives in Washington, D.C. depends on the state's population. Oregon has five representatives. Each represents the people in a different district of our state. Representatives are elected for two-year terms.

Oregon, like each of the 50 states, elects 2 senators to represent it in the United States Senate. Senators are elected for six-year terms.

The voters of Oregon also help to choose the President of the United States. Presidential elections are held every four years in the month of November.

HOW THE NATIONAL GOVERNMENT WORKS

In many ways the national government—generally called the federal government—is much like the government of the state. But it is different, too.

The federal government handles matters that go beyond state borders. If you write to a friend in Florida, the United States Postal Service carries your letter.

The federal government works with other countries. For example, it might sign an agreement with Canada that neither country will hunt whales. The federal government also maintains the armed forces to protect our nation's interests.

SOME IMPORTANT OREGONIANS

In the earlier chapters you have read about some important Oregonians who helped to make a difference in our state and in our country. Abigail Scott Duniway was one of the people who made a difference. She helped Oregon women gain the right to vote and helped women across the country to gain their rights. Who are some of the other important Oregonians who helped shape our state and nation?

Oregonians today continue to serve Oregon and the nation. Two examples are our senators, Mark Hatfield and Bob Packwood. While

The United States House of Representatives and the Senate meet to make laws in the United States Capitol Building in Washington, D.C.

Bob Packwood (*above*) and Mark Hatfield (*below*) represent Oregon in the United States Senate.

working as a tour guide at our state capitol building in Salem, the young Hatfield was determined to sit in the governor's chair some day. After many years of hard work, he

did just that. He was elected and served as Oregon's governor from 1959–1967. In 1967 he was elected to the United States Senate.

Our other senator, Bob Packwood, has been in the United States Senate since 1969. He serves on important committees. His great-grandfather was an Oregon pioneer who took part in the convention that drafted the state's first constitution!

THE FUTURE

As you have read, Oregonians have shaped not only the history of our state but of our country, too. As future voters you will have the right and the responsibility to help elect the leaders who will work for a bright future for our state and country. You might even want to run for government office. With your help Oregon will continue to be a state that makes a difference.

 Check Your Reading

1. In what ways are Oregon's government and the government of the United States similar?
2. How many senators does Oregon send to the United States Senate? How many representatives does it send to the House of Representatives?
3. **THINKING SKILL:** In what ways have Oregonians helped shape our state and nation?

4 Oregon and the Pacific Rim

READ TO LEARN

Key Vocabulary

international trade   interdependent

Read Aloud

We are in a unique situation in Oregon to develop a good working trade relationship with our neighbors across the Pacific Ocean, because they need wheat, wood products, and other things that grow in abundance on Oregon soil.

This is what Senator Mark Hatfield from Oregon had to say about trade with the Pacific Rim nations. In this lesson you will read about how Oregon has started to build important relationships with its neighbors around the Pacific Ocean.

Read for Purpose

1. **WHAT YOU KNOW:** In what ways do you depend on other people to meet your daily needs?
2. **WHAT YOU WILL LEARN:** How is Oregon's relationship with its Pacific Rim neighbors expanding?

WHAT IS THE PACIFIC RIM?

As you have read in Chapter 1, the Pacific Rim is made up of the nations that border the Pacific Ocean, the earth's largest ocean.

There are nearly 30 nations in the Pacific Rim, including the United States, New Zealand, Canada, Japan, the Soviet Union, China, and Korea. Since one of Oregon's borders is the Pacific Ocean, Oregon is part of the Pacific Rim. Locate the Pacific Rim countries on the map on page 256.

INTERNATIONAL TRADE

Oregon's location makes possible international trade with nations that border the Pacific Ocean. International trade is the buying and selling of products among nations. The governments of many Pacific

Rim nations have worked together to establish good trade relations. Oregon's government, for example, has a department that was created just to handle international trade.

One of the ways in which the different Pacific Rim countries are interdependent is through trade. *Interdependent* means "depending on one another in order to meet needs and wants." The coming years are sometimes called the "Pacific Century" because trade among the countries that border the Pacific Ocean is growing so fast.

Look around your classroom. How many items do you think came from one of our Pacific Rim neighbors? Calculators or tape recorders in your classroom might have come from Japan. The sneakers you are wearing or the ball in your classroom closet might have been made in South Korea. Perhaps the plants your teacher has placed on the window sill were grown in Australia.

If you were to visit some of our Pacific Rim neighbors, you would find products from Oregon. In grocery stores in South Korea you might see bread that was made from wheat or corn that was grown in Oregon. In China you might see students doing their homework with

MAP SKILL: Name one country to the north and one to the south of the United States that are part of the Pacific Rim.

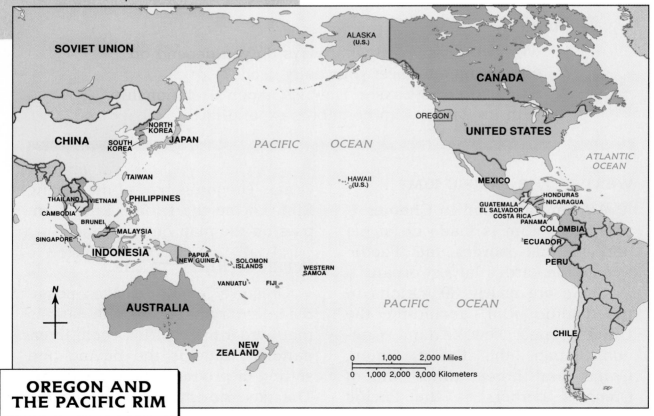

OREGON AND THE PACIFIC RIM

the help of calculators that were made in Oregon. They might also be using paper produced from Oregon's trees.

Not only products are traded among Pacific Rim neighbors, however. The people of these nations also exchange thoughts and ideas.

Several Oregon cities have "sister cities" along the Pacific Rim. Sister cities help to build bridges of friendship between different cultures. One of Beaverton's three sister cities is Gotemba, Japan.

Students at Hazeldale Elementary School in the Beaverton School District are involved in many activities with students at Gotemba Elementary School in Japan. Students at these two schools send photographs, posters, videos, musical tapes, and spoken letters on cassettes to one another. Many of the students have also become pen pals. In special classes these American and Japanese students learn words from one another's language and study one another's culture.

BUILDING BRIDGES

As Oregon looks to the future, some of its most exciting challenges will be found in building bridges to the nations of the Pacific Rim. But these bridges are only a part of Oregon's future.

Throughout this book you have read about a growing, changing Oregon. And Oregon faces even

This origami box and daruma doll were made by Hazeldale students while learning about Japanese culture.

greater challenges as it continues to grow. As you grow, you too will be a part of Oregon's continuing story.

✔ Check Your Reading

1. What is the Pacific Rim?
2. Name two products that come from our Pacific Rim neighbors.
3. In what ways has Oregon become better acquainted with its Pacific Rim neighbors?
4. **GEOGRAPHY SKILL:** Look at the map on page 256. Name five Pacific Rim nations not mentioned in this lesson.
5. **THINKING SKILL:** Name three products of the future that Oregon might trade with the Pacific Rim nations.

Oregon Traditions

READ TO LEARN

Key Vocabulary

landfill

Read for Purpose

1. **WHAT YOU KNOW:** How can Oregonians make a difference in their environment?
2. **WHAT YOU WILL LEARN:** What do you think life might be like in the future?

"Grandpa, I need your help."

"Sure, Arnie. What is it?" Mr. Driscoll switched off the video screen on which he was watching telecasts of his local newspaper.

Arnie held up his parents' video camera. "I have to record a report about the changes in Oregon since the old days. We're supposed to talk to someone who remembers. Do you think you're old enough?"

Mr. Driscoll laughed. "I think I'm as old as I need to be. Pull up a chair, Arnie. Got the camera focused? Let's begin. . . .

"When I was your age, back in the early 1990s, things were a lot different. Every school had some computers, but it wasn't like today. Now you have all your lessons cabled to your own classroom workstations directly from the Office of Education. And if my parents wanted to know how I was doing in school, they

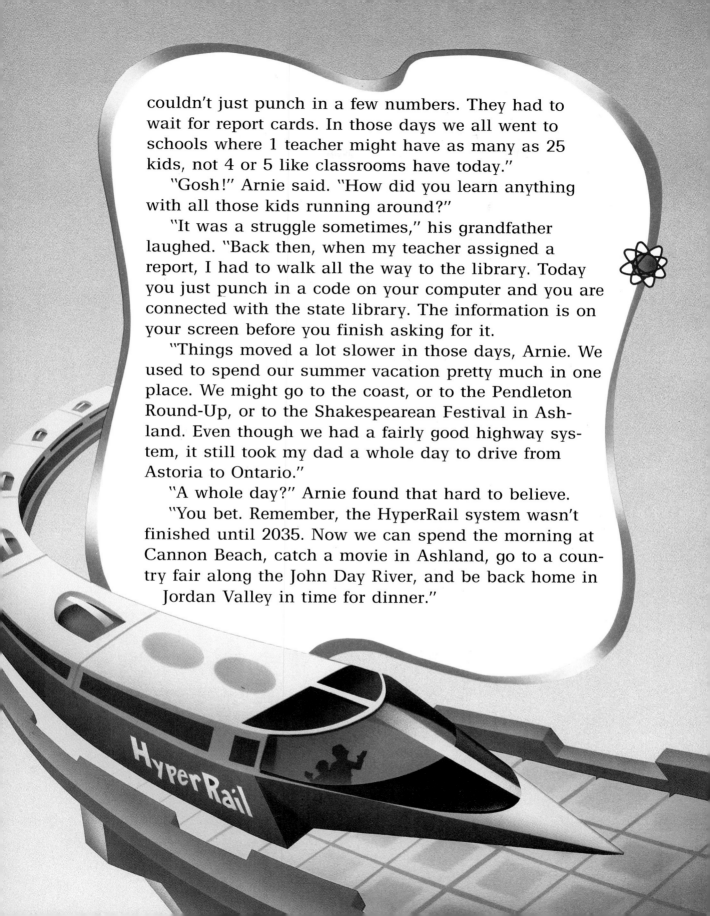

couldn't just punch in a few numbers. They had to wait for report cards. In those days we all went to schools where 1 teacher might have as many as 25 kids, not 4 or 5 like classrooms have today."

"Gosh!" Arnie said. "How did you learn anything with all those kids running around?"

"It was a struggle sometimes," his grandfather laughed. "Back then, when my teacher assigned a report, I had to walk all the way to the library. Today you just punch in a code on your computer and you are connected with the state library. The information is on your screen before you finish asking for it.

"Things moved a lot slower in those days, Arnie. We used to spend our summer vacation pretty much in one place. We might go to the coast, or to the Pendleton Round-Up, or to the Shakespearean Festival in Ashland. Even though we had a fairly good highway system, it still took my dad a whole day to drive from Astoria to Ontario."

"A whole day?" Arnie found that hard to believe.

"You bet. Remember, the HyperRail system wasn't finished until 2035. Now we can spend the morning at Cannon Beach, catch a movie in Ashland, go to a country fair along the John Day River, and be back home in Jordan Valley in time for dinner."

"I know," said Arnie. "That's what we did last summer. Dad says HyperRail was invented in Oregon."

"He's right," Mr. Driscoll said. "The extra-fast electricity and the new kind of cold-water power that run HyperRail were developed by scientists in Oregon. We owe those scientists a lot, Arnie. Without them life in Oregon wouldn't be much fun."

"How come, Grandpa?"

"Well, by the end of the twentieth century we were in big trouble. Our cities produced more garbage than they could get rid of. Portland had no more room in its landfills. You know what a landfill is—a place where garbage is dumped and then covered with soil.

"Gasoline fumes were polluting the air. Hydroelectric power was cheap and clean, but we'd run out of places to build dams.

"So we were stuck, until scientists discovered how to make energy by using cold water and copper wire. No waste to worry about. No danger to anyone. Oregon became a leading producer of energy because if there's one thing we have, it's water. We learned to recycle our trash. Cars and trucks began to run on water and didn't dirty the air. The smog over Portland gradually disappeared. We took down the hydroelectric dams along the Columbia River.

"So, Arnie, I guess it comes down to this. You better take care of your environment, because if you mess it up, you end by messing up your own life. The big difference between now and the old days is that we understand this now."

Arnie switched off the camera. "Gee, Grandpa! When you were my age, did you ever think you would see so many changes?"

Mr. Driscoll smiled. "Arnie, the changes you're going to see in your lifetime will make those that happened during mine seem like those of the covered-wagon days. Who knows what lies ahead? Someday Oregonians may be living on the moon. Oregon's barely 200 years old. Our best is yet to come."

Check Your Reading

1. By talking about his or her past, how can an older relative help us to understand the present time and perhaps to plan for the future?
2. How does Arnie's grandfather's description of the 1990s compare to your life today?
3. What are some other problems of our time that you think might be better when you are older?
4. **THINKING SKILL:** Name some ways in which Arnie's schooling differs from his grandfather's.

You can make a difference

In this book you have read about some people who make a difference. By finding families to adopt orphaned children, Grandma Holt has given thousands of needy children around the world a better chance for a happy life. With their beach clean-up project the children at the Neskowin Valley School are helping to preserve the beauty of their town.

These are only a few of the many people who have made an effort to help others. Chances are that there is someone who has worked hard to solve a problem in your own community. Perhaps it was an adult. Perhaps it was a young person like you.

You may be too young to help find families that want to adopt children, but there are many other ways in which you can help your community. Is there a park nearby with litter on the ground? A clean park is more pleasant for everybody. Is there a senior citizen in your neighborhood who might enjoy a visit from a young person? Do you have a neighbor who needs help carrying groceries?

You might be able to help out in instances like these, or you might think of other ways in which to help your community. The important thing is always to remember that *you*, too, can make a difference.

REVIEWING VOCABULARY

bill	Senate
city manager	taxes
international	trade

Number a sheet of paper from 1 to 5. Beside each number write the word or term from the list above that best matches the definition.

1. The plan for a law
2. Along with the House of Representatives, makes up Congress
3. The buying and selling of products between nations
4. Money that people pay to the government so that the government can provide services to the people
5. A person who is appointed to take care of a city's business

REVIEWING FACTS

1. What does the judicial branch of government do?
2. How does the government get money to provide people with the services they need and want?
3. What is a county? What is a county seat?
4. Why is Oregon considered to be part of the Pacific Rim?
5. Describe some of the connections between Beaverton and its sister city of Gotemba, Japan.

WRITING ABOUT MAIN IDEAS

1. **Writing a Diary Entry:** Imagine that you are a member of the Camp Fire group that worked to make the hazelnut the Oregon state nut. Write a diary entry about the day that you appeared before the House committee giving reasons supporting Bill SCR5. What happened? What did you say? How did you feel?
2. **Planning an Interview:** What would you ask the mayor or city manager of your town or city if you were to interview him or her? What would you like to know about his or her background, election experience, work, and so on? Plan at least five questions that you would ask.

BUILDING SKILLS: READING A NEWSPAPER

1. Name four parts of a news story.
2. Which part of a news story is supposed to catch the reader's interest?
3. What does a headline do?
4. Choose an event that took place at school during the last few days. Write a short newspaper story about the event. Be sure to include the *Who*, *What*, *When*, and *Where* of the story in the first paragraph. Then write a headline for the story.

REVIEWING VOCABULARY

Number a sheet of paper from 1 to 5. Beside each number write **C** if the underlined word is used correctly. If it is not, write the word that would complete the sentence correctly.

1. Another word for the business of farming is <u>manufacturing</u>.
2. People pay <u>bills</u> to the government so it can provide services.
3. The nations of the Pacific Rim trade with one another. These nations are <u>interdependent</u>.
4. Skiing and attending concerts are examples of <u>tourism</u>.
5. Oregon's State Legislature is made up of the <u>Congress</u> and the House of Representatives.

WRITING ABOUT THE UNIT

Interpreting Song Lyrics: Read the words from the Oregon state song, "Oregon, My Oregon," found on page 2. Then write a paragraph that tells the main ideas of the song in your own words.

ACTIVITIES

1. **Researching Local Government:** Find out what kind of positions your city or town government includes. Make a chart that shows the duties of each position and the names of the people who hold these positions today.

2. **Working Together to Make a Mural:** With a group of your classmates, choose a topic about Oregon, such as its famous people. Then have each group member draw part of a mural about that topic.

BUILDING SKILLS: READING CIRCLE GRAPHS

Use the graph on page 245 to answer these questions.

1. How many cents of each state tax dollar go to natural resources?
2. Which service receives the least amount of money?

LINKING PAST, PRESENT, AND FUTURE

The government of Oregon does not have enough money to pay for all the services that people need or want. Which services do you think are important today? Which do you think will be important in the future? List your choices and explain why each is important.

REFERENCE SECTION

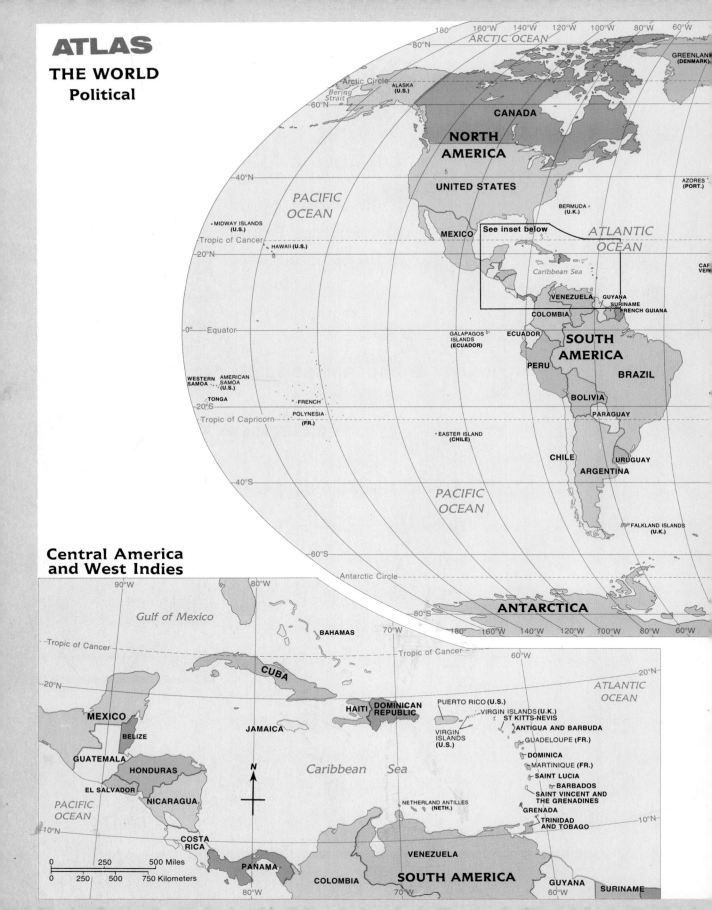

ATLAS
THE WORLD
Political

ARCTIC OCEAN

180° 160°W 140°W 120°W 100°W 80°W 60°W

80°N

GREENLAND
(DENMARK)

Arctic Circle

ALASKA
(U.S.)

60°N

CANADA

**NORTH
AMERICA**

40°N

UNITED STATES

AZORES
(PORT.)

*PACIFIC
OCEAN*

BERMUDA
(U.K.)

*ATLANTIC
OCEAN*

See inset below

MEXICO

CAP
VER

· MIDWAY ISLANDS
(U.S.)

Tropic of Cancer

20°N

Caribbean Sea

HAWAII (U.S.)

VENEZUELA   GUYANA
SURINAME
FRENCH GUIANA

COLOMBIA

0° Equator

GALAPAGOS
ISLANDS
(ECUADOR)

ECUADOR

**SOUTH
AMERICA**

PERU

BRAZIL

WESTERN   AMERICAN
SAMOA   SAMOA
(U.S.)

· TONGA

· FRENCH

20°S

BOLIVIA

PARAGUAY

POLYNESIA
(FR.)

Tropic of Capricorn

· EASTER ISLAND
(CHILE)

CHILE   URUGUAY

ARGENTINA

40°S

*PACIFIC
OCEAN*

FALKLAND ISLANDS
(U.K.)

60°S

Central America
and West Indies

Antarctic Circle

80°S

ANTARCTICA

180° 160°W 140°W 120°W 100°W 80°W 60°W

90°W   80°W

Gulf of Mexico

70°W

BAHAMAS

60°W

20°N

Tropic of Cancer

Tropic of Cancer

*ATLANTIC
OCEAN*

20°N

CUBA

PUERTO RICO (U.S.)

VIRGIN ISLANDS (U.K.)
ST KITTS-NEVIS

MEXICO

HAITI

DOMINICAN
REPUBLIC

ANTIGUA AND BARBUDA

BELIZE

JAMAICA

VIRGIN
ISLANDS
(U.S.)

GUADELOUPE (FR.)

GUATEMALA

DOMINICA

HONDURAS

Caribbean   Sea

MARTINIQUE (FR.)

EL SALVADOR

N

SAINT LUCIA

BARBADOS

*PACIFIC
OCEAN*

NICARAGUA

NETHERLAND ANTILLES
(NETH.)

SAINT VINCENT AND
THE GRENADINES

GRENADA

10°N

TRINIDAD
AND TOBAGO

10°N

COSTA
RICA

VENEZUELA

0   250   500 Miles

PANAMA

0   250   500   750 Kilometers

COLOMBIA

SOUTH AMERICA

GUYANA

80°W   70°W   60°W

SURINAME

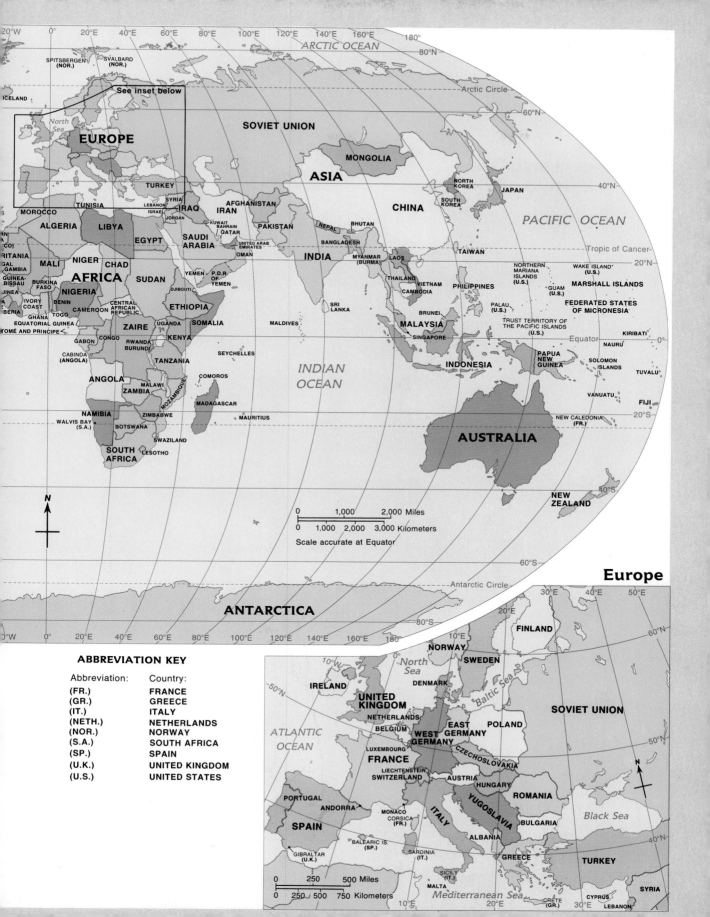

ABBREVIATION KEY

Abbreviation:	Country:
(FR.)	FRANCE
(GR.)	GREECE
(IT.)	ITALY
(NETH.)	NETHERLANDS
(NOR.)	NORWAY
(S.A.)	SOUTH AFRICA
(SP.)	SPAIN
(U.K.)	UNITED KINGDOM
(U.S.)	UNITED STATES

THE WORLD
Physical

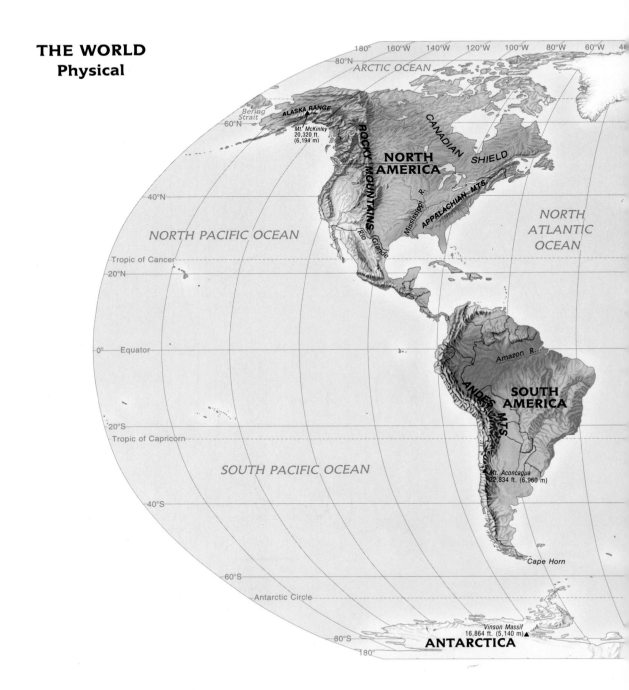

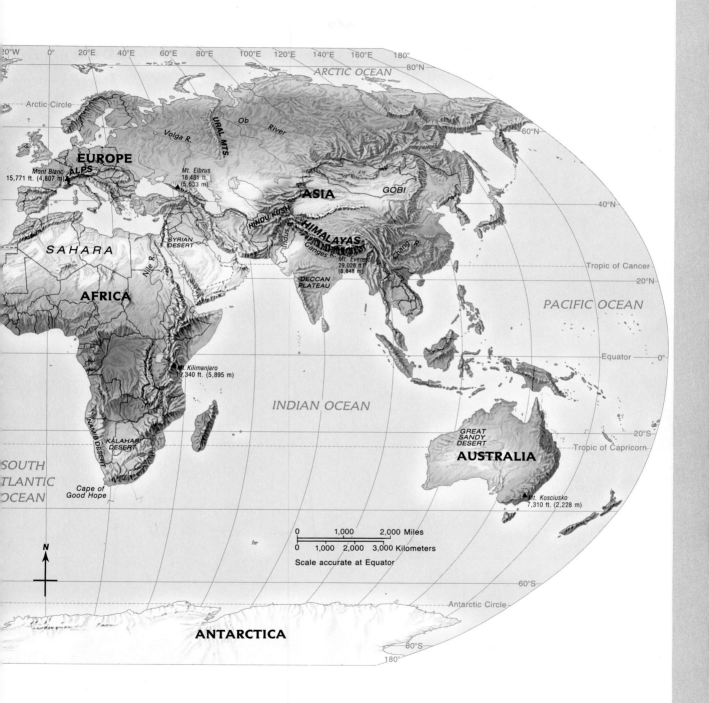

ARCTIC OCEAN

80°N

20°W 0° 20°E 40°E 60°E 80°E 100°E 120°E 140°E 160°E 180°

60°N

Arctic Circle

URAL MTS.

Ob   River

Volga R.

EUROPE

Mont Blanc ALPS
15,771 ft. (4,807 m)

Mt. Elbrus
18,481 ft.
(5,633 m)

ASIA

GOBI

40°N

HINDU KUSH

HIMALAYAS

SAHARA

SYRIAN
DESERT

Nile R.

AFRICA

DECCAN
PLATEAU

Ganges R. Mt. Everest
29,028 ft.
(8,848 m)

Chang R.

Tropic of Cancer

20°N

PACIFIC OCEAN

Mt. Kilimanjaro
19,340 ft. (5,895 m)

Equator 0°

INDIAN OCEAN

GREAT
SANDY
DESERT

20°S

NAMIB DESERT

KALAHARI
DESERT

AUSTRALIA

Tropic of Capricorn

Cape of
Good Hope

Mt. Kosciusko
7,310 ft. (2,228 m)

SOUTH
ATLANTIC
OCEAN

N

0   1,000   2,000 Miles
0   1,000 2,000 3,000 Kilometers
Scale accurate at Equator

60°S

ANTARCTICA

Antarctic Circle

80°S

180°

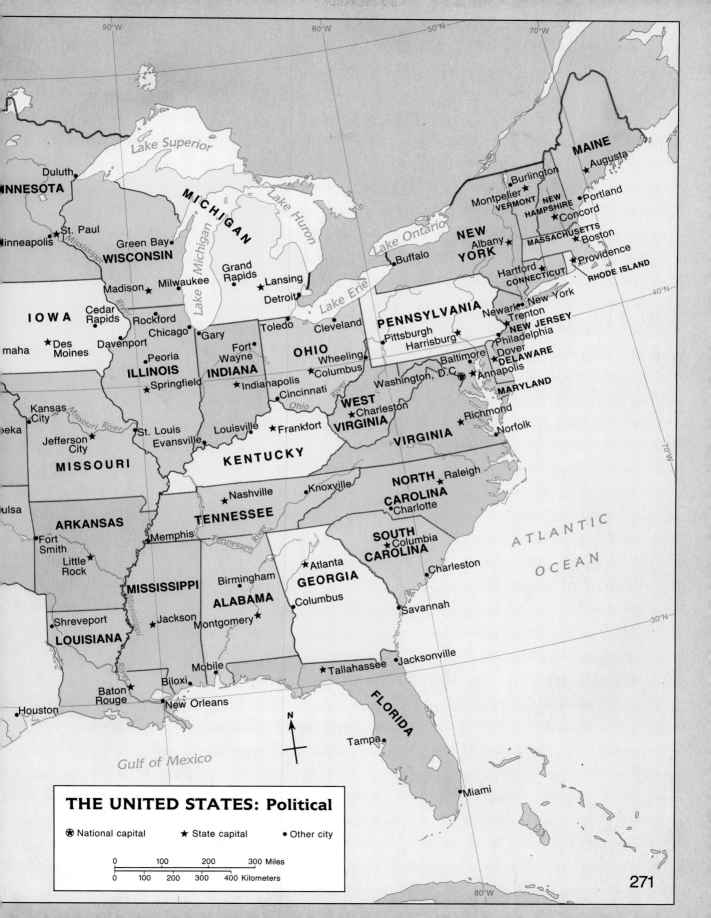

THE UNITED STATES: Political

⊗ National capital   ★ State capital   • Other city

0   100   200   300 Miles
0 100 200 300 400 Kilometers

271

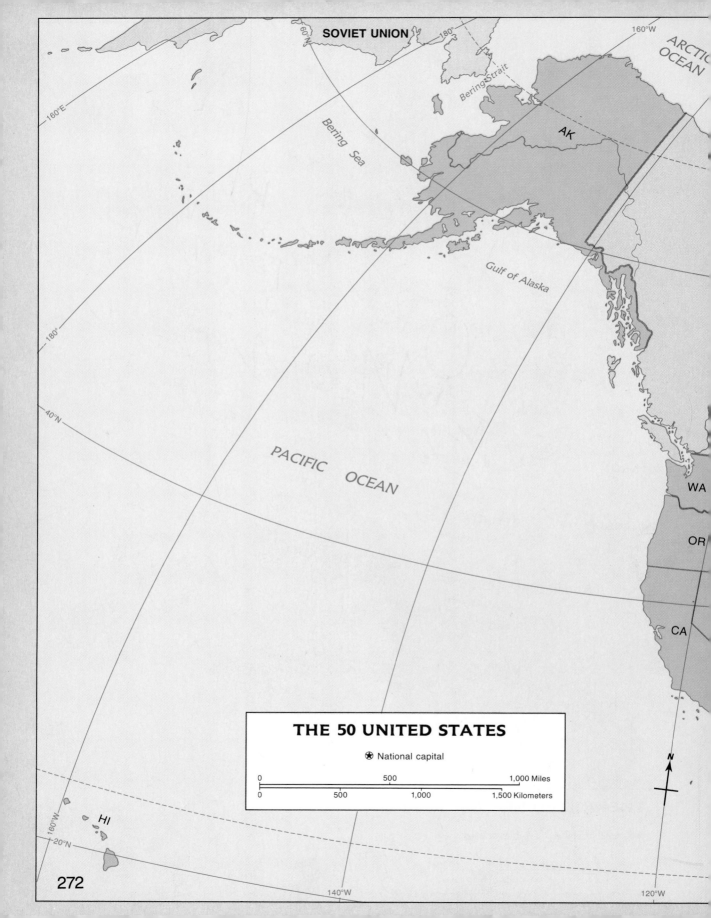

SOVIET UNION

ARCTIC
OCEAN

Bering Strait

AK

Bering Sea

Gulf of Alaska

PACIFIC   OCEAN

WA

OR

CA

160°E

180°

40°N

160°W

160°E

180°

40°N

160°W

20°N

HI

THE 50 UNITED STATES

✪ National capital

| 0 | 500 | 1,000 Miles |
| 0 | 500 | 1,000 | 1,500 Kilometers |

N

140°W

120°W

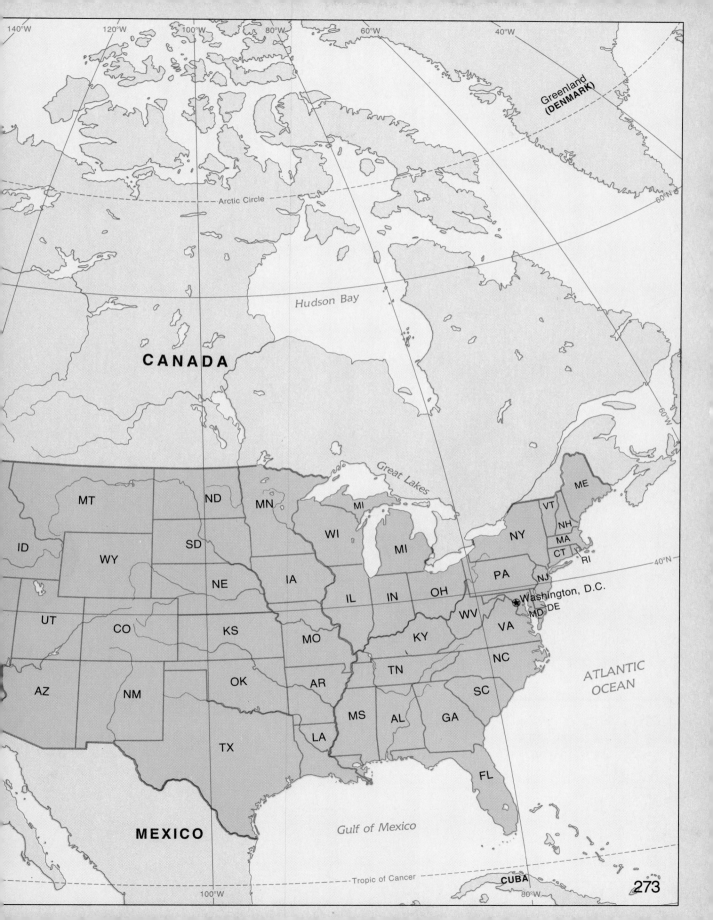

140°W 120°W 100°W 80°W 60°W 40°W

Greenland
(DENMARK)

Arctic Circle

60°N

Hudson Bay

CANADA

Great Lakes

ME

MT ND MN MI VT

WI NH

ID SD MI NY MA

WY IA CT RI

40°N

NE IL IN OH PA NJ

UT Washington, D.C.

CO KS MO WV MD DE

AZ NM OK AR KY VA

TN NC ATLANTIC OCEAN

MS AL GA SC

TX LA FL

MEXICO Gulf of Mexico

Tropic of Cancer CUBA 80°W

100°W

273

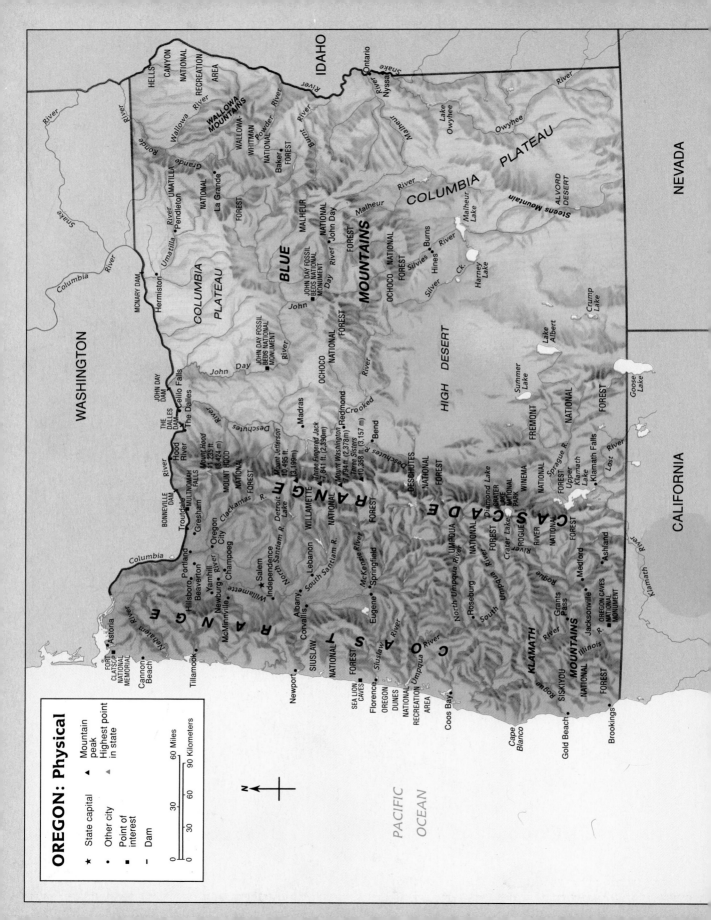

OREGON: Physical

- ★ State capital
- • Other city
- ■ Point of interest
- – Dam
- ▲ Mountain peak
- ▲ Highest point in state

60 Miles
90 Kilometers

WASHINGTON

IDAHO

NEVADA

CALIFORNIA

PACIFIC OCEAN

HELLS CANYON NATIONAL RECREATION AREA

WALLOWA MOUNTAINS

WALLOWA WHITMAN NATIONAL FOREST

COLUMBIA PLATEAU

BLUE MOUNTAINS

MALHEUR NATIONAL FOREST

OCHOCO NATIONAL FOREST

HIGH DESERT

COLUMBIA PLATEAU

ALVORD DESERT

Steens Mountain

CASCADE RANGE

WILLAMETTE NATIONAL FOREST

DESCHUTES NATIONAL FOREST

FREMONT NATIONAL FOREST

WINEMA NATIONAL FOREST

COAST RANGE

SIUSLAW NATIONAL FOREST

UMPQUA NATIONAL FOREST

ROGUE RIVER NATIONAL FOREST

KLAMATH MOUNTAINS

SISKIYOU NATIONAL FOREST

Snake River
Grande Ronde River
Wallowa River
Powder River
Burnt River
Malheur River
Lake Owyhee
Owyhee River
Umatilla River
Columbia River
John Day River
Silvies River
Silver Ck.
Harney Lake
Malheur Lake
Burns
Hines
Crump Lake
Lake Albert
Summer Lake
Goose Lake
Crooked River
Deschutes River
Sprague R.
Upper Klamath Lake
Lost River
Klamath Falls
Klamath River
Diamond Lake
Crater Lake
CRATER LAKE NATIONAL PARK
Rogue River
Illinois R.
North Umpqua River
South Umpqua River
McKenzie River
South Santiam R.
North Santiam R.
Detroit Lake
Clackamas R.
Willamette River
Yamhill River
Nestucca River
Columbia River
Siuslaw River
Umpqua River

Ontario
Nyssa
Pendleton
La Grande
Baker
Hermiston
The Dalles
Celilo Falls
Hood River
Troutdale
Gresham
Portland
Hillsboro
Beaverton
Oregon City
Newberg
McMinnville
Champoeg
★ Salem
Independence
Albany
Corvallis
Lebanon
Springfield
Eugene
Newport
Florence
Coos Bay
Roseburg
Grants Pass
Medford
Jacksonville
Ashland
Gold Beach
Brookings
Cape Blanco
Madras
Redmond
Bend
Astoria
Cannon Beach
Tillamook

MCNARY DAM
JOHN DAY DAM
THE DALLES DAM
BONNEVILLE DAM

JOHN DAY FOSSIL BEDS NATIONAL MONUMENT
MULTNOMAH FALLS
MOUNT HOOD NATIONAL FOREST
Mount Hood 11,235 ft. (3,424 m)
Mount Jefferson 10,495 ft. (3,199 m)
Three Fingered Jack 7,841 ft. (2,390 m)
Mount Washington 7,794 ft. (2,378 m)
Three Sisters 10,358 ft. (3,157 m)
FORT CLATSOP NATIONAL MEMORIAL
SEA LION CAVES
OREGON DUNES NATIONAL RECREATION AREA
OREGON CAVES NATIONAL MONUMENT

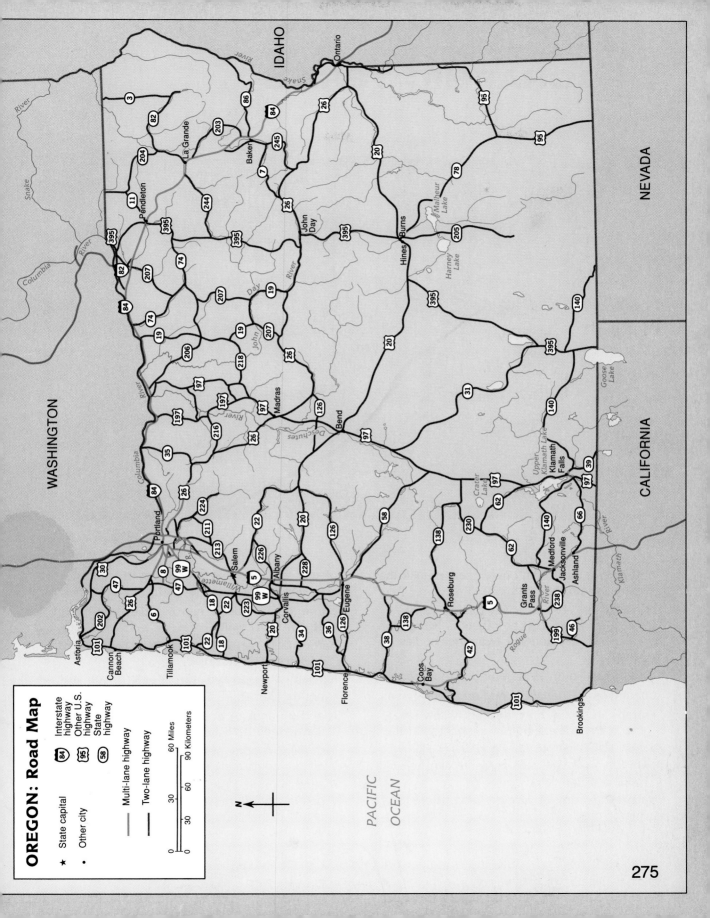

OREGON: Road Map

★ State capital
• Other city

(84) Interstate highway
(95) Other U.S. highway
(58) State highway

—— Multi-lane highway
—— Two-lane highway

0   30   60 Miles
0   30   60   90 Kilometers

N

PACIFIC OCEAN

WASHINGTON

IDAHO

NEVADA

CALIFORNIA

Snake River
Columbia River
Snake River
Columbia River
Willamette River
Deschutes River
John Day River
Day River
Malheur Lake
Harney Lake
Goose Lake
Upper Klamath Lake
Klamath Lake
Klamath River
Rogue River
Crater Lake

Astoria
Cannon Beach
Tillamook
Newport
Florence
Coos Bay
Brookings
Portland
Salem
Albany
Corvallis
Eugene
Roseburg
Grants Pass
Medford
Jacksonville
Ashland
Klamath Falls
Bend
Madras
John Day
Burns
Hines
Ontario
Baker
La Grande
Pendleton

3   82   86   84   26   95
203   245   95
204   7
11   244   26   78
82   395   395   205
207   74   19   207
84   74   19   207   395   20
19   206   218   19   207   26
97   197   197   126   20   31
197   216   26   97   140
35   26   140
84   224   22   20   126   58   138   230   62   97   39
211   213   226   228   5   66   140
8   99W   47   223   99W   228   138   62   5   238   199   46
30   47   18   22   20   34   36   126   38   42
26   202   101   22   18   101   20
6   101

275

DICTIONARY OF
GEOGRAPHIC TERMS

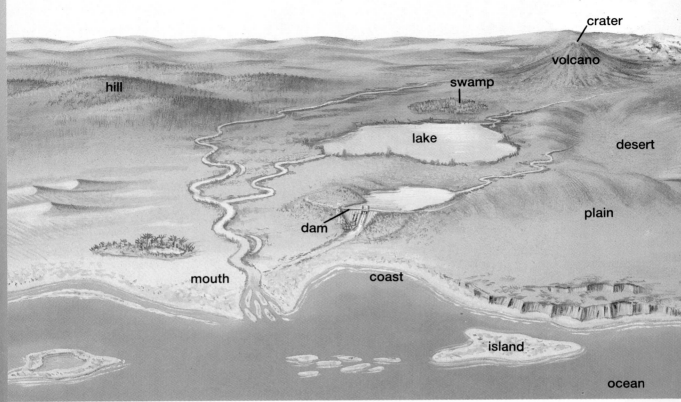

bay (bā) A part of an ocean, sea, or lake that extends into the land.

canal (kə nal′) A waterway built to carry water for navigation or irrigation. Navigation canals usually connect two other bodies of water.

cavern (kav′ ərn) A large underground cave.

coast (kōst) The land along an ocean or sea.

crater (krā tər) A bowl-shaped hollow area, made by an explosion or impact, as at the top of a volcano.

dam (dam) A wall built across a river to hold back flowing water.

desert (dez′ ərt) A very dry area where few plants grow.

glacier (glā′ shər) A huge sheet of ice that moves slowly over the land.

gorge (gôrj) A deep, narrow valley that has steep, rocky walls.

harbor (här′ bər) A safe place along a coast where ships can dock.

hill (hil) A rounded, raised landform, that is not as high as a mountain.

island (ī′ lənd) A body of land completely surrounded by water.

lake (lāk) A body of water completely or almost completely surrounded by land.

mountain (moun′ tən) A high, rounded, or pointed landform with steep sides. A mountain is higher than a hill.

276

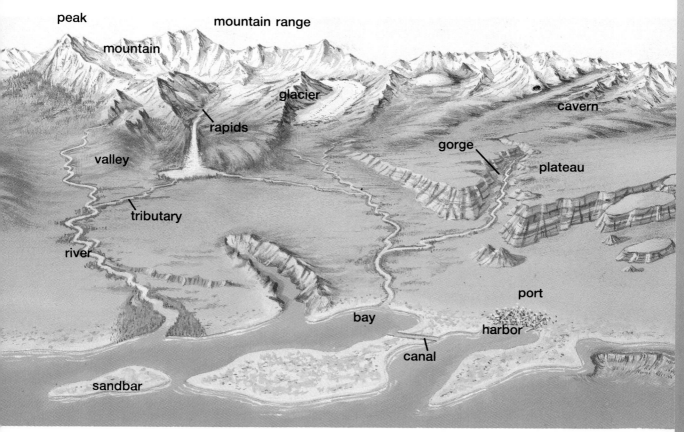

peak

mountain range

mountain

glacier

cavern

rapids

gorge

valley

plateau

tributary

river

port

bay

harbor

canal

sandbar

mountain range (moun′ tən ranj) A row or chain of mountains.

mouth (mouth) The place where a river empties into another body of water.

ocean (ō′ shən) One of the earth's four largest bodies of salt water. The four oceans are really a single body of salt water that covers three fourths of the earth's surface.

peak (pēk) The pointed top of a mountain or hill.

plain (plān) A large area of flat or nearly flat land.

plateau (pla tō′) A high, flat landform raised above the surrounding country.

port (pôrt) A place where ships can load and unload goods.

rapids (rap′ idz) A part of a river where the water flows swiftly and roughly.

river (riv′ ər) A large stream of water that flows in a natural channel across the land and empties into a lake, ocean, or another river.

sandbar (sand′ bär) A ridge of sand built up from the floor of a body of water by the action of waves.

swamp (swomp) An area of wet land.

tributary (trib′ yə târ ē) A river or stream that flows into a larger river or stream.

valley (val′ ē) An area of low land between hills or mountains.

volcano (vol kä′ nō) An opening in the earth through which lava, rock, and gases are forced out.

GAZETTEER

This Gazetteer is a geographical dictionary that will help you to pronounce and locate the places discussed in this book. Latitude and longitude are given for cities and some other places. The page number tells you where each place appears on a map.

PRONUNCIATION KEY

a	cap	hw	where	oi	coin	ü	moon
ā	cake	i	bib	ôr	fork	ū	cute
ä	father	ī	kite	ou	cow	ûr	term
är	car	îr	pierce	sh	show	ə	about, taken,
âr	dare	ng	song	th	thin		pencil, apron,
ch	chain	o	top	th	those		helpful
e	hen	ō	rope	u	sun	ər	letter, dollar,
ē	me	ô	saw	ù	book		doctor

A

Albany (ôl′ bə nē) An important city on the banks of the Willamette River; 45°N, 123°W. (p. 40)

Alvord Desert (al vərd′ dez′ ərt) The hottest and driest part of Oregon. (p. 49)

Ashland (ash′ lənd) The home of the yearly Oregon Shakespearean Festival; 42°N, 123°W. (p. 23)

Astoria (as tōr′ ē ə) A harbor city located at the mouth of the Columbia River; 46°N, 124°W. (p. 36)

B

Barlow Road (bär′ lō rōd) The road cleared through the Cascade Mountains in 1846 by pioneer Samuel Barlow. (p. 124)

Bend (bend) A city in Eastern Oregon; 44°N, 121°W. (p. 49)

Bering Strait (bîr′ ing strāt) The narrow waterway between Asia and North America. (p. 266)

Blue Mountains (blü moun′ tənz) A row of mountains in the northeast corner of Eastern Oregon. (p. 49)

Bonneville Dam (bon′ ə vil dam) A dam built on the Columbia River in the 1930s to provide hydroelectric power and water for irrigation; 46°N, 122°W. (p. 45)

C

Cannon Beach (kan′ ən bēch) A beach along the rugged Oregon Coast, about 20 miles (32 km) south of Astoria; 46°N, 124°W. (p. 36)

Cascade Range (kas kād′ rānj) A row of mountains that stretches from Canada south through Oregon to California. (p. 36)

Celilo Falls (sə li′ lō fôlz) A good location for catching fish on the Columbia River; (p. 274)

Champoeg (cham pō′ eg) A town in the Willamette valley; the site of early settlers' efforts to set up a government; 45°N, 123°W. (p. 274)

Coast Range (cōst rānj) A row of mountains located just inland from the Oregon Coast. (p. 36)

Columbia Plateau (kə lum′ bē ə pla tō′) A large area of flat land that makes up most of the northern section of Eastern Oregon. (p. 49)

Columbia River (kə lum′ bē ə riv′ ər) A major river in Oregon that flows from Canada through the Cascade Range to the Pacific Ocean. (p. 23)

Columbia River Gorge (kə lum′ bē ə riv′ ər gôrj) The deep-sided opening in the Cascade Range through which the Columbia River flows to the ocean. (p. 23)

Coos Bay (küs bā) The largest city on the Oregon coast; a center for shipping forest products; 43°N, 124°W. (p. 36)

Corvallis (kôr val′ əs) A university town on the banks of the Willamette River; 45°N, 123°W. (p. 40)

Crater Lake (krā′ tər lāk) A lake at the top of Mount Mazama; 43°N, 122°W. (p. 23)

E

Eugene (ū jēn′) A university town on the banks of the Willamette River; 44°N, 123°W. (p. 40)

F

Florence (flôr′ əns) A city on the Oregon Coast near the Sea Lion Caves; 44°N, 124°W. (p. 36)

Fort Clatsop (fôrt klat′ səp) The small fort built near the mouth of the Columbia River by the members of the Lewis and Clark expedition; 46°N, 124°W. (p. 87)

Fort Hall (fôrt hôl) A trading post built by Nathaniel Wyeth in the 1830s; 43°N, 111°W. (p. 124)

Fort Laramie (fôrt lar′ ə mē) A stopping-off place on the Oregon Trail in Wyoming; 41°N, 106°W. (p. 124)

Fort Vancouver (fôrt van kü′ vər) The fort built under the direction of John McLoughlin at the mouth of the Willamette River in 1825; 46°N, 123°W. (p. 124)

French Prairie (french prâr′ ē) The site of a mission built by Jason Lee in the Willamette Valley in 1834; 45°N, 123°W. (p. 133)

G

Green River (grēn riv′ ər) A river that flows south from the Rocky Mountains through Wyoming and Utah into the Colorado River. (p. 108)

H

Hood River (hùd riv′ ər) A town near the Columbia River Gorge; a center for windsurfing; 46°N, 121°W. (p. 45)

K

Klamath Mountains (klam′ əth moun′ tənz) The steep, tree-covered mountains at the southern end of the Coast Range. (p. 36)

L

Lapwai (lap′ wī) The site of the mission built among the Nez Percé by Henry and Eliza Spalding in 1836; 46°N, 117°W. (p. 115)

Lewis and Clark Trail (lü′ is ənd klärk trāl) The route followed by the Lewis and Clark expedition from St. Louis to the Pacific Ocean. (p. 87)

Louisiana Territory (lü ē zē an′ ə ter′ i tôr ē) The land between the Mississippi River and the Rocky Mountains that the United States bought from France in 1803. (p. 86)

M

Mission Bottom (mish′ ən bot′ əm) The area near the Willamette River where Jason Lee built his mission in 1834; 45°N, 123°W. (p. 115)

Missouri River (mi zür′ ē riv′ ər) A river in the Middle West that flows east from the Rocky Mountains to join the Mississippi River near St. Louis, Missouri. (p. 86)

Mount Hood (mount hùd) A snow-covered volcano in the Cascade Range; the highest peak in the Cascade Range; 46°N, 122°W. (p. 45)

Mount Hood National Forest (mount hùd nash′ ə nəl fôr ist) A national forest, used especially for skiing and other winter sports. (p. 274)

Mount Jefferson (mount jef′ ər sən) The second-highest peak in the Cascade Range; 45°N, 122°W. (p. 45)

N

Newberry Crater (nü′ ber ē krā′ tər) A crater near Bend with a surface like that of the moon; 44°N, 121°W. (p. 49)

North Platte River (nôrth plat riv′ ər) A river that runs from Wyoming into Nebraska, where it joins the Platte River. (p. 124)

Nyssa (nis′ ə) A town with factories in which sugar is made from sugar beets; 44°N, 117°W. (p. 229)

O

Oregon (ôr′ i gon) A state in the northwestern United States; the subject of this textbook. (p. 23)

Oregon Caves (ôr′ i gon cāvz) The caves in the Klamath Mountains with unusual rock formations. (p. 36)

GAZETTEER

Oregon City (ôr′ i gon sit′ ē) A city in the Willamette Valley near the western end of the Oregon Trail; 45°N, 123°W. (p. 40)

Oregon Country (ôr′ i gon kun′ trē) The name given to the region between the Rocky Mountains and the Pacific Ocean in the 1800s. (p. 86)

Oregon Trail (ôr′ i gon trāl) The main route used by pioneers to travel west from Missouri to Oregon Country in the 1800s. (p. 124)

Owyhee River (ō wī′ hē riv′ ər) A river in Eastern Oregon that is excellent for fishing. (p. 23)

P

Pacific Ocean (pə sif′ ik ō′ shən) The ocean that borders the western coast of the United States and forms Oregon's western border. (p. 23)

Pacific Rim (pə sif′ ik rim) The countries that border the Pacific Ocean. (p. 256)

S

South Pass (south pas) An opening through the Rocky Mountains, discovered by Mountain Man Jedediah Smith with the help of some Native Americans. (p. 108)

Springfield (spring′ fēld) An important Oregon city, located on the banks of the Willamette River; 44°N, 123°W. (p. 40)

St. Louis (sānt lü′ is) A city in the state of Missouri, located on the Mississippi River; 39°N, 90°W. (p. 87)

T

Three Fingered Jack (thrē fin′ gərd jak) The jagged-topped mountain in the Cascade Range; 44°N, 122°W. (p. 45)

Three Sisters (thrē sis′ tərz) Three mountains in the Cascade Range that are close together; 44°N, 122°W. (p. 45)

Tillamook (til′ ə mək) A city on the Oregon Coast known for its cheese; 45°N, 124°W. (p. 36)

Timberline Lodge (tim′ bər līn loj) A recreational building on Mount Hood that was built during the Great Depression; 45°N, 122°W. (p. 40)

U

United States (ū nī′ tid stātz) The country located in North America, made up of 50 states, that includes Oregon. (pp. 270–271)

W

Waiilatpu (wy ee′ lat pu) The site of the Whitman's mission, built in 1836; 46°N, 118°W. (p. 115)

Wallowa Mountains (wo lou′ ə mount′ tənz) A row of mountains in the northeast corner of Eastern Oregon. (p. 40)

Washington, D.C. (wô′ shing tən dē sē) The capital of the United States; 39°N, 77°W. (pp. 270–271)

Willamette National Forest (wə lam′ ət nash′ ə nəl fôr ist) Oregon's largest forest, used for hiking, camping, and other recreational activities. (p. 274)

Willamette River (wə lam′ ət riv′ ər) An important tributary of the Columbia River that flows between the Coast Range and the Cascade Range. (p. 40)

Y

Yamhill (yam′ hil) The community southwest of Portland in which author Beverly Cleary grew up; 45°N, 123°W. (p. 274)

a cap; ā cake; ä father; är car; âr dare; ch chain; e hen; ē me; hw where; i bib; ī kite; îr pierce; ng song; o top; ō rope; ô saw; oi coin; ôr fork; ou cow; sh show; th thin; th those; u sun; u̇ book; ü moon; ū cute; ûr term; ə about, taken, pencil, apron, helpful; ər letter, dollar, doctor

GAZETTEER

BIOGRAPHICAL DICTIONARY

This Biographical Dictionary will help you to pronounce and identify the Key People in this book. The page number will tell you where each person first appears in the text.

PRONUNCIATION KEY

a	cap	hw	where	oi	coin	ü	moon
ā	cake	i	bib	ôr	fork	ū	cute
ä	father	ī	kite	ou	cow	ûr	term
är	car	îr	pierce	sh	show	ə	about, taken,
âr	dare	ng	song	th	thin		pencil, apron,
ch	chain	o	top	th	those		helpful
e	hen	ō	rope	u	sun	ər	letter, dollar,
ē	me	ô	saw	u̇	book		doctor

A

Abernethy, George (ab ər nē′ thē), Governor of the provisional government of the Oregon Country in 1843. (p. 139)

Ashley, William (ash′ lē), 1778?–1838 Conducted fur trading in the Northwest in the 1820s. (p. 107)

Astor, John Jacob (as′ tər), 1763–1848 Founder of the Pacific Fur Company, which built Fort Astoria. (p. 93)

B

Barlow, Samuel (bär′ lō), 1795–1867 Cleared the Barlow Road in 1846, making it safer to travel to the Oregon Country. (p. 127)

Belluschi, Pietro (bə lü′ shē), 1899– Architect who designed the Oregon Art Institute. (p. 218)

Black, William (blak), British sea captain sent to capture Fort Astoria during the War of 1812. (p. 95)

Blanchet, Father (blan shā′), 1795–1883 Catholic missionary; came to the Oregon Country in 1838; built St. Paul's mission on French Prairie. (p. 115)

Broughton, William (brôt′ ən), 1762–1821 British lieutenant under Captain Vancouver; explored the Columbia River in 1792. (p. 83)

C

Clark, William (klärk), 1770–1838 Coleader of the expedition to explore the Louisiana Territory. (p. 86)

Cleary, Beverly (klî′ rē), 1916– Author from Oregon who wrote the Ramona books. (p. 192)

Cook, James (ku̇k), 1728–1779 English explorer; searched for the Northwest Passage. (p. 82)

Crawford, Medorem (krô′ fərd), 1819–1891 Pioneer; kept a journal of his trip on a wagon train going west in 1842. (p. 126)

D

Demers, Father (də mär′), 1808–1877 Catholic missionary; came to the Oregon Country in 1838; built St. Paul's mission on French Prairie. (p. 115)

DePreist, James (də prēst′), 1936– Conductor of the Oregon Symphony Orchestra. (p. 207)

Duniway, Abigail Scott (dun′ ə wā), 1834–1915 Leader of the women's suffrage movement in Oregon. (p. 170)

F

Fosbury, Dick (foz′ ber ē), 1947– Olympic high jumper. (p. 213)

G

Goldschmidt, Neil (gōld′ shmit), 1940– Elected governor of Oregon in 1987. (p. 244)

Gray, Robert (grā), 1755–1806 United States sea captain; explored and named the Columbia River in 1792. (p. 83)

H

Hatfield, Mark (hat' fēld), 1922– Oregon senator since 1967. (p. 253)

Heceta, Bruno (e ze' tə, brü' no) 1751–1807 Spanish explorer; searched for the Northwest Passage. (p. 82)

Henry, Andrew (hen' rē), 1775?–1833 Fur trader in the Northwest in the 1820s. (p. 107)

J

Jack, Captain (jak) 1837?–1873 Modoc leader; returned with his people to their homeland, rather than live on a reservation; fought against the United States Army. (p. 158)

Jefferson, Thomas (jef' ər sən), 1743–1826 United States President; agreed to the Louisiana Purchase in 1803. (p. 85)

Joseph, Chief (jō' zəf), 1832–1904 Nez Percé chief; tried to help his people flee to Canada rather than live on a reservation. (p. 159)

K

Kaiser, Henry (kī' zər), (1882–1967) Portland shipbuilder; during World War II he built record numbers of Liberty Ships. (p. 183)

L

Lane, Joseph (lān), 1801–1881 Appointed governor of the Oregon Territory in 1848. (p. 146)

Le Guin, Ursula (lə gwin'), 1929– Oregon author of science fiction books. (p. 205)

Lee, Daniel (lē), 1806–1895 Protestant missionary; helped to set up the first Christian mission in the Oregon Country. (p. 112)

Lee, Jason (lē), 1803–1845 Protestant missionary; helped to set up the first Christian mission in the Oregon Country; led the group that became known as the Great Reinforcement. (p. 112)

Lewis, Meriwether (lü' is), 1774–1809 Coleader of the expedition to explore the Louisiana Territory. (p. 86)

Lovejoy, Asa L. (luv' joi), 1808–1882 Helped to found and name Portland. (p. 216)

M

McCall, Tom (mə kôl), 1913–1983 Governor of Oregon from 1967 to 1975; fought for laws to protect the environment. (p. 189)

McLoughlin, John (mə klôf' lən), 1784–1857 Leader of Fort George for the Hudson's Bay Company in 1824; moved the trading post to Fort Vancouver in 1825; member of the 1845 provisional government. (p. 98)

Meek, Joseph (mēk), 1810–1875 Mountain Man; convinced Congress to make Oregon a territory. (p. 134)

Meier, Julius (mī' ər), 1874–1937 Governor of Oregon from 1931 to 1935. (p. 178)

Morey, Walt (mô' rē), 1907– Oregon author. (p. 205)

Murphy, Dale (mûr' fē), 1956– Famous professional baseball outfielder. (p. 212)

O

Ogden, Peter Skene (ôg' dən), 1794–1854 Canadian fur trapper; convinced the Cayuse to turn in the Indians responsible for the Whitman Massacre. (p. 145)

P

Packwood, Bob (pak' wŭd), 1932– Important senator from Oregon since 1969. (p. 253)

Pettygrove, Francis W. (pet' ē grōv), 1812–1887 Helped to found and name Portland. (p. 216)

Polk, James K. (pōk), 1795–1849 United States President; helped to bring Oregon under American control in 1846. (p. 140)

R

Roosevelt, Franklin D. (rōz' velt), 1882–1945 United States President during the Great Depression and World War II. (p. 178)

S

Sacajawea (sak ə jə wē' ə), 1787?–1812 Shoshone Indian; served as translator and guide during the Lewis and Clark expedition. (p. 87)

Schollander, Don (shōl lan' dər), 1946– In 1964, the first swimmer to win four gold medals at one Olympic game. (p. 213)

Slacum, William A. (slā' kəm), ?–1839 Arranged for Ewing Young to bring cattle to the Oregon Country in 1838. (p. 118)

Slaney, Mary Decker (slā' nē), 1958– Olympic runner; set five American and world records. (p. 213)

Smith, Jedediah (smith), 1799–1831 Famous Mountain Man. (p. 108)

BIOGRAPHICAL DICTIONARY

Spalding, Eliza (spôld′ ing), 1807–1851 Protestant missionary; came to the Oregon Country with the Whitmans in 1836. (p. 112)

Spalding, Henry H. (spôld′ ing), 1803?–1843? Protestant missionary; came to the Oregon Country with the Whitmans in 1836. (p. 112)

T

Thorn, Jonathan (thôrn), 1779–1811 United States sea captain; led the sea expedition to Oregon for the Pacific Fur Company in 1810. (p. 93)

U

U'Ren, William (ûr en′), 1859–1949 Member of the Oregon legislature; proposed the initiative, referendum, and recall. (p. 169)

V

Vancouver, George (van kü′ vər), 1757–1798 British sea captain; explored the Columbia River and claimed it for Great Britain. (p. 83)

Villard, Henry (və lärd′), 1855–1900 Promoted the railroad that, in 1883, connected Oregon with the East. (p. 164)

W

White, Elijah (hwīt), 1806–1879 Member of Jason Lee's mission who returned east hoping to encourage others to move to the Oregon Country. (p. 125)

Whitman, Marcus (hwit′ mən), 1802–1847 Protestant missionary; came with his wife to the Oregon Country in 1836. (p. 112)

Whitman, Narcissa (hwit′ mən), 1808–1847 Protestant missionary; came with her husband to the Oregon Country in 1836. (p. 112)

Winnemucca, Sarah (win′ ə mŭk′ ə), 1844?–1891 Paiute Indian; acted as translator and scout for the United States Army; started a school for Indians; the first Indian to publish a book in English. (p. 157)

Wyeth, Nathaniel J. (wī′ əth), 1802–1856 Built Fort Hall. (p. 110)

Y

York, Ben (yôrk), about 1770–? Slave of William Clark. (p. 87)

Young, Ewing (yung), 1812–1841 Mountain Man; the leader of the men who brought cattle to the Oregon Country in 1838. (p. 119)

BIOGRAPHICAL DICTIONARY

a cap; ā cake; ä father; är car; âr dare; ch chain; e hen; ē me; hw where; i bib; ī kite; îr pierce; ng song; o top; ō rope; ô saw; oi coin; ôr fork; ou cow; sh show; th thin; <u>th</u> those; u sun; u̇ book; ü moon; ū cute; ûr term; ə about, taken, pencil, apron, helpful; ər letter, dollar, doctor

GLOSSARY

This glossary will help you to pronounce and understand the meanings of the Key Vocabulary in this book. The page number at the end of the definition tells where the word first appears.

PRONUNCIATION KEY

a	cap	hw	where	oi	coin	ü	moon
ā	cake	i	bib	ôr	fork	ū	cute
ä	father	ī	kite	ou	cow	ûr	term
är	car	îr	pierce	sh	show	ə	about, taken,
âr	dare	ng	song	th	thin		pencil, apron,
ch	chain	o	top	th	those		helpful
e	hen	ō	rope	u	sun	ər	letter, dollar,
ē	me	ô	saw	u̇	book		doctor

A

agriculture (ag′ ri kul chər) The science and business of raising crops and farm animals. (p. 230)

amendment (ə mend′ mənt) A change or addition to a constitution. (p. 169)

ancestors (an′ ses tərz) Relatives who lived long ago. (p. 29)

archaeologists (är kē ol′ ə jists) Scientists who search for and study artifacts. (p. 62)

architecture (är′ ki tek chər) The art of designing buildings. (p. 217)

artifacts (är′ tə fakts) Objects left behind by people who lived long ago. (p. 62)

B

bill (bil) A plan for a law. (p. 245)

bracero (bro ser′ ō) Mexican workers who worked temporarily in the United States during World War II. (p. 185)

byline (bī′ līn) The words at the beginning of a news story that tell who wrote the story. (p. 246)

C

canyon (kan′ yən) A deep, narrow valley with steep sides. (p. 49)

cardinal directions (kär′ də nəl di rek′ shənz) The main directions—north, east, south, and west. (p. 9)

cause (kôz) Something that makes something else happen. (p. 116)

circle graph (sûr′ kəl graf) A type of graph that shows how the parts of something are related to the whole. (p. 232)

city council (sit′ ē koun′ səl) The legislature of a city government. (p. 251)

city manager (sit′ ē man′ i jər) A person appointed by a city council to take care of the day-to-day business of the city. (p. 251)

climate (klī′ mit) The pattern of weather over a long period of time. (p. 23)

commissioners (kə mish′ ə nərz) The elected members of a board who run a county government. (p. 250)

compass rose (kum′ pəs rōz) A small drawing included on a map that shows directions. (p. 9)

compromise (kom′ prə mīz) The settlement of a dispute by having each side agree to give up part of its demands. (p. 140)

Congress (kong′ gris) The branch, or part, of the United States government that makes the laws. (p. 146)

conservation (kon sər vā′ shən) The protection of natural resources. (p. 177)

constitution (kon sti tü′ shən) A plan of government. (p. 154)

constitutional convention (kon sti tü′ shə nəl kən ven′ shən) A meeting held to write or agree on a new constitution. (p. 155)

continent (kon′ tə nənt) A very large body of land; there are seven continents on the earth. (p. 7)

county (koun′ tē) A division of a state. (p. 250)

county seat (koun′ tē sēt) The town or city in which a county government is located. (p. 250)

culture (kul′ chər) The way of life of a group of people, including their beliefs, customs, and activities. (p. 66)

D

dateline (dāt′ līn) The words at the beginning of a news story that tell when and where the story was written. (p. 246)

decision (di sizh′ ən) The act of making a choice. (p. 64)

degree (di grē′) A unit of measurement for latitude and longitude. (p. 42)

desert (dez′ ərt) A hot, dry land where less than 10 inches (25 cm) of rain falls per year. (p. 25)

discrimination (di skrim ə nā′ shən) The unfair difference in treatment of one group over another. (p. 184)

Donation Land Act (dō nā′ shən land akt) A law passed by Congress in 1850 that allowed settlers in Oregon to claim land; white men who had lived on the land for at least four years could claim 320 acres (130 ha); white men who had lived on the land for fewer than four years could claim 160 acres (65 ha); married couples could claim twice as much land as single men. (p. 153)

E

economy (i kon′ ə mē) The use of resources, money, and goods to meet people's needs and wants. (p. 221)

effect (i fekt′) What happens as the result of something else. (p. 116)

elevation (el ə vā′ shən) The height of land above sea level. (p. 26)

environment (en vī′ rən mənt) Surroundings, including plants, animals, climate, and soil. (p. 66)

equator (i kwā′ tər) An imaginary line that lies halfway between the North Pole and the South Pole. (p. 8)

executive branch (eg zek′ yə tiv branch) The part of government that makes sure that the laws are carried out. (p. 245)

expedition (ek spi dish′ ən) A journey made for a special purpose. (p. 86)

explorer (ek splôr′ ər) A person who travels to unknown lands. (p. 81)

F

folk art (fōk ärt) Any type of creative art that has been passed down from one generation to another. (p. 206)

frontier (frun tîr′) A settled region lying along the border of an unsettled area. (p. 87)

fur brigade (fûr bri gād′) Groups of fur trappers, working for the Hudson's Bay Company, who traveled on horseback. (p. 100)

fur trapper (fûr trap′ ər) Someone who traps wild animals for their fur. (p. 92)

G

geography (jē og′ rə fē) The study of the earth's land and water, plants and animals. (p. 18)

geologist (jē ol′ ə jist) A person who studies the earth to learn how it changes over time. (p. 18)

ghost town (gōst toun) A town that has been deserted; especially, a mining town that was deserted after the mines near by closed down. (p. 154)

glacier (glā′ shər) A huge, slowly moving sheet of ice. (p. 19)

graph (graf) A diagram that shows facts so that they can be easily understood and compared. (p. 232)

Great Depression (grāt di presh′ ən) The hard times that began in 1929 when many businesses closed and many people lost their jobs. (p. 178)

greenway (grēn′ wā) A strip of land in fields or forests where no businesses or houses may be built. (p. 190)

grid (grid) A set of crisscrossing lines on a map or globe. (p. 43)

grid map (grid map) A map on which a grid is used to locate places. (p. 12)

H

harbor (här′ bər) A place along a coastline where ships can dock safely. (p. 37)

hatchery (hach′ ə rē) A place in which fish eggs are hatched. (p. 231)

headline (hed′ līn) The words printed in large type at the top of a news story to catch the reader's attention. (p. 246)

hemisphere (hem′ i sfîr) Half a sphere. (p. 7)

heritage (her′ i tij) The ways and beliefs that are handed down from one generation to another. (p. 202)

House of Representatives (hous əv rep ri zen′ tə tivz) One of the two houses of Congress that makes up the legislative branch of the United States government. (p. 252)

Hudson's Bay Company (hud′ sənz bā kum′ pə nē) A British fur trading company that had trading posts all across Canada during the 1800s. (p. 97)

hydroelectric (hī drō i lek′ trik) The power that is created by the force of falling water. (p. 178)

I

Ice Age (īs āj) The period in prehistoric times when glaciers covered much of the earth. (p. 19)

industry (in′ də strē) All the businesses that make one kind of product or provide one kind of service. (p. 221)

initiative (i nish′ ə tiv) A procedure by which voters can make their own state laws without involving the legislature. (p. 169)

interdependent (in tər di pen′ dənt) Depending on and needing one another. (p. 256)

intermediate directions (in tər mē′ dē it di rek′ shənz) Directions that lie halfway between the cardinal directions—northwest, southeast, etc. (p. 9)

international trade (in tər nash′ ə nəl trād) The buying and selling of goods among nations. (p. 255)

irrigation (ir i gā′ shən) The watering of dry land by means of canals, pipes, or ditches. (p. 45)

J

joint occupation (joint ok yə pā′ shən) Shared control of an area. (p. 96)

judicial branch (jü dish′ əl branch) The part of government that decides the meaning of laws and whether they agree with the constitution; the part of government made up of the courts. (p. 246)

L

land-use map (land ūs map) A map that shows how people in different areas earn a living. (p. 186)

landfill (land′ fil) A place where garbage is dumped and then covered with soil. (p. 260)

landform (land′ form) A shape on the earth's surface, such as a mountain or plateau. (p. 22)

landmark (land′ märk) A familiar object that serves as a guide. (p. 124)

latitude (lat′ i tüd) The imaginary lines on a map or globe that measure degrees north or south of the equator. (p. 42)

lead (lēd) The first paragraph of a news story, which tells the most important facts and is written so as to catch the reader's interest. (p. 246)

legislative branch (lej′ is lā tiv branch) The part of government that makes laws. (p. 244)

legislature (lej′ is lā chər) A group of elected leaders who make laws. (p. 168)

Liberty Ship (lib′ ər tē ship) One of the many ships built in Henry Kaiser's shipyards in Portland during World War II. (p. 183)

Liberty Train (lib′ ər tē trān) One of the trains that brought workers to Portland during World War II to work for the Kaiser Company. (p. 183)

line graph (līn graf) A type of graph that shows changes over time. (p. 233)

livestock (līv′ stok) Animals raised on a farm or ranch to be sold at a market. (p. 228)

locks (loks) Narrow, concrete passages like canals, in which the water level can be raised or lowered. (p. 44)

logging (lô′ ging) The business of cutting down trees, cutting them into logs, and transporting them to a mill. (p. 221)

GLOSSARY

longitude (lon′ ji tüd) The imaginary lines on a map or globe that show degrees east or west of the prime meridian. (p. 42)

Louisiana Purchase (lü ē zē an′ ə pûr′ chəs) The territory that the United States purchased from France in 1803. (p. 86)

lumbering (lum′ bər ing) The business of cutting and preparing logs. (p. 221)

M

manufacturing (man yə fak′ chər ing) The making of goods. (p. 234)

map key (map kē) A diagram or box on a map that explains what the symbols mean. (p. 10)

mayor (mā′ ər) The elected head of the executive branch of a city government. (p. 251)

meridian (mə rid′ ē ən) A line of longitude. (p. 42)

migrate (mī′ grāt) To move from one place to another in order to settle there. (p. 62)

mission (mish′ ən) A settlement started by missionaries whose purpose was to teach their religion and convert the surrounding people. (p. 112)

missionary (mish′ ə ner ē) A person who teaches his or her religion to others who have different beliefs. (p. 112)

Mountain Men (moun′ tən men) Fur trappers who hunted for beaver in the Rocky Mountains during the early 1800s. (p. 108)

mouth (mouth) The place where a river empties into a large body of water. (p. 37)

N

natural feature (nach′ ər əl fē′ chər) Any part of the earth that is formed by nature. (p. 22)

natural resource (nach′ ər əl rē′ sôrs) Something found in nature that is useful to people. (p. 24)

New Deal (nü dēl) President Roosevelt's plan for helping people who were hurt by the Great Depression. (p. 178)

O

ocean (ō′ shən) A large body of water; there are four oceans on the earth. (p. 7)

P

Pacific Fur Company (pə sif′ ik fûr kum′ pə nē) A company formed by John Jacob Astor in 1810 that built Fort Astoria as a trading post. (p. 93)

parallel (par′ ə lel) A line of latitude. (p. 42)

petition (pə tish′ ən) A formal request to someone in authority. (p. 119)

pioneer (pī ə nîr′) A person who is among the first to settle in a region. (p. 123)

plateau (pla tō′) A large area of high, flat land. (p. 25)

point of view (point əv vū) The way in which a person looks at something. (p. 214)

pollution (pə lü′ shən) The dirtying of the air, soil, or water. (p. 188)

population (pop yə lā′ shən) The number of people living in a place. (p. 132)

population map (pop yə lā′ shən map) A map that shows the number of people who live in different areas. (p. 186)

Portland Rose Festival (pôrt′ lənd rōz fes′ tə vəl) The second-largest rose parade in the United States; it takes place yearly in Portland. (p. 217)

powwow (pou′ wou) A present-day gathering of Indians in which they take part in activities that celebrate their heritage. (p. 202)

precipitation (pri sip i tā′ shən) Any form of water that falls to earth, such as rain or snow. (p. 37)

precipitation map (pri sip i tā′ shən map) A map that shows the amount of precipitation that falls in different areas. (p. 186)

prime meridian (prīm mə rid′ ē ən) The starting line for measuring longitude. (p. 42)

progressive (prə gres′ iv) Describing a state in which citizens may participate in the making of laws. (p. 170)

a cap; ā cake; ä father; är car; âr dare; ch chain; e hen; ē me; hw where; i bib; ī kite; îr pierce; ng song; o top; ō rope; ô saw; oi coin; ôr fork; ou cow; sh show; th thin; th those; u sun; ú book; ü moon; ū cute; ûr term; ə about, taken, pencil, apron, helpful; ər letter, dollar, doctor

GLOSSARY

provisional government (prə vizh′ ə nəl guv′ ərn mənt) A temporary government, such as the one set up in Oregon in 1843 that strengthened the American claim to the Oregon Territory. (p. 138)

R

rain shadow (rān shad′ ō) The side of a mountain on which little rain falls. (p. 48)

rapids (rap′ idz) The parts of a river where the water flows swiftly. (p. 53)

recall (ri kôl′) A procedure by which voters can remove state leaders from government office. (p. 169)

recreation (rek rē ā′ shən) Any activity that people take part in for enjoyment or relaxation. (p. 211)

referendum (ref ə ren′ dəm) A procedure by which voters can change state laws. (p. 169)

region (rē′ jən) A large area with common features that set it apart from other areas. (p. 22)

religion (ri lij′ ən) The way people worship the god or gods they believe in. (p. 111)

rendezvous (rän′ də vü) A large meeting of fur trappers, traders, and Indians from the entire Rocky Mountain region that took place during the 1800s. (p. 109)

reservation (rez ər vā′ shən) A piece of public land set aside for Native Americans to live on. (p. 157)

Rocky Mountain Fur Company (rok′ ē moun′ tən fûr kum′ pə nē) The fur trading company set up by William Ashley and Andrew Henry in 1822. (p. 108)

S

sandbar (sand′ bär) A ridge of sand built up from the ocean floor by the action of waves; sandbars can be difficult for ships to cross. (p. 83)

scale (skāl) The relationship between the distances shown on a map and the real distances on the earth. (p. 11)

segregation (seg ri gā′ shən) The separation of one group from another. (p. 184)

self-sufficient (self′ sə fish′ ənt) Able to provide for one's own needs. (p. 125)

Senate (sen′ it) One of the two houses of Congress that makes up the legislative branch of the United States government. (p. 252)

service industries (sûr′ vis in′ də strēz) Businesses that do useful work that people need and want. (p. 240)

slave (slāv) A person who is owned by another person. (p. 87)

stagecoach (stāj′ kōch) A horse-drawn carriage, common in the 1800s, that carried passengers from place to place. (p. 161)

steamboat (stēm′ bōt) A riverboat, powered by a steam engine, that could travel against the flow of the river's current. (p. 162)

suffrage (suf′ rij) The right to vote. (p. 170)

sweat lodge (swet loj) A small hut, used by the Nez Percé, in which cold water is poured on heated rocks to make steam. (p. 76)

symbol (sim′ bəl) Something that stands for something else. (p. 10)

T

taxes (taks′ əz) The money that people pay to the government. (p. 244)

technology (tek nol′ ə jē) The use of new ideas and tools to meet people's needs. (p. 163)

temperature (tem′ pər ə chər) How hot or cold a place is. (p. 36)

tepee (tē′ pē) A cone-shaped tent that can be put up and taken down quickly. (p. 72)

territory (ter′ i tôr ē) An area of land that is protected by the national government but does not have the rights of a state. (p. 145)

The Great Reinforcement (thə grāt rē in fôrs′ mənt) The group of 50 missionaries who arrived in Oregon in 1840 and added to the strength of the settlement. (p. 119)

timber (tim′ bər) A group of trees growing in a continuous area. (p. 222)

time line (tīm līn) A diagram that shows when and the order in which events took place. (p. 90)

tourist (tûr′ ist) A person who travels to learn about and enjoy other places. (p. 238)

GLOSSARY

trading post (trād′ ing pōst) A place where trappers and Indians could bring their furs and exchange them for goods or money during the early 1800s. (p. 93)

transportation (trans pər tā′ shən) A way to move goods and people from one place to another. (p. 40)

transportation map (trans pər tā′ shən map) A map that shows the different ways to travel from one place to another. (p. 13)

treaty (trē′ tē) A formal agreement, especially between nations. (p. 157)

tributary (trib′ yə ter ē) A river or stream that flows into a larger river. (p. 39)

V

veto (vē′ tō) To refuse to sign a bill. (p. 245)

volcano (vol kā′ nō) An opening in the earth's surface from which hot fiery rock, ash, and gas are forced out. (p. 18)

voyageurs (voi′ ə zhərz) The French-speaking Canadian fur trappers who transported furs along streams and rivers to the trading posts of the Hudson's Bay Company. (p. 97)

W

wagon train (wag′ ən trān) A group of covered wagons that follow one another. (p. 125)

weather (weth′ ər) How hot, cold, wet, or dry the air in a place is. (p. 23)

white water (hwīt wô′ tər) Churning rapids, filled with whirlpools. (p. 129)

Wolf Meetings (wùlf mēt′ ingz) The meetings held in 1843 to discuss the problem of wild animals killing settlers' cattle. (p. 133)

World War I (wûrld wôr wun) The war that broke out in Europe in 1914 in which Germany, Austria-Hungary, Turkey, and other countries fought against England, France, Russia, and the United States. (p. 175)

a cap; ā cake; ä father; är car; âr dare; ch chain; e hen; ē me; hw where; i bib; ī kite; îr pierce; ng song; o top; ō rope; ô saw; oi coin; ôr fork; ou cow; sh show; th thin; th those; u sun; ù book; ü moon; ū cute; ûr term; ə about, taken, pencil, apron, helpful; ər letter, dollar, doctor

GLOSSARY

INDEX

Page references in italic type which follow an *m* indicate a map. Those following a *p* indicate photographs, artwork, or charts.

INDEX

INDEX

INDEX

CREDITS